Transport Law in Japan

Transport Law in Japan

Noboru Kobayashi
Makoto Hiratsuka
Shinichiro Yamashita
Yuji Miyazaki
Yoichiro Tadano

This book was originally published as a monograph in the International Encyclopaedia of Laws/Transport Law.

Founding Editor: Roger Blanpain
General Editor: Frank Hendrickx
Volume Editor: Eric Van Hooydonk

Wolters Kluwer

Published by:
Kluwer Law International B.V.
PO Box 316
2400 AH Alphen aan den Rijn
The Netherlands
E-mail: lrs-sales@wolterskluwer.com
Website: www.wolterskluwer.com/en/solutions/kluwerlawinternational

Sold and distributed by:
Wolters Kluwer Legal & Regulatory U.S.
7201 McKinney Circle
Frederick, MD 21704
United States of America
E-mail: customer.service@wolterskluwer.com

ISBN 978-94-035-1716-2

e-Book: ISBN 978-94-035-1456-7
web-PDF: ISBN 978-94-035-1466-6

The Authors

Prof. Noboru Kobayashi, PhD, is a Professor Emeritus of Seikei University, Tokyo and a Counsellor of Law, Hiratsuka & Co. Tokyo. He studies and teaches commercial law, especially maritime law and insurance law, as a Professor of Law at Seikei University. He taught Japanese commercial law at the Katholieke Universiteit Leuven, Belgium in 1992. He is now a Titulary Member of Comite Maritime International.

Makoto Hiratsuka is Senior Partner of Hiratsuka & Co., Tokyo. He graduated from Faculty of Law (LLB) at the University of Tokyo and got Diploma in Shipping Law at the University College of London. He is a Fellow of International Academy of Trial Lawyer and is a board member of the Japanese Maritime Law Association.

The Authors

Shinichiro Yamashita is a Partner of Hiratsuka & Co., Tokyo. He graduated from the University of Tokyo (LLB) and is now a Member of Daiichi Tokyo Bar Association. He attended the Maritime Law Short Course offered by the Institute of Maritime Law at the University of Southampton. He is a member of the Japanese Maritime Law Association.

Yuji Miyazaki is a Partner of Hiratsuka & Co., Tokyo. He graduated from the University of Tokyo (BA) and Waseda Law School (JD) and is currently a member of the Tokyo Bar Association. He attended the 40th Maritime Law Short Course offered by the Institute of Maritime Law at the University of Southampton in 2013.

Yoichiro Tadano is an Associate of Hiratsuka & Co., Tokyo. He graduated from Waseda University (BE) and Tokyo Metropolitan University (JD). He is now a Member of the Daiichi Tokyo Bar Association.

Table of Contents

The Authors 3

List of Abbreviations 21

General Introduction 23

Chapter 1. General Background Information 23

§1. Geography and Demography 23

§2. Political and Legal System 23

§3. Commerce and Industry 24

§4. Ministry of Land, Infrastructure, Transport and Tourism (MLIT) 24

Chapter 2. Statistical Data on Transport in Japan 26

§1. Maritime Transport 26

§2. Railway Transport 26

§3. Road Transport 26

§4. Air Transport 27

Part I. Transport Laws in Japan 29

Chapter 1. Laws in General 29

Chapter 2. Laws on Each Mode of Transport 30

§1. Maritime Transport 30

§2. Railway Transport 31

§3. Road Transport 31

§4. Air Transport 31

§5. Combined Transport 32

Chapter 3. Case Law 33

Chapter 4. Private International Law 34

§1. Introduction 34

§2. Consumer Protection 34

Chapter 5. Jurisdiction 35

§1. Legislation 35

§2. Jurisdiction Clause 35

Chapter 6. Arbitration 37

Part II. Maritime Law 39

Chapter 1. The Vessel 39

§1. Definition and Legal Nature of Ships 39
I. The General Concept of a Ship 39
II. Ships under Japanese Law and Regulations 39
III. Ships under Maritime Law 40
IV. The Legal Nature of a Ship 41

§2. Nationality, Ship Registry and Ship's ledger 41
I. Japanese Ships 41
II. Port of Registry 42
III. Public Notice System for Ships 42
A. Ship Registry 43
B. Ship's Ledger 43
C. Register of Small-Sized Vessels 43

§3. Ownership of a Ship 44
I. Acquisition or Loss of Ownership 44
A. Transfer of Ownership by Sale 44
B. Newbuilding of a Ship 45
II. The Shipowner 45
III. Co-ownership of a Ship 46

Chapter 2. Maritime Liens, Mortgages and Other Security Interests 48

§1. Maritime Liens 48
I. General Remarks 48
II. Law Governing Maritime Liens 48
III. Claims Giving Rise to Maritime Liens 49
A. Maritime Liens Arising under the Commercial Code 49
B. Maritime Lien Arising under Limitation of Shipowners' Liability Act 50
C. Maritime Lien Arising under the Liability for Oil Pollution Damage Act 50
IV. Order of Priority Between Maritime Liens and Other Security Interests 50
A. Priority Among Maritime Liens 50
B. Priority Among Other Security Interests 51
V. Object of a Maritime Lien 51
VI. Extinguishment of a Maritime Lien 51

§2. Ship Mortgage 52
I. General Remarks 52
II. Object of a Ship Mortgage 52
III. Asserting a Ship Mortgage Against Third Parties 53
IV. Order of Priority Between Ship Mortgages and Other Security Interests or Bareboat Charters 53
V. Special Ship Mortgages 54

§3. Enforcement of Maritime Liens and Ship Mortgages 55

§4. Carrier's Right of Retention Against the Goods 55

Chapter 3. Ship's Captain and Other Seamen 56

§1. The Captain 56
I. Definition and Qualifications of a Ship's Captain 56
II. Regulations under the Seamen's Act 56
A. Authority of the Captain 56
B. Duties of the Captain 57
III. The Legal Status of a Ship's Captain under Maritime Law 59
A. The Appointment of a Captain 59
B. The Substitute Captain and Acting Captain 59
C. The Captain's Authority of Representation 59
D. The Captain's Right to Dispose of and Use Carried Goods 60
E. The Captain's Liability for the Acts of Seamen 60
F. Dismissal and Termination of the Captain 60

§2. SEAMEN 61
I. General Remarks 61
II. The Hiring Contract 61
A. The Parties 61
B. Conditions 61
C. Termination 62
D. Statutory Compensation and Allowance for Termination 62
E. Obligation of the Captain to Give Notice Regarding the Contract 63
III. Provisions for the Protection of Reserve Seamen under Employment Contracts 63
IV. Rights and Duties of Seamen, Etc. 64

Chapter 4. Contracts for the Carriage of Cargo by Sea 65

§1. CONTRACT FOR THE CARRIAGE OF GOODS BY SEA 65
I. Relevant Statutes 65
II. Overview and Definitions 66

§2. THE CARRIER 66
I. The Obligations of the Carrier 66
A. Warranty of Seaworthiness 67
B. Obligations Related to the Loading of Goods 67
C. Obligation to Perform the Voyage 67
D. Obligation to Keep Custody of the Goods with Due Care 68
E. Obligation to Comply with the Instructions of the Shipper or Charterer 68
F. Obligation to Discharge and Deliver the Goods 68
II. The Liability of the Carrier 69
A. Liability for Want of Due Care 69
B. Liability for Unseaworthiness 69
C. Loss, Damage or Delay 69
D. Title to Sue 70
E. Exclusions of the Carrier in International Carriage 70
F. Valuation of Claim 70
G. High Value Goods 71
H. Limitation of Liability in International Carriage 71
I. Objection Against Damage or Partial Loss 71
J. Time Bar 72
K. Prohibition of Certain Special Agreements 73
L. Application to Liabilities in Tort 73
III. Rights of the Carrier 74
A. Rights Related to the Carriage of Illegal or Dangerous Goods 74
B. Right of Retention and Time Bar for Claims by the Carrier 74

§3. THE SHIPPER 74
I. Obligations of the Shipper 74

A. Obligation to Pay Freight 74
B. Obligation to Deliver Documents 75
C. Obligation to Deliver a Shipping Label 75
D. Obligations Related to Dangerous Goods 75
II. Rights of the Shipper 76
A. Right to Dispose of the Goods 76
B. Right to Cancel the Carriage 76

§4. THE CONSIGNEE 77
I. Identifying the Consignee 77
II. Obligations of the Consignee 77
A. Obligation to Pay Freight and Other Costs 77
B. Lack of Obligation to Take Receipt of the Goods and Carrier's Remedy 78
III. Right of the Consignee to Demand Delivery and Claim Compensation 78

Chapter 5. Shipowners' Limitation of Liability 79

§1. GENERAL REMARKS 79
I. Japan as a Party to the Limitation Conventions 79
II. The Limitation Conventions and Japanese Law 79

§2. PARTIES ENTITLED TO LIMIT LIABILITY 80
I. Shipowner, Etc. 80
II. Salvor 80
III. Servants, Etc. 81

§3. LIMITATION OF LIABILITY 81

§4. SHIPS FOR WHICH LIABILITY MAY BE LIMITED 81

§5. CLAIMS SUBJECT TO LIMITATION 82
I. Claims Against the Shipowner, Etc. or Their Servants, Etc. 82
II. Claims Against the Salvor or Their Servants, Etc. 83
III. Claims for Bunker Oil Pollution 83

§6. CLAIMS WHICH CANNOT BE LIMITED 83
I. Claims for Wreck Removal, Etc. 83
II. Claims for Loss of Life or Personal Injury to Passengers 84
III. Claims Based on Salvage or General Average Contributions and Claims by the Servants of the Ship or Salvage Ship and Their Heirs, Etc. 84
IV. Claims for Tanker Oil Pollution 84
V. Claims for Nuclear Damage 84

§7. COUNTERCLAIMS 85

§8. Breaking Limitation 85

§9. Limit of Liability 85
I. Limits of Liability for Property Damage Only 85
II. Limits of Liability for Claims including Personal Injury 86
III. Apportionment of Dividends when Both Types of Claims Are Limited 86

§10. Limitation of Liability Proceedings and the Limitation Fund 86
I. Jurisdiction 87
II. Application and Deposit 87
III. Commencement of Proceedings 88
IV. Filing and Investigation of Claims 88
V. Distribution and Close of Proceedings 89

Chapter 6. Charter Parties 90

§1. Definition and Types of Charter Parties 90

§2. Voyage Charters 90
I. Definition 90
II. Carriage of Goods under a Voyage Charter 90
A. The Parties 90
B. Warranty of Seaworthiness 91
C. Loading and Laytime 91
D. Departure and Voyage 91
E. Disposal of the Goods 92
F. Discharge 92
G. Cancellation of the Charter 92

§3. Bareboat Charters 93
I. Overview 93
II. Effect Against Third Parties 93
III. Responsibility for Repairs 94
IV. Liability to Third Parties 94

§4. Time Charters 94
I. Overview 94
II. Right to Give Instructions and Collision Liability 95
A. Time Charterer's Right to Give Instructions 95
B. Precedents on Time Charterer's Collision Liability 95
C. Discussion 97
III. Responsibility to Pay Costs 97
IV. Application of Provisions Relating to Carriage of Goods and Ship Leases 97

Chapter 7. Transport under a Bill of Lading 99

§1. Definition and Function of a Bill of Lading 99
I. Definition 99
II. Three Functions of a Bill of Lading 99
III. Characteristics of a Bill of Lading 99

§2. Types of Bills of Lading and Similar Transport Documents 100
I. To-Order, Straight, and Bearer Bills of Lading 100
II. Received and Shipped Bills of Lading 102
III. Clean and Foul Bills of Lading 102
IV. Master and House Bills of Lading 103
V. Surrendered and Other Bills of Lading 103
VI. Sea Waybills 103
VII. Electronic Bills of Lading 104
VIII. Charter Parties and Bills of Lading 104

§3. The Contents of a Bill of Lading 105

§4. Carriage under a Bill of Lading 106
I. Overview 106
II. Choice of Governing law and Jurisdiction 106
A. Choice of Governing Law 106
B. Jurisdiction Agreements 107
C. Arbitration Agreements 107
III. Liabilities of the Carrier, Exclusions and Burden of Proof 108
A. First Cause of Claim: Carrier's Liability for Want of Due Care 108
B. Defence for Error in Navigation or Management, or Fire 108
C. Defence for Exercise of Due Care 109
D. Defence for Excepted Causes 109
E. Second Cause of Claim: Unseaworthiness 110
F. Defence for Exercise of Due Diligence 110
IV. Amount of Compensation 110
A. Method of Valuation 110
B. Limits of Liability 111
C. High Value Goods 112
V. Title to Sue, Notice, Time Bar 112
A. Title to Sue 112
B. Notice 112
C. Time Bar 113
VI. Dangerous and Illegal goods 113
VII. Semi-mandatory Provisions and Exceptions 114
A. Semi-mandatory Provisions 114
B. Exceptions 114
VIII. Application to Liabilities in Tort 115

Chapter 8. Pilotage 116

§1. General Remarks 116

§2. Legal Provisions Regarding Pilotage 116

§3. The Relationship Between the Pilot and Captain 117

§4. The Relationship Between the Pilot and the Shipowner 117

Chapter 9. Tug and Tow 118

§1. General Remarks 118

§2. Legal Provisions Regarding Towage 118

§3. Internal Relationships of a Towage Contract 118

§4. External Relationships of a Towage Contract 119

Chapter 10. Salvage and Assistance 121

§1. Definition 121
I. The 1910 Convention 121
II. Commercial Code 121

§2. Statutory Provisions 122
I. Governing Law 122
II. 1910 Salvage Convention 122
III. Japanese Law 123

§3. Salvage Remuneration 125
I. 1910 Salvage Convention 125
A. Outline 125
B. Amount of Remuneration 125
C. Proportion of Remuneration (Distribution) 126
II. Japanese Law 126
A. Outline 126
B. Amount of Remuneration 127
C. Proportion of Remuneration (Distribution) 128

§4. Remuneration of the Crew 128
I. The 1910 Convention 128
II. Japanese Law 129
A. Proportion of Remuneration Between Vessel Owner and Crew (Distribution) 129

B. Proportion (Distribution) Among Crews 129

§5. SPECIAL COMPENSATION 130
I. The 1910 Salvage Convention 130
II. Japanese Law 130
A. General Comments 130
B. Requirements and Effects 130
C. Amount of Special Compensation 130

§6. LIABILITY AND LIMITATION OF LIABILITY OF SALVORS 131
I. Liability of Salvors 131
II. Limitation of Liability of Salvors 131

§7. SALVAGE CONTRACTS 132
I. Governing Law 132
II. 1910 Salvage Convention 133
III. Japanese Law 134

Chapter 11. General Average 135

§1. THE CONCEPT OF GENERAL AVERAGE 135

§2. STATUTORY PROVISIONS 136
I. General 136
II. Requirements 136
III. Effects 137

§3. THE RECEIVING FUND 138

§4. THE CONTRIBUTING FUND 139

§5. SETTLEMENT 141

§6. QUASI GENERAL AVERAGE 142

§7. PARTICULAR AVERAGE 142

Chapter 12. Collisions 143

§1. DEFINITIONS 143
I. 1910 Collision Convention 143
II. Commercial Code 143

§2. STATUTORY PROVISIONS 144
I. Application of Conventions and National Laws 144
II. Damages and Procedure 145
A. Basic Rules on Liability, Japanese Law: Negligence 145

B. Basic Rules on Liability, Japanese Law: Creditors 146
C. Basic Rules on Liability, Japanese Law: Debtors 147
D. Basic Rules on Liability, Japanese Law: Extinctive Prescription of Claims 149
E. Basic Rules on Liability, 1910 Collision Convention 149
F. Evaluation of Fault 149
G. Liability for Damage to Other Vessels Where the Japanese Law Applies 150
H. Liability for Damage to Other Vessels Where 1910 Collision Convention Applies 150
I. Liability for Cargo Claims Where Japanese Law Applies 151
1. Claims Against the Owner of Vessel A 151
2. Claims Against the Owner of Vessel B 152
J. Liability for Cargo Claims Where the 1910 Collision Convention Applies 152
1. Claims Against the Owner of Vessel A 152
2. Claims Against the Owner of Vessel B 153
K. Liability for Personal Injury (Crew) Where Japanese Law Applies 153
L. Liability for Personal Injury (Crew) Where the 1910 Collision Convention Applies 154
M. Procedure, Especially the Determination of Damages 154
III. Limitation of Liability 155
IV. Tugs and Collisions 155

Chapter 13. Marine Pollution 157

§1. Introduction 157

§2. Statutory Provisions 157

§3. Sources of Pollution 158
I. Pollution from Vessels 158
A. Regulations on Discharge of Oil from Vessels 158
B. Regulations on Discharge of Hazardous Liquid Substances from Vessels 159
C. Regulations on Discharge of Wastes from Vessels 159
D. Regulations on Discharge of Harmful Water Ballast from Vessels 160
E. Regulations on the Emission of Exhaust Gas from Vessels 160
F. Prohibition of Disposal of Vessels 162
G. Penalties 162
H. Ordinance for Enforcement of the Vessel Safety Act 162
II. Pollution from Land-Based Sources 162
A. Regulations on Discharged Water 162
B. Total Volume Control in Designated Areas 163
C. Regulations on Underground Seepage Water 164

D. Designated Facilities and Measures to Be Taken in the Event of an Accident 164
E. Oil Storage Facilities and Measures to Be Taken in the Event of an Accident 165
F. Compensation for Damages 165
G. Criminal Penalties 165
H. Regulations of the Waste Management and Public Cleaning Act 166
III. Pollution from Seabed Activities 166
A. Outline 166
B. Regulation of the Discharge of Oil, Hazardous Liquid Substances and Wastes from Offshore Facilities 166
C. Regulations on the Disposal of Oil, Hazardous Liquid Substances and Wastes under the Seabed 167
D. Regulation of Disposal of Offshore Facilities 167
E. Penalties 167
IV. Prevention of Marine Pollution and Marine Disaster 168
A. Duty to Report 168
B. Measures to Be Taken in the Event of Discharge, Etc. 169
C. Authority of the Director-General of the Japan Coast Guard 169
D. Penalties 172
V. Tanker Oil Pollution Damage 173
A. Tanker Owner's Liability for Damages 173
B. Compulsory Conclusion of Security Contract and Insurer's Responsibility 174
C. Limitation of Liability of Tanker Owners and Insurers, Etc. 176
D. Claims Against the International Fund 177
E. Claims Against the Additional Fund 178
VI. Oil Pollution Damage of General Vessel, Etc. 179
A. Liability for Compensation for Damages of the Owner of Tanker or General Vessel 179
B. Compulsory Conclusion of Security Contract and Insurer's Responsibility 180
C. Limitation of Liability of Owners, Etc. of the Vessel and Insurers, Etc. 182
VII. Wreckage Removal Damage 183
A. Liability for Compensation for Damages of Owner of Tanker or General Vessel 183
B. Compulsory Conclusion of Security Contract and Insurer's Responsibility 184
C. Limitation of Liability of Insurer, Etc. 186

Chapter 14. The Arrest of Vessels 187

§1. Sources of Law 187

§2. Vessel Auction Based on a Statutory Lien 187

I. Requirement for an Arrest of Vessels 187
II. Judicial Procedure 187
III. Security and Counter Security 189
IV. Enforcement of the Arrest Order 189
V. Appeal by Debtor 189
A. Outline 189
B. Rescission of Auction Procedure by Provision of Security 190
C. Court's Permission for Navigation 191
D. Settlement with Creditor 191
VI. Remedies for Wrongful Arrest 191
VII. Costs 192

§3. Vessel Auction Based on Vessel Mortgages 192
I. Requirement for an Arrest of Vessels 192
II. Judicial Procedure 193
III. Security and Counter Security 193
IV. Enforcement of the Arrest Order 194
V. Appeal by Debtor 194
A. Outline 194
B. Rescission of Auction Procedure by Provision of Security 195
C. Court's Permission for Navigation 196
D. Settlement with Creditor 196
VI. Remedies for Wrongful Arrest 196
VII. Costs 196

§4. Vessel Auction Based on a Final and Binding Judgment 197
I. Requirement for an Arrest of Vessels 197
II. Judicial Procedure 197
III. Security and Counter Security 198
IV. Enforcement of the Arrest Order 198
V. Appeal by Debtor 199
A. Outline 199
B. Rescission of Auction Procedure by Provision of Security 200
C. Court's Permission for Navigation 200
D. Settlement with Creditor 201
VI. Remedies for Wrongful Arrest 201
VII. Costs 201

§5. Provisional Seizure of Vessels 202
I. Requirement for an Arrest of Vessels 202
II. Judicial Procedure 202
III. Security and Counter Security 203
IV. Enforcement of the Arrest Order 203
V. Appeal by Debtor 204
A. Outline 204
B. Appeal Against an Order of Provisional Seizure 204

C. Revocation of the Execution of an Order of Provisional Seizure 206
VI. Remedies for Wrongful Arrest 207
VII. Costs 207

Chapter 15. Carriage of Passengers by Sea 208

§1. Introduction 208

§2. Statutory Provisions 208
I. Formation of Passenger Carriage Contract 208
II. Carrier's Obligations 209
III. Carrier's Rights 210
IV. Termination of Transportation Contract 211

§3. Liability and Limitation of Liability 211
I. Carrier's Liability in General 211
II. Liability for Injury of the Life or Body of a Passenger 212
III. Carrier's Liability in Respect of Delivered Baggage (Checked Baggage) 212
IV. Carrier's Liability in Respect of Not-delivered Baggage (Unchecked Baggage) 213
V. Limitation of Liability of Owners, etc. of Vessel 213

Part III. Other Transport 215

Chapter 1. Transport by Road and Rail 215

§1. General 215

§2. Source of Law 215
I. The Commercial Code 215
II. International Conventions 216

§3. Liability of the Carrier 216
I. Compensation for Damages 216
II. Amount of Compensation for Damages 217
III. Special Provisions for Expensive Goods 218
IV. Liability of the Carrier in Multimodal Transport 219

§4. The Legal Status of Consignor 220
I. Obligation to Issue an Invoice 220
II. Duty to Give Notice Regarding Dangerous Goods 221
III. Right of Consignor 221

§5. The Legal Status of the Consignee 222

§6. Transport Document 222

§7. Time Bar 223
I. General 223
II. Extinguishment of Liability of Carrier by Lapse of Time 223
III. Extinguishment of Liability of Carrier by Receiving the Goods Without Reservation 223
IV. Extinguishment of Carrier's Claim 224

§8. Successive Carriage 224
I. Definition 224
II. Right and Obligation of Successive Carriers 224
III. Liability of Successive Carriers 224

§9. Cause of Action 225

§10. Passenger Transportation 225
I. Definition 225
II. Liability of Carrier with Regard to Passengers 226
III. Liability of the Carrier with Regard to Checked Baggage 226
IV. Liability of the Carrier with Regard to Unchecked Baggage 227
V. Right to Demand Fares 227
VI. Extinguishment of Liability of Carrier 228
VII. Extinguishment of Carrier's Claim 229

Chapter 2. Air Transportation 230

§1. Introduction 230

§2. Definition 230

§3. Source of Law 231
I. The Commercial Code 231
II. The Montreal Convention 231

§4. Domestic Carriage of Goods by Air 231
I. Introduction 231
II. Liability of the Carrier 231
III. Amount of Compensation for Damages 232
IV. Exemption of Liability 233
V. Provisions for Expensive Goods 233
VI. Extinguishment of Liability 234
VII. Obligation to Issue an Invoice 234
VIII. Right of Consignor 235

§5. International Carriage of Goods by Air 235
I. Introduction 235

II. Air Waybill 236
III. Liability of the Carrier 237
IV. Timely Notice of Complaints (Article 30 of the MC) 239
V. Jurisdiction (Article 33 of the MC) 239
VI. Limitation of Actions (Article 35 of the MC) 240

§6. Domestic Carriage of Passengers by Air 241
I. Introduction 241
II. Liability of the Carrier with Regard to the Passengers 242
III. Amount of Damages with Regard to Passengers 243
IV. Liability of the Carrier with Regard to Checked Baggage 243
V. Liability of the Carrier with Regard to Unchecked Baggage 244
VI. Amount of Compensation for Damages with Regard to Baggage 245
VII. Deposit and Disposal of the Baggage 245

§7. International Carriage of Passengers by Air 246
I. Liability of the Carrier with Regard to Passengers 246
II. Liability of the Carrier with Regard to Baggage 247
III. Liability of the Carrier with Regard to Delay 247
IV. Jurisdiction 248
V. Limitation of Actions 248

Chapter 3. Multimodal Transportation 249

§1. General 249
I. Definition 249
II. Types 249

§2. Source of Law 249

§3. Multimodal Transport B/L 250

§4. Liability of the Carrier 250
I. In Case the Section Is Identified 250
II. In Case the Section Is Not Identified 251
III. Terms and Conditions 251

Selccted Bibliography 253

Index 255

List of Abbreviations

AA	Arbitration Act
ANA	All Nippon Airways Co.
APMPMD	Act on Prevention of Marine Pollution and Maritime Disaster
APR	Act on Port Regulations
B/L	Bill of Lading
BIMCO	Baltic and International Maritime Council
C.A.	Court of Appeal
CIF	Cost Insurance Freight
Civ. A.A.	Civil Aeronautics Act
Com. Code	Commercial Code
CEA	Civil Execution Act
CER	Civil Execution Rule
CCP	Code of Civil Procedure
COGSA	Carriage of Goods by Sea Act
Civ. Code	Civil Code
D.C.	District Court
DEC	deposit entrustment contract
H.R.	Hague Rules
H.V.R.	Hague Visby Rules
JAL	Japan Airlines Co. Ltd.
Limit. Act	Limitation of Shipowners' Liability Act
MLIT	Ministry of Land, Infrastructure, Transport and Tourism
ML	Maritime Law
NVOCC	Non-vessel Owing Common Carrier
NYPE	New York Produce Exchange Time Charter
OPDA	Liability for Oil Pollution Damage Act
PHA	Port and Harbour Act
PHTBA	Port and Harbour Transportation Business Act
PRA	Civil Provisional Remedy Act
PRP	Civil Provisional Remedy Rule

List of Abbreviations

ROA	Railway Operation Act
RRT	Regulations on Railway Transport
SWB	Sea Waybill
SDR	Special Drawing Right
US	United States of America
WPA	Water Pollution Prevention Act

General Introduction

Chapter 1. General Background Information

§1. Geography and Demography

1. Japan is an island country situated beyond the eastern end of the Asian continent. The area extends to 378,000 km^2 with more than 126,167,000 inhabitants (in 2019). The largest city in Japan is Tokyo, its capital, and the cities of Yokohama, Osaka and Nagoya follow.

Japan is fundamentally a country of one-nation which speaks the language Japanese. But nowadays, especially after World War II, many people can speak and write English due to the educational system introduced by the United States of America (US).

§2. Political and Legal System

2. The Constitution of Japan, which entered into force on 3 May 1947, stipulates the fundamental political system of Japan in addition to the principle of renunciation of war (Article 9).

3. The Emperor of Japan, unlike under the old Constitution, has become just a symbol of the state and of the unity of the people. Sovereign power is bestowed upon the people of Japan. Therefore, the Emperor of Japan can only perform the formal state acts provided for in the Constitution and does not have powers related to government (Articles 1, 4, 7).

4. The Diet of Japan is the highest organ of state power and is the sole law-making organ of the state (Article 41). It consists of two Houses, namely the House of Representatives and the House of Councillors (Article 42). Both Houses consist of elected members, representatives of all the people (Article 43).

5. Executive power is vested in the Cabinet (Article 65). The Cabinet, in the exercise of executive power, is collectively responsible to the Diet. The Cabinet consists of the Prime Minister, who is its head, and other ministers of state (Article 66). The Prime Minister is designated from among the members of the Diet (Article 67). The Prime Minister appoints the ministers of state. However, a majority of their number must be chosen from among the members of the Diet (Article 68).

6. Judicial power is vested in the Supreme Court and in inferior courts as are established by law. No extraordinary tribunal can be established, and no organ or agency of the executive may be given final judicial power (Article 76). The Supreme Court is the court of last resort with power to determine the constitutionality of any law, order, regulation or official Act (Article 81).

§3. Commerce and Industry

7. Japan is a country with a free economy and the Japanese economy depends very largely on trade with the US, European Union (EU) and other Asian countries. Until recently, Japan enjoyed rapid economic development; but in the 1990s the Japanese economy was faced with many problems caused by the collapse of the bubble economy from which the country recovered at last from the year 2005. At the same time, the economy also experienced several years of financial recession caused by bankruptcy of Lehman Brothers Holding Inc. in 2008. In 2018, the Japanese economy had a gross domestic product of Japanese Yen (JPY) 548,367 billion (nominal) and a national income of JPY 568,431 billion (nominal), and both figures are plus 0.1% and plus 0.3% compared with those of the preceding year.

8. In 2019, the amounts of exports from Japan and imports to Japan were JPY 76,932 billion and JPY 78,600 billion respectively. The major items of export consisted of machines, automobiles, steel and chemical products and imports consisted of machines, petroleum, clothes, meat and fishery products. Japan exports mainly high-technical products such as computers or precision machines while it imports machinery in addition to oil and food.

§4. Ministry of Land, Infrastructure, Transport and Tourism (MLIT)

9. Following the restructuring national administrative organs done by the Central Government Reform in 2001, the Ministry of Land, Infrastructure, Transport and Tourism (MLIT) was newly established which merged the former Ministry of Transport, the Ministry of Construction, the Hokkaido Development Agency and the National Land Agency.

10. The Ministry of Transport was established in 1945 which succeeded the Ministry of Railways and was in charge of the administrative control and policy making over all kinds of transport in Japan for a long time. In 2008, the Japan Tourism Agency and the Transport Safety Committee were established and both were merged into the MLIT.

11. The MLIT has many sections within it and there are four main bureaus which handle the administrative policy concerning transport business in Japan.

12. The Maritime Bureau handles both international shipping and coastal shipping. Its main policies regarding maritime business are, for example, maritime transport business, shipping building business, safety of ships and conservation of maritime environment, and training and employment of seafarers.

13. The Railway Bureau handles transport business by train in general which includes Shinkansen (bullet train). Its policies regarding railway transportation business includes, conserving safety of train transport, maintaining preventive measures for traffic noise or environmental problems.

14. The Road Transport Bureau handles registration of automobiles, policy making for automobile transport, making prevention for traffic noise or environmental problems.

15. The Civil Aviation Bureau handles both domestic and international air transports and its main policy are to enregister aircrafts, issue certificates for pilots and make preventive measures for noise or environmental problems.

Chapter 2. Statistical Data on Transport in Japan[1]

§1. Maritime Transport

16. In Japan more than 99% of trade cargos are transported by ships; but the number of Japanese ships have been decreasing since 1970 (1970–2018: from 7867 to 4003 ships), which is caused to the increase in the flag of conveniences and foreign seafarers.

17. The main maritime cargos in export by weight in 2018 are steel (22.3%), machines (8.4%), cements (6.6%), cars (3.8%), electric goods (0.9%) and those in import are coals (25.0%), crude oil (19.0%), iron ore (16.3%), and liquid natural gas (12.3%).

18. The gross tonnage of ships entered in main Japanese ports in 2018 are Yokohama (296,656,000 t), Nagoya (237,614,000 t), Kobe (189,183,000 t), Tokyo (182,980,000 t), Chiba (143,206,000 t) and Osaka (112,957,000 t).

The number of passengers by ship who enter into Japanese port have been increasing following the boom of cruising travel, but it decreased drastically from the year of 2019, due to the problems of new corona virus.

§2. Railway Transport

19. The railway transport is the essential means for moving between the grand cities and the network of the Shinkansen (bullet train) covers almost all of the area of Japan. The volume of cargo transport by railway has been decreasing after the years of 1970s, compared with the road transport.

20. The volume of cargos by railway transport in Japan were 87 million ton (1990), 45 million ton (2017) and 42 million ton (2018) and the number of passengers by railway transport were 21,939 million person (1990), 24,973 million person (2017)and 25,269 million person (2018).

§3. Road Transport

21. The road transport is the most voluminous means of transport in both cargo and passenger transport in Japan. Especially after the latter half of the 1970s, following the increase of the internet transactions, the cargo transport by road expanded rapidly.

22. The volume of cargos by road transport in Japan was 6,114 million ton (1990), 4,509 million ton (2017) and 4,453 million ton (2018) and the number of

1. The Tsuneta Yano Memorial Society, *Nihon Kokusei Zu-e* (Graphs and Tables of Japan National Census), 2020/2021.

passengers by road transport was 55,767 million persons (1990), 69,402 million persons (2017) and 70,220 million persons (2018).

§4. Air Transport

23. The volume of transport by air is increasing recently in Japan, due to the development of low cost carrier (LCC) which expands their routes worldwide. In Japan there are many airports, but most of the passengers or cargos utilize the airports in the big cities and many airports in the local cities meet financial problems nowadays.

24. The volume of cargos by air transport in Japan were 691 million ton (domestic 1990), 622 million ton (international 2018), 823 million ton (domestic 1990), and 1,447 million ton (2018). The passengers by air were 65,252 million persons (domestic 1990), 10,318 million persons (international 1990) and 103,903 million persons (domestic 2018), 23,396 million persons (international 2018).

Part I. Transport Laws in Japan

Chapter 1. Laws in General

25. The Civil Code (Civ. Code) of 1896 (Law No. 89, 27 April 1896) has, in its Book III, Chapter 2, provisions concerning the civil contract in general, and these provisions are applied to transport contracts. The articles of obligations in Civ. Code was revised fundamentally in 2019 and those admitting the binding force of standard contract terms were newly prescribed. The Com. Code 1899 (Law No. 48, 9 March 1899) had, in its Book II (Commercial Transactions), Chapter 8 (Transport), provisions on transport (Articles 569–594) which are to apply to all types of transport, and in its Book III (Maritime Commerce) had provisions which are to apply to maritime transactions and maritime incidents, i.e., collision, salvage, General Average (Articles 684–850) including marine insurance (Articles 815–830) and maritime lien and mortgage (Articles 842–850). By the recent Revision of the Commercial Code concerning transport law and maritime law in 2018 (Law No. 29, 2018), contents of the provisions of Commercial Code are modernized fundamentally.

26. Formerly, in Japan, there was a controversy over whether contract clauses should be regarded as a kind of law concerning each contract. For example, it was discussed how we could explain the effect that insurance contractors or assureds were bound by the insurance contract clauses when they might not be well informed about them. Some scholars wished to explain this by the idea that the insurance contract clauses were a kind of law. But today most scholars and judicial cases also admit that insurance contract clauses have binding force due to the general concept of usage. Therefore, insurance contract clauses are not to be regarded as law.[2] Anyway, as mentioned above, the 2019 revision of Civ. Code resolved this problem by explicitly admitting the binding force of contract clauses.

2. Supreme Court Judgment, 24 Dec. 1915, *Minroku*, Vol. 21, 2182.

Chapter 2. Laws on Each Mode of Transport

§1. Maritime Transport

27. The Marine Transportation Act (Act No. 187 of 1949) regulates marine transport business in Japan. The purpose of this Act is to ensure transportation safety and protect the interests of marine transportation users through a fair and reasonable operation of marine transportation business (Article 1). In this Act, marine transportation business denotes the ship-operation business, the ship-leasing business, the ship-broking business and the shipping agency business (Article 2).

28. Book III of the Commercial Code (hereinafter the 'Com. Code') prescribes the Maritime Law, particularly in its Chapter I 'Ships' (section 1 'General', section 2 'Shipowner', section 3 'Bareboat charter', section 4 'Timecharter'), Chapter II 'Captain', and Chapter III 'Carriage of Goods by Sea' (section 1 'Carriage of Goods in General Ship', section 2 'Voyagecharter', section 3 'Bills of Lading etc.', section 4 'Sea Waybills').

The Com. Code of Japan is based essentially on the German ADHGB of 1861 and has been influenced by German Law; but nowadays it introduced in fact the contents of international treaties within it (ex. 1989 Salvage Convention).

29. Japan has ratified many international maritime conventions which include maritime transport treaties and codified several of them into Japanese law as follows:

- as regards the International Carriage of Goods by Sea, Japan has the special law for it named the International Carriage of Goods by Sea Act (Law No. 172, 1957) which was codified by ratifying the 1924 international B/L convention and 1968 and 1979 protocols thereto (Hague-Visby Rules, 'H.V.R.');
- International Convention for the Collision and Salvage 1910;
- the Conventions of Shipowners' Limitation of Liability 1957; the Limitation of Maritime Claims 1976 as amended by 1996 protocol was codified to the Shipowners' Limitation of Liability Act (Law No. 94, 1975) as amended;
- International Convention on Civil Liability for Oil Pollution Damage 1969, as modified by the amending Protocol of 1992 and International Convention on the Establishment of an International Fund for the Compensation for Oil Pollution Damage 1971 as modified by the amending Protocol of 1992 and additional Protocol of 2003 which were codified by the Oil Pollution Damage Act (Law No. 95, 1975) as amended;
- International Convention on Civil Liability for Bunker Oil Pollution Damage 2001 (Bunker Convention) and the Nairobi International Convention on the Removal of Wrecks 2007 which were codified by amending the Oil Pollution Damage Act in 2019;
- Convention on the International Regulations for Preventing Collisions at Sea 1972 as amended (COLREG 1972);
- International Convention for the Prevention of Pollution from Ships 1973 as modified by the amending Protocols of 1978 and 1997 (MARPOL 1978/97); and

- International Convention for the Safety of Life at Sea, London 1974 as amended (SOLAS 1974) and the additional Protocols of 1978 and 1988 and the Agreement 1996.

§2. Railway Transport

30. The main Acts concerning the Railway transportation in Japan are as follows:

- Railway Business Act (Law No. 92, 1986): The purpose of this Act is to secure the safety of transportation and protect the benefit of users of railways as well as to ensure the sound advancement of railway business. The person who intends to operate Railway Business shall obtain a licence of the Minister of Land, Infrastructure, Transport and Tourism (Article 3).
- Railway Operation Act (Law No.65, 1900): This Act prescribes the Railway Operation in several aspects. For example, Chapter 1 Railway Equipment and Facilities, and Railway Transportation, Chapter 2 Railway Staff, Chapter 3 Passengers and Public. In Chapter 1, Article 3 prescribes Fare and Other Transportation Terms, and Article 11-2 prescribes Compensation for Damage.

§3. Road Transport

31. The main Act concerning Road Transport in Japan is as follows:

- Motor Truck Transportation Business Act (Law No. 83, 1989). The purpose of this Act is to ensure the safety of transportation and sound development of the motor truck transportation business. Those who wish to manage the general motor truck transportation business must obtain a permission of the Minister of Land, Infrastructure, Transport and Tourism (Article 3).

§4. Air Transport

32. The Civil Aeronautics Act ((hereinafter the 'Civ. A.A.') (Act No. 231 of 1952) has the purpose to promote the development of civil and general aviation and enhance public welfare by providing for the methods to ensure the safety of aircraft and to prevent problems arising from the navigation of aircraft, and by ensuring transportation safety and improving convenience for users through proper and rational management of business for operating aircraft, in conformity with both provisions of the Convention on International Civil Aviation as well as the Standards, practices and procedures adopted as Annexes hereto.

Any person who operates air transport services shall obtain a licence from the Minister of Land, Infrastructure, Transport and Tourism (Article 100), and any domestic air carrier shall establish conditions of carriage and obtain approval from the Minister of Land, Infrastructure, Transport and Tourism (Article 106).

33. Japan has long been a Contracting Party of the Warsaw Convention 1929 modified by Hague Protocol 1995; in 2000, it ratified the Montreal Convention 1999 (Convention for the Unification of Certain Rules for International Carriage by Air, hereinafter 'MC') concerning international air transport, and therefore as regards the liability of international air carrier the MC shall now be applied directly.

§5. Combined Transport

34. The Consigned Freight Forwarding Business Act (Act No. 82 of 1989) is the Act which has the purpose to aim the sound development of consigned freight forwarding business and ensure the smooth provision of freight forwarding business (Article 1).

Those who wish to manage the first class consigned freight forwarding business shall obtain a registration from the Minister of Land, Infrastructure, Transport and Tourism(Article 3), and shall prepare the consigned forwarding contract and obtain an approval of the Minister of Land, Infrastructure, Transport and Tourism (Article 8).

35. Japan has not ratified the United Nation's International Treaty for Combined Transport 1980, but at the revision of the Com. Code in 2018, two new articles concerning the combined transport, i.e., Article 578 (Liability of Combined Transport Operator) and Article 769 (Combined Transport Document) was prescribed.

Chapter 3. Case Law

36. Compared with the Anglo-American Legal System, Japan has not taken the case law system, and has put the weight rather on the construction of legislated codes.

Therefore, in Japan, we cannot admit in the judicial judgments the binding effect of *ratio decidendi* in the strict meaning. However, we can find the effect of the binding force de facto in the precedents especially sentenced by the Supreme Court.

37. In the field of ML, the Judgment of Supreme Court has a very important role as regards the construction of law. For example, before the revision of the Com. Code in 2018, there was no article for the time charter in it, and the Supreme Court of Japan in 1928 (Supreme Court Decision 28 June 1928, *Minshu*, Vol. 7 No. 8, p. 519) construed the time charter as a contract of the lease of a ship with employment of seamen and introduced the conclusion that the charterer bears the liability of ship's collision for long time since before the World War II while there was many controversies against this conclusion within scholars.

Chapter 4. Private International Law

§1. Introduction

38. The private international law of Japan has been prescribed by the law concerning the application of laws (*Horei*, Law No. 10, 21 June 1898) which is now replaced by the new law under the name of the Act on General Rules for Application of Laws (Law No. 78, 21 June 2006).

According to Article 7 of this Law, the formation and effect of a contract is governed by the law which has been chosen by the parties (paragraph 1). However, if the intention of the parties is not clear, the law of the place which has the most intimate contact will govern (Article 8 paragraph 1).

This Article 7 is construed to permit the autonomy of the concerned parties as regards the choice of law in respect of contract law, and in effect most contracts include a governing law clause which prescribes the law to be applied to the contract. Japanese judicial courts admit the validity of these governing law clauses within contracts in general as they consider that these clauses explicitly indicate the intention of the parties.

§2. Consumer Protection

39. However, recently, there has been an argument in Japan about whether we should admit the principle of autonomy of the parties in full, especially in contracts of adhesion such as contracts. Some scholars insist that the application of the principle of autonomy of the parties should be restricted when the balance of economic power of the parties is not equivalent as in contracts of adhesion. The Act on General Rules for Application of Laws 2006 prescribes that when the parties of a consumer contract have not chosen the applicable law, the law of the habitual residence of the consumer will govern the contract (Article 11, paragraph 2).

Therefore, in the cases of transport contract of passenger, there is a room where the principle of consumer protection will be applied, but as regards the cases of transport of the goods, the principle of autonomy of the parties will be maintained.

Chapter 5. Jurisdiction

§1. Legislation

40. In Japan, the provisions on jurisdiction are contained in Articles 4–22 of the Code of Civil Procedure (CCP) 1996 (Law No. 109, 1996) which has modernized the old law, the CCP 1890 (Law No. 29, 1890).

These articles stipulate as general jurisdictions, the domicile of the defendant (Article 4(2)) or the principal place of office or business of the defendant legal entity (Article 4(4)). In addition, as regards property claims, the place of the performance of obligations (Article 5(1)), the place of the payment of bills or cheques (Article 5(2)), the place of registry of a ship (Article 5(3)), the place where the act for the tort was committed (Article 5(9)), the place where real estate is located (Article 5(12)), etc., are to be selected as jurisdictions.

41. These articles on jurisdiction stipulate originally those within Japan, that is, domestic jurisdictions, and not international jurisdictions. However, according to the prevailing theory of judgments and scholars, international jurisdictions may be inferred from these articles of the CCP. Consequently, the international jurisdiction of Japanese courts will be fundamentally admitted if the domestic jurisdiction prescribed by articles of the CCP exists within Japan. However, in cases when the international jurisdiction of Japanese courts would be contrary to the properness of the judgment, the equality of the parties or the promptness of the judicial process, it might be denied.[3] In 2011, the articles concerning the international jurisdiction of Japanese courts were newly added in the CCP (Articles 3*bis* to 3-12, Law No. 36, 2011) which mostly embody the above-mentioned prevailing theory of international jurisdictions.

§2. Jurisdiction Clause

42. The parties may choose and decide the jurisdiction of the court by contractual agreement so far as the Court of First Instance is concerned (Article 11(1)). The agreement is not valid unless it is made in writing and is made in respect of a suit concerning a particular legal relation (Article 11(2)).

Thus, Article 11 of the CCP admits the validity of the jurisdiction clause and prescribes the necessary conditions for its validity. However, the courts may reject the validity of the jurisdiction clause for the reason of forum non conveniens or other reasons depending on the circumstances of individual cases even if they satisfy the conditions of Article 11.[4]

3. Supreme Court Judgment of 16 Oct. 1981, *Minshu*, Vol. 35, No. 7, 1224. Tokyo District Court Judgment of 20 Jun. 1986, *Hanji*, Vol. 1196, 87.
4. Supreme Court Judgment of 28 Nov. 1975, *Minshu*, Vol. 29, No. 10, 1554.

43. The validity of the international jurisdiction clause of transport contracts, which in most cases stipulates the court of the place of principal office of the transport companies as the exclusive jurisdiction, is also judged by the above-mentioned standard which is now stipulated by Article 3-7 of the CCP. But, unlike transport contracts of goods which are often made between companies and have international elements in the contracts, transport contracts of passengers are usually made between individuals and transport companies; therefore, the validity of the jurisdiction clauses in the transport contracts of passengers will be more severely checked than those of goods (Article 3-7(5)).

Chapter 6. Arbitration

44. Legal disputes about transport contracts are ordinarily settled in the judicial courts.

According to the Judicial Code (Law No. 59, 16 April 1947), Japanese judicial courts are composed of the Supreme Court and inferior courts, which are the Appellate Courts, the District Courts, the Small Claims Courts and the Family Courts (Article 2). With the exception of the exclusive jurisdiction of the Small Claims Courts for those matters in which the claim's amount is less than JPY 1,400,000 (approximately US Dollars (USD) 12,500), disputes concerning insurance contracts are ordinarily brought to the District Courts as first instance (Articles 24 and 33).

45. The parties of transport contract may prefer to settle legal problems by arbitration instead of judicial judgment. Earlier, in Japan, there were not many legal cases which were brought to be settled by arbitration in transportation; but in 2003, the Arbitration Act (Law No. 138, 1 August 2003) was codified and as this Act does not exclude disputes concerning transport contracts, the number of the cases to be settled by arbitration has increased.

As regards the commercial arbitration for transportation cases, the International Chamber of Commerce, Japan or the Japan Shipping Exchange, Inc will accept them as a permanent arbitration courts.

Part II. Maritime Law

Chapter 1. The Vessel

§1. Definition and Legal Nature of Ships

I. The General Concept of a Ship

46. Japanese law does not provide an overarching definition of a 'ship'. Therefore, its legal definition must be determined in accordance with its general meaning in the Japanese language. In this respect, a ship is understood to be a particular structure purposed for and having the capacity to be used for navigation on water.

47. 'Navigation on water' includes underwater navigation. Thus, submarines are considered ships. Hovercrafts are also ships. Airships and seaplanes do not qualify because they are not 'purposed for navigation on water'. Fixed structures such as buoys, floating docks, platforms, and wrecks that have lost their ability to sail altogether fall outside the definition due to their lack of 'capacity to be used for navigation'. The ability to self-navigate is not essential, and barges and hoist ships which cannot sail on their own are not excluded from the concept of a ship (Tokyo C.A. Judgment of 23 August 1972, Osaka C.A. Decision of 10 March 2010). A ship must also possess a specific buoyant structure to withstand the dangers of the seas and be capable of carrying persons or goods. It follows that water skis and rafts which lack that 'certain buoyant structure to withstand the dangers of the seas' are not ships.

48. A ship under construction generally falls outside the category of ships, because it is yet to be 'purposed for and having and capacity to be used for navigation'. However, when construction progresses to the point where the structure may be used for such a purpose, the newbuild becomes classified as a ship. The launching ceremony is considered one of the divides between a newbuild under construction and a ship.

II. Ships under Japanese Law and Regulations

49. Despite the lack of a formal definition, Japanese law makes numerous references to ships. However, the concept of a ship is not uniform among the various statutes, such as the Com. Code, the Act on Preventing Collision at Sea, and the

Limitation of Shipowners' Liability Act (hereinafter 'Limit. Act'). Therefore, the varying concepts of a ship within these statutes must be construed by considering the purpose and wording of the respective laws and regulations, while not departing too far from the general meaning.

50. For example, as explained above, seaplanes do not fall under the general meaning of a ship (*see* paragraph 47). However, the Act on Preventing Collision at Sea specifically includes seaplanes in its definition of ships (§3(5) Act on Preventing Collision at Sea) after the Convention (Rule 3(a) Convention on the International Regulations for Preventing Collisions at Sea 1972). Wrecks, which fall outside the general meaning of ships, do not qualify as ships under the Act on Preventing Collision at Sea, and the rules of navigation stipulated therein (based on the Convention on the International Regulations for Preventing Collisions at Sea, 1972 (COLREGS)) cannot be applied to them. However, wrecks may qualify as ships under the Com. Code if its navigational capacity may be recovered after salvage, meaning that any transfer of its ownership may require registration to take effect against third parties (§687 Com. Code, *see* paragraph 71).

51. The concept of a ship under the Maritime Law section of the Com. Code ('ML') will be discussed further in the following paragraphs.

III. Ships under Maritime Law

52. Ships to which the ML applies are defined as 'ships used in a voyage at sea to conduct a commercial activity (but excluding ship's tenders and other boats steered solely or mainly using oars or paddles)' (§684 Com. Code). In other words, a ship must be (a) intended for 'commercial activity', (b) 'used in a voyage at sea', and (c) must not be a 'ship's tender [or] other boats steered solely or mainly using oars or paddles' for the ML provisions regarding ships to apply.

53. According to this definition, a ship must be used 'to conduct a commercial activity'. However, the Vessel Act provides that the ML 'shall apply *mutatis mutandis* to all ships that are used in a voyage at sea even if they are not used to conduct commercial activity, provided that they are not owned by government or public agencies' (§35(1) Vessel Act). As a result, all non-public ships may qualify as ships under the ML. The determining factor of whether a ship is public or not under the wording of the Vessel Act is ownership. However, the actual criterion is usage rather than ownership. Accordingly, a state-owned ship used exclusively for private purposes by a private corporation is not a public ship and may be subject to the ML. Conversely, a private-owned vessel operated by the state is a public ship and cannot be subject to the ML.

54. A ship must also be 'used in a voyage at sea' for the ML to apply. One issue in this context is whether ships engaging only in voyages through inland waters, i.e., lakes, rivers, and harbours, fall under this category. To answer this, the 2018 revision of the Com. Code instated a new clause stating that the provisions of the ML relating to contracts of carriage by sea and salvage are applied *mutatis mutandis* to 'non-ocean-going vessels' navigating in lakes, harbours, and other non-ocean waters (§§747, 807 Com. Code). As a result, the distinction between ocean-going and non-ocean-going vessels in the context of the ML has lessened in importance.

55. 'Ship's tenders and other boats steered solely or mainly using oars or paddles' were excluded from ships under the ML because it was deemed impractical to include them given their small size and scope of activity. Despite this legislative intent, the size of a ship per se has no direct bearing. A precedent has held that the ML applies even to ships of less than 20 tons gross tonnage (Supreme Court Judgment of 8 December 1937).

IV. The Legal Nature of a Ship

56. The Japanese Civil Code ('Civ. Code') divides tangible properties into real properties and movable properties (§§85, 86 Civ. Code). Ships are categorized as movable properties. However, many provisions concerning the compulsory execution against and auctions of real properties are applied *mutatis mutandis* to similar proceedings against ships (§121 Civil Execution Act (CEA)). In addition, Japan has a registration system for ships of 20 tons or more in gross tonnage (*see* paragraph 60), which is similar to the registration system for real properties.

57. Under Japanese law, a ship does not have the legal capacity to hold rights or obligations. Therefore, there are no actions in rem or other anthropomorphic treatments of ships as seen in the common law jurisdictions.

§2. Nationality, Ship Registry and Ship's ledger

I. Japanese Ships

58. A ship has Japanese nationality in any of the following cases (§1 Vessel Act):

- when owned by the Japanese government or public agency;
- when owned by a Japanese citizen;
- when owned by a commercial corporation incorporated under the laws of Japan and which all its legal representatives and two-thirds or more of its executive officers are Japanese nationals; or
- when owned by a non-commercial corporation incorporated under the laws of Japan and which all its legal representatives are Japanese nationals.

59. The privileges granted to Japanese ships include the ability to 'call at non-opened ports or engage in the carriage of goods or passengers between Japanese ports' (§3 Vessel Act). 'Non-opened ports' are ports where the import/export of cargo and entry/exit of foreign ships is not permitted (§2(1)(xiii) Customs Act) and comprised of all ports and equivalent locations which are not included in the 119 'open ports' at the time of this writing.

60. Ships of Japanese nationality must fly the Japanese flag (§§2, 7 Vessel Act). Japanese ships with a gross tonnage of 20 tons or more (but not ship's tenders and other boats steered solely or mainly using oars or paddles) must have a port of registry within Japan and must be registered with the ship registry at the local legal affairs bureau (§§5, 34 Vessel Act, §§2(i), 4 Ship Registration Order). Such ships must also be registered with the ship's ledger in the regional transport bureau with jurisdiction over the port of registry and obtain a certificate of nationality (§§5, 20 Vessel Act). Non-ocean-going ships are exempted from registration with the ship registry, but not from registration with the ship's ledger (§2(i) Ship Registration Order). Japanese ships with less than 20 tons gross tonnage must be registered with the register of small-sized vessels to be used for voyages (§2, 3 Act on Registration etc. of Small-Sized Vessels). Fishing boats, boats steered solely or mainly using oars and paddles, and moored ships are excluded from this requirement. The registration systems will be discussed later (*see* paragraphs 63 et seq.).

II. Port of Registry

61. The 'port of registry' must be 'in a municipality touching the waters where the ship can sail' and must be located 'in the municipality where the shipowner resides unless the shipowner's domicile is overseas or there are other compelling circumstances' (§3 Vessel Act Enforcement Regulations). These requirements outline the formal concept of a ship's port of registry.

62. Under law, the port of registry functions as the place of registry (*see* paragraph 60) and the place of jurisdiction for (a) 'actions against the shipowner or other users of the ship which arise in connection with a ship or voyage' (§5(vi) CCP), (b) 'actions against seamen involving an economic right' (§5(iii) CCP) and (c) shipowners' limitation of liability proceedings for Japanese ships (§9 Limit. Act). In addition, the captain has a general right to represent the shipowner outside the port of registry regarding any actions necessary for a voyage (§708 Com. Code). In the context of the captain's right of representation, the port of registry is understood to mean the commercial home port of the ship, which may or may not coincide with the formal concept (*see* paragraph 61).

III. Public Notice System for Ships

63. Japan has three systems for public notice regarding Japanese ships. They are the ship registry, the ship's ledger, and the register of small-sized vessels.

A. *Ship Registry*

64. The ship registry provides public notice regarding the status of private rights existing over a ship. Only ocean-going ships with a gross tonnage of 20 tons or more (but not ship's tenders and other boats steered solely or mainly using oars or paddles) may be registered with the ship registry (§2(i) Ship Registration Order). Like the Japanese real estate registry, it is possible to register the preservation, establishment, transfer, alteration, restrictions, or extinction of ownership and mortgages, leaseholds, and appointments or dismissals of a ship's husband when she is co-owned (*see* paragraph 81). A ship under construction may also be registered with the ship registry regarding her future owner or the establishment, transfer, modification, restriction on disposition and extinction of mortgages (§3 Ship Registration Order). The registry records are kept at the local legal affairs bureau or their branch or sub-branch offices that have jurisdiction over the port of registry (§4 Ship Registration Order). Any person is entitled to request the issuance of a document certifying the recorded contents of the ship registry by paying a fee (§33 Ship Registration Order).

B. *Ship's Ledger*

65. The ship's ledger is run by the MLIT for administrative supervision over ships. As with the ship registry, only ships with a gross tonnage of 20 tons or more (but not ship's tenders and other boats steered solely or mainly using oars or paddles) must be registered, although non-ocean-going ships are also subject to registration. The ledger is primarily concerned with the determination of Japanese nationality. As with the ship registry, any person is entitled to request a document certifying the recorded contents of the ship's ledger by paying a fee (§29 Vessel Act Enforcement Regulations).

C. *Register of Small-Sized Vessels*

66. The register of small-sized vessels is a hybrid system for providing public notice regarding the ownership over small ships as well as administrative supervision. Ships with less than 20 tons gross tonnage which are of (a) Japanese flag or (b) non-Japanese flag and engaged solely in coastal navigation but not involved in carriage, are subject to registration in order to sail within Japanese waters (§2, 3 Act on Registration etc. of Small-Sized Vessels). Fishing boats, boats which are steered solely or mainly using oars and paddles, and moored ships are excluded from this requirement.

§3. OWNERSHIP OF A SHIP

I. Acquisition or Loss of Ownership

67. Under Japanese law, a ship is a movable property (*see* paragraph 56). In principle, the acquisition and loss of ownership over a ship operate similar to general movable properties under the Civ. Code (*see* paragraph 70).

68. Ownership of a ship may be acquired or lost in many ways. The following are a few examples which are peculiar to ships:

- capture or seizure as an act of war;
- sinking due to a maritime casualty;
- demolition by scrapping;
- confiscation of a non-Japanese ship which flies the Japanese flag or presents a false certificate of Japanese nationality (§§22, 22-2, 23 Vessel Act);
- exercise of a dissenting co-owner's statutory right to demand a buy-out of their shares in a ship when it is decided that the ship should (a) embark on a new voyage not planned initially or (b) carry out a major repair (§694 Com. Code; *see also* paragraph 79); and
- exercise of the statutory right to buy out another co-owner's shares to prevent the loss of the ship's nationality because of that co-owner's (a) personal loss of nationality or (b) intended transfer of their shares to a non-Japanese entity (§700 Com. Code; *see also* paragraph 79).

69. In practice, the most important causes of the acquisition and loss of ships are (a) transfers of ownership by sale and (b) new buildings, which shall be discussed below.

A. Transfer of Ownership by Sale

70. Under the Civ. Code, the transfer of a property right occurs when the relevant parties manifest their intent (§176 Civ. Code). Furthermore, contracts of sale do not need to be in writing to take effect (§555 Civ. Code). Accordingly, it is not legally required to prepare a written ship sale agreement. However, in practice, a contractual document with detailed provisions is almost always prepared, often relying on standard forms such as the NIPPONSALE forms by the Japan Shipping Exchange or the SALEFORM by the Norwegian Shipbrokers' Association.

71. When ownership is transferred during a voyage, the profits and losses arising from that voyage are credited to the transferee (§688 Com. Code). This rule is voluntary and only applies in the absence of a contractual provision.

72. If a ship is subject to registration with the ship registry (*see* paragraph 60), the transfer does not take effect against a third party unless it is entered into both the ship registry and the certificate of nationality (§687 Com. Code). If a ship is not subject to registration, the transfer becomes effective against third parties solely by her delivery, as per the general rule for movables (§178 Civ. Code). Generally, ships under construction generally do not qualify as ships (*see* paragraph 48) and may be transferred without registration.

73. Japanese law provides for the good faith acquisition of movables (§192 Civ. Code), whereby a person who peacefully and openly obtains possession of a movable by a transactional act will immediately acquire full rights thereon, provided the acquirer was in good faith and faultless in believing that the previous possessor had legitimate rights. Precedent holds that good faith acquisition does not apply to ships subject to registration with the ship registry (Supreme Court Judgment of 1 December 1903). Good faith acquisition does apply to ships which are not subject to registration.

74. The minister of the MLIT must be given notice when ownership of a Japanese ship of 2,000 gross tons or more that meet certain requirements (such as liquefied natural gas carriers and roll-on roll-off ships) is transferred outside Japan (§44-2 Marine Transportation Act, §43 Marine Transportation Act Enforcement Regulations).

B. Newbuilding of a Ship

75. When a shipyard receives an order and builds a ship using its own materials, the contract is academically categorized as a 'contract for the supply of a product', which is a hybrid between a sale contract (§555 et seq. Civ. Code) and a contract for work (§632 et seq. Civ. Code). As with the transfer of ownership, there is no legal requirement for shipbuilding contracts to be in writing. In practice, however, a contract is almost invariably prepared by modifying in-house forms often derived from the standard form of the Shipbuilders' Association of Japan (the so-called SAJ form), where the rights and obligations of the parties are specified in detail.

II. The Shipowner

76. In general terms, a 'shipowner' is simply an entity who owns a ship. In the narrower meaning, they are entities who own and use a ship for voyages at sea to conduct commercial activities. It is this narrower meaning that is relevant in the context of the ML. The shipowner is the principal actor in a maritime commercial endeavour, who owes a special vicarious liability for the actions of seamen onboard a ship (*see* paragraph 77) and who is entitled to a special limitation of liability (*see* paragraphs 213 et seq.).

77. When the captain or other seamen of a ship cause damage or loss to third parties by intention or negligence in the course of their duties, the shipowner is liable to compensate such damage or loss (§690 Com. Code). 'Seamen' in this context is understood to mean persons who the shipowner employs to continuously perform duties onboard a particular ship. Judicial precedents have held that seamen in this context include a non-mariner engaged in seafood processing onboard the ship (Kobe D.C. Judgment of 20 November 1964) and a pilot (Tokyo D.C. Judgment of 19 September 2013). The requirement for the loss or damage to have been caused 'in the course of their duties' is satisfied if the relevant act was (a) committed while performing work which was reasonably connected to the ship and (b) objectively fell within the scope of the specific seaman's onboard duties (Kobe D.C. Judgment of 20 November 1964). Because this is a vicarious liability, this provision requires that the seaman be at fault for a tortious act or to have played an assisting role in a shipowner's breach of contract. The shipowner's responsibility under this provision is strict liability. They may not be exempted by reason of their having exercised due care in the selection and supervision of the seamen.

III. Co-ownership of a Ship

78. Most ships are owned by a single entity, but ships may also be co-owned. In general terms, a 'co-owner of a ship' is simply an entity with joint ownership over a ship. In the narrower meaning, they are understood to be an entity that jointly owns and uses a ship for voyages at sea to conduct commercial activities. As was the case with the shipowner, it is this narrower meaning that is relevant in the context of the ML.

79. The internal relationship between the co-owners of a ship is determined by an agreement between the parties. In the absence of an agreement, matters relating to the use of a ship must be determined by a majority of the co-owners in accordance with the value of their shares, except for a disposal of the ship in which case the consent of all co-owners is required (§692 Com. Code). 'Disposal' includes actions that physically alter the ship, such as destruction and modification, and actions which change the ship's legal status, such as sale or mortgage. A dissenting co-owner may demand the other co-owners to buy out their shares if it is decided that (a) the ship will embark on a new voyage not originally planned, or (b) the ship will undergo significant repairs (§694 Com. Code). Costs for fuel, outfitting and other matters associated with the use of the ship are also borne by the ship's co-owners in proportion to the value of their shares (§693 Com. Code). In principle, the consent of the other co-owners is not required for the transfer of a share (§696 Com. Code). However, if a co-owner's loss of nationality or intended transfer of their shares to a third party would result in the ship losing her nationality, the other co-owners have a statutory right to buy out that co-owner's shares (§700 Com. Code).

80. Externally, the ship's co-owners are liable to third parties for claims arising from the use of the ship in proportion to the value of their shares (§695 Com. Code). Claims may be in either tort or contract. The co-owners are also entitled to limit their liabilities arising from the ship (*see* paragraph 220).

81. The co-owners of a ship must appoint a ship's husband (§697(1) Com. Code). The ship's husband represents the co-owners regarding the use of the ship. The co-owners may restrict the powers of a ship's husband, but such restrictions do not have effect against a third party in good faith. Powers to lease the ship, grant a mortgage over the ship, buy insurance, embark the ship on a new voyage, make major repairs on the ship or borrow monies are not included in the general powers of a ship's husband, and must be granted by special agreement (§698 Com. Code). The appointment of a ship's husband and the extinction of their power of representation must be entered into the ship registry (§697(3) Com. Code). The ship's husband is obligated to keep books with all information concerning the use of the ship. They must also settle the voyage accounts and request approval from the co-owners at regular intervals (§699 Com. Code).

Chapter 2. Maritime Liens, Mortgages and Other Security Interests

§1. Maritime Liens

I. General Remarks

82. Under Japanese law, a maritime lien is a security interest in a ship and her equipment, securing certain types of claims arising in relation to that ship. By way of real subrogation, the lien also extends to rents (bareboat charter hire) and claims for damages or insurance money in the event of loss or damage to the ship or equipment.

83. Japan has yet to ratify the International Convention for the Unification of Certain Rules of Law Relating to Maritime Liens and Mortgages, 1926 or the International Convention on Maritime Liens and Mortgages, 1993. Therefore, maritime liens under Japanese law are governed exclusively by domestic law.

84. The claims giving rise to the Maritime Lien are set out in the Com. Code (§842 Com. Code), the Limit. Act (§95 Limit. Act) and the Liability for Oil Pollution Damage Act ('OPDA') (§55 OPDA). The order of priority between maritime liens and other security interests is prescribed by statute.

II. Law Governing Maritime Liens

85. The Japanese courts do not automatically apply Japanese substantive law to maritime liens. Instead, the applicable governing law is determined according to the conflict-of-laws' provisions in the Act on General Rules for Application of Laws. Under the act, 'rights in rem are governed by the law of the place where the subject property is located', while 'the acquisition and loss of such rights are governed by the law of the place where the subject property was located at the time when the underlying cause is completed' (§13 Act on General Rules for Application for Laws).

86. The courts are uniform in applying Japanese law as 'the law of the place where the subject property is located' to determine the effects of a maritime lien executed in Japan. However, there is a dispute regarding the governing law of its formation, i.e., 'acquisition'. The first question is whether the 'place where the subject property is located at the time when the underlying cause is completed' should be determined according to the ship's geographical position, her flag state or *lex fori*. The second question is whether the governing law of the underlying claim should also be considered when considering the formation of security rights. Court precedents are not uniform regarding these questions, and there is no Supreme Court judgment. As such, the question of what law should govern the formation of maritime liens is still open to interpretation.

87. Many recent precedents cumulatively apply (a) the law governing the secured claim and (b) the law governing the geographical location of the ship at the time when the underlying cause was perfected. According to these precedents, a bunker lien would have to satisfy both the law governing the supply contract and the law of the bunkering port to be formed validly (Tokyo C.A. Decision of 30 June 2017, Kobe D.C. Decision of 21 January 2016, Fukuoka D.C. Kokura Branch Decision of 4 December 2015 and Mito D.C. Decision of 20 March 2014).

88. However, there are other precedents which have (a) cumulatively applied the law governing the secured claim and *lex fori* (Fukuoka D.C. Decision of 8 September 2008, Yokohama D.C. Decision of 4 June 2007), (b) cumulatively applied the law governing the secured claim and the law of the flag state (Osaka D.C. Decision of 31 March 2008), (c) applied only the law of the secured claim (Fukuoka D.C. Kokura Branch Decision of 18 July 2008) or (d) applied only *lex fori* (Tokyo D.C. Decision of 15 December 1992, Tokyo D.C. Decision of 19 August 1991).

89. Since Japanese law allows for a wide range of causes that give rise to maritime liens (*see* paragraphs 90 et seq.), it is usually the non-Japanese laws that limit their formation. Since Japanese courts are wary of allowing wrongful arrests (*see* paragraph 737), a claimant asserting a maritime lien may be requested to explain that the lien would form according to most if not all the positions described above.

III. Claims Giving Rise to Maritime Liens

A. Maritime Liens Arising under the Commercial Code

90. The following claims give rise to maritime liens under the Com. Code.

91. First, there are claims for personal injury arising in direct relation to the operation of the ship (§842(i) Com. Code). Claims for injuries on a ship that has been in dock for an extended period, injuries caused by disputes between passengers and visitors who just happened to be on the ship, or injuries to stevedores engaged in cargo work do not fall under this category because they lack a 'direct relation to the operation of the ship'. The personal injury may occur outside the ship as long as it arose directly in relation to her operation (e.g., injuries onboard the opposing ship in a collision).

92. Second, there are claims for salvage charges and general average contributions to be borne by a ship (§842(ii) Com. Code). 'Salvage' in this context may be either contractual or voluntary.

93. Third, there are claims arising in connection with port entry, port usage or other navigation which may be collected under national tax procedures and claims for pilotage charges and towage (§842(iii) Com. Code). Examples of claims that may be collected under national tax procedures include tonnage tax, port entry tax, and lighthouse tax.

94. Fourth, there are claims for necessaries to continue a voyage (§842(iv) Com. Code). 'Necessaries' includes repairs and replacements, provisions and equipment, and bunker supplies. 'Voyage' in this context refers to the entire voyage from the time the ship leaves its commercial home port to the time it returns there, and not to individual voyages between each port of call (Supreme Court Judgment of 24 March 1983).

95. Fifth, there are claims held by the ship's captain or other seaman arising from an employment contract (§842(v) Com. Code). This includes repatriation expenses, medical treatment and nursing expenses, and wages.

B. Maritime Lien Arising under Limitation of Shipowners' Liability Act

96. The following claim gives rise to a maritime lien under the Limit. Act:

- Claims for property damage that are subject to limitation (§95 Limit. Act). Claims covered under this provision are those relating to loss or damage to property other than the ship in question, which loss occurred either onboard the ship or in direct connection with the operation of the ship (§3(1) (i) Limit. Act).

C. Maritime Lien Arising under the Liability for Oil Pollution Damage Act

97. The following claims give rise to maritime liens under the OPDA:

- claims for oil pollution caused by fuel oil from tankers and general ships, which are subject to limitation under the Limit. Act (§40 OPDA, §95 Limit. Act); and
- claims for tanker oil pollution which are subject to limitation under the OPDA (§55(1) OPDA).

IV. Order of Priority Between Maritime Liens and Other Security Interests

A. Priority Among Maritime Liens

98. The order of priority among maritime liens arising under the Com. Code follows the order in which they are listed under statute (*see* paragraphs 91–95). However, liens arising for salvage charges take priority over all maritime liens that arose prior to their occurrence (§843 Com. Code).

99. Maritime liens under the Limit. Act and the OPDA have second priority after those arising under the Com. Code (§95(2) Limit. Act, §55(2) OPDA).

100. If there are multiple maritime liens with the same rank of priority, the respective creditors are entitled to payment in proportion to the amount of their claim. However, if there are multiple maritime liens among those arising from (a) salvage charges and general average contributions (§842(ii) Com. Code), (b) taxes/pilotage/towage (§842(iii) Com. Code) or (c) necessaries to continue the voyage (§842(iv) Com. Code), then those arising more recently have priority (§843(2) Com. Code).

B. Priority Among Other Security Interests

101. Maritime liens have priority over general liens arising under the Civ. Code (§844 Com. Code, §95(3) Limit. Act, §55(3) OPDA). General liens over movables may arise for costs of preservation (§320 Civ. Code) and may be established by reason of ship repairs (Supreme Court Judgment of 5 February 2002).

102. When there is a conflict between a maritime lien and a ship mortgage, the maritime lien takes precedence (§848(1) Com. Code).

103. The Civ. Code also grants a right of retention over goods when the claimant has possession of a good and the claim arose in relation to that good (§295 Civ. Code). This right of retention entitles the claimant to retain possession of the goods until payment. For example, a repair dock may have a right of retention over a repaired ship. If there is a conflict between a maritime lien and a right of retention over a ship, the maritime lien takes precedence in theory. This is because the latter does not grant the right to auction the ship by judicial sale and collect from the proceeds. However, the right of retention survives a judicial sale, and the buyer needs to reimburse the holder of the right of retention to receive delivery (§§59(4), 121, 189 CEA). Because of this, it may be said that the right of retention has de facto priority over maritime liens.

V. Object of a Maritime Lien

104. The object of a maritime lien is a ship and her equipment (§842 Com. Code). Although ships under construction are not ships (*see* paragraph 48), the Com. Code provisions for maritime liens are applied *mutatis mutandis* (§850 Com. Code). A ship need not be the property of the debtor of the claim giving rise to the lien, and a lien arising in relation to the use of a ship by a lessee (bareboat charterer) or time charterer has effect against the shipowner (§§703(2), 707 Com. Code). This applies not only to maritime liens but also to general liens against ships. Thus, a shipyard or dock may have a general lien on a ship to secure the repair costs, even if the work was ordered by the bareboat charterer (Supreme Court Judgment of 5 February 2002).

VI. Extinguishment of a Maritime Lien

105. A maritime lien is extinguished one year after its formation (§846 Com. Code, §95(3) Limit. Act, §55(3) OPDA). This is a statutory limitation period and cannot be interrupted, suspended, or extended. The commencement of the limitation period is not delayed or otherwise affected by whether the claimant knew of the right or whether the right could have been exercised.

106. If there is a maritime lien over a ship subject to registration with the ship registry (*see* paragraph 60) and ownership is subsequently transferred, the transferee must register the transfer and give public notice so that the lien holder may file their claim within a certain period not less than one month. If no claim is filed within that period, the maritime lien is extinguished (§845 Com. Code).

107. A maritime lien survives the transfer of the ship only to the extent described in the previous paragraph. Maritime liens over ships that are not subject to registration with the ship registry are extinguished upon the transfer of ownership (§333 Civ. Code).

108. The extinguishment of a maritime lien does not affect the underlying claim. Further, general liens under the Civ. Code, such as those which may arise by reason of repairs to a ship (§320 Civ. Code), are also unaffected by the extinguishment of a maritime lien. General liens do not have a statutory limitation period and are only extinguished with the underlying claim. Ordinary claims that may give rise to general liens under the Civ. Code are subject to a statutory limitation period of either (a) five years from the time when the claimant knew that they could exercise the claim, or (b) ten years from the time when the claim could have been exercised, whichever the shorter (§166(1) Civ. Code). As such, general liens can last a long time after maritime liens are extinguished by the one-year limitation period.

§2. Ship Mortgage

I. General Remarks

109. A ship mortgage is a mortgage on a ship and her equipment. Ship mortgages are established by a contract between the shipowner and a creditor (§847 Com. Code). The statutory provisions relating to real estate mortgages apply *mutatis mutandis* to ship mortgages, and thus its effect, priority and extinguishment are governed by the general provisions of the Civ. Code (§847(3) Com. Code). The mortgagee is entitled to receive satisfaction of their claim from the object of the mortgage according to their order of priority (§369(1) Civ. Code).

II. Object of a Ship Mortgage

110. The object of a ship mortgage is a ship and her equipment. The ship to be mortgaged must be registered with the ship registry (§847 Com. Code; *see also* paragraph 60). Ships not subject to registration cannot be mortgaged. Although ships under construction are not ships (*see* paragraph 48), the ship mortgage provisions are applied *mutatis mutandis*, allowing them to be mortgaged in the same manner (§850 Com. Code).

111. There is an ongoing dispute over whether a ship mortgage covers equipment added to the ship after the mortgage was created. The mortgage applies regardless of whether the shipowner owns the equipment is owned by the shipowner or not, and regardless of whether the equipment has been attached to and has become an integral part of the ship.

112. If the mortgaged ship is lost or damaged by a third party, the mortgagee may subrogate the shipowner's claim against the third party or the insurance claim. The mortgagee may also subrogate the shipowner's right to receive hire for a bareboat charter. In such cases, the mortgagee receives satisfaction by seizing the claim before it is paid to the shipowner (§§304, 372 Civ. Code).

III. Asserting a Ship Mortgage Against Third Parties

113. For a ship mortgage to take effect against a third party, it must be entered into the ship registry (§847(3) Com. Code, §177 Civ. Code). The existence of a mortgage can be confirmed by applying for a document certifying the recorded contents of the ship registry (*see* paragraph 64).

IV. Order of Priority Between Ship Mortgages and Other Security Interests or Bareboat Charters

114. The order of priority between multiple ship mortgages is determined according to the order in which they were entered into the ship registry (§847(3) Com. Code, §373 Civ. Code). This order of priority may be changed by agreement between the mortgagees subject to the consent of any interested parties, but any such change must be registered to take effect (§847(3) Com. Code, §374 Civ. Code).

115. Ship mortgages rank behind maritime liens in order of priority, and rank *pari passu* with the top rank of general liens under the Civ. Code (§848 Com. Code).

116. If there is a conflict between a ship mortgage and a right of retention over a ship, the right of retention will effectively prevail, as with the case of maritime liens (*see* paragraph 103).

117. In principle, the order of priority between a ship lease (bareboat charter) and a ship mortgage depends on the order of registration (§701 Com. Code). Accordingly, a bareboat charter registered before the mortgage will survive the execution of the mortgage, but one registered after the mortgage will be extinguished. However, short leases not exceeding six months have effect against a ship mortgagee even if they were registered after the mortgage or never registered at all (§847(3) Com. Code, §395 Civ. Code).

V. Special Ship Mortgages

118. A 'blanket mortgage' occurs when multiple items are mortgaged to secure a claim (§§392, 393 Civ. Code). A 'revolving mortgage' secures a particular category of claim within a specific limit but with an undetermined amount (§398-2 Civ. Code). The four allowed categories of claim for revolving mortgages are (1) claims arising from continuous transactions between the claimant and debtor, (2) claims arising from a specific type of transaction between the claimant and debtor (such as purchase and sale, supply of goods, banking and loan, and guarantees), (3) claims arising from specific causes between the claimant and debtor (such as claims for pollution damage from leaked chemicals from a factory) and (4) claims for promissory notes, cheques and electronic instruments issued by the debtor and transferred to the claimant.

119. The two methods may be combined by mortgaging multiple items to secure a particular category of claim within a specific limit. This is accomplished as either a 'pure blanket revolving mortgage' or a 'cumulative revolving mortgage'. A pure blanket revolving mortgage occurs when multiple revolving mortgages are created on multiple items to secure a single category of claim within a specific limit, and the mortgages are registered as blanket mortgages at the time of formation (§398-16 Civ. Code). In this case, the mortgagee may only collect up to the total limit of the revolving mortgage from all the mortgaged items combined, and thus the mortgages are not cumulative. A cumulative revolving mortgage occurs when (a) multiple revolving mortgages are created on multiple items to secure multiple categories of claims, or (b) multiple revolving mortgages are created on multiple items to secure the same category of claims without registering the mortgages as blanket mortgages. In cumulative revolving mortgages, a mortgagee may collect up to the limit of the revolving mortgage from each of the mortgaged items (§398-18 Civ. Code).

120. Ordinary ship mortgages are used for regular term loans, instalment loans and margin loans where the secured claim is pre-defined. However, a revolving mortgage may be useful when a bank provides the shipowner with a line of credit where multiple loans may be made within a specific limit and the amount of the payable balance may fluctuate.

121. In a standard mortgage, the mortgagee may assert preferential repayment for interest and delayed damages only up to the final two years (§375 Civ. Code). However, in a revolving mortgage, however, such limit does not automatically apply if the principal amount and any interest or delayed damages, etc. remain within the secured limit. Further, it is impossible to effect variable interest rates with standard mortgages, because the registry only allows the registration of fixed interest rates. In contrast, it is not necessary to register interest rates in a revolving mortgage, making it possible to collect variable interest so long as the combined principal and interest remain within the limit.

§3. Enforcement of Maritime Liens and Ship Mortgages

122. A creditor who holds a maritime lien or a ship mortgage over a ship may execute against the ship by reason of their security interest and receive priority payment from the proceeds of a judicial sale (§189 CEA).

123. Execution against a ship is not allowed against a ship underway on a voyage and not at anchor (§689 Com. Code). 'Voyage' in this context refers to individual voyages between each port of call (contrast with paragraph 94).

124. Only the enforcement of security interests against ships of 20 tons or more gross tonnage (excluding ship's tenders and other boats steered by oars and paddles) are subject to the provisions regarding execution against ships (§§112, 189 CEA). Ships not meeting this criterion and ships under construction would be executed against according to the provisions regarding general movables. Detailed procedures regarding execution against ships are discussed in Chapter 15.

§4. Carrier's Right of Retention Against the Goods

125. A carrier has the right to retain consigned goods under their custody until they receive payment of freight, ancillary costs, monies paid on the shipper or consignee's behalf, and any other amounts due in respect of the goods for general average contributions or salvage (§§574, 741 Com. Code, §15 Carriage of Goods by Sea Act (COGSA)). Only those goods in relation to which the secured claims arose may be retained, but they need not be owned by the shipper (or consignee or other person liable to pay freight, etc.). The carrier can also auction the goods in a judicial sale to recover the above-mentioned claims. Although the right to judicial auction survives delivery of the goods to the consignee, it may no longer be exercised after the goods are transferred to a third party (§742 Com. Code, §15 COGSA).

Chapter 3. Ship's Captain and Other Seamen

§1. The Captain

I. Definition and Qualifications of a Ship's Captain

126. Japanese law does not define the 'captain'. As such, its legal meaning must be sought in the general meaning under the Japanese language, as was the case with ships (*see* paragraph 46). It is generally understood that the captain is a member of the ship's crew who commands the ship and who has certain statutory powers to represent the shipowner. The ship's captain must hold a maritime licence appropriate to the purpose, navigational area, and size of the commanded ship (§§5, 18 Seaman and Small Craft Operator Act).

II. Regulations under the Seamen's Act

127. The Seamen's Act is primarily concerned with labour conditions and labour protection regulations. However, it also contains administrative provisions for safe navigation, the captain's authority, and onboard rules of conduct. The Seamen's Act applies to seamen onboard (a) Japanese ships, (b) ships owned by Japanese corporations which cannot own Japanese ships (*see* paragraph 58), (c) ships leased (bareboat chartered) by any Japanese corporation or any entity who may own Japanese ships (*see* paragraph 58), (d) ships contracted to sail from Japanese ports to foreign ports, (e) ships manned by the Japanese government, and (f) ships that sail only between domestic ports (§1 Seamen's Act, §1 Seamen's Act Enforcement Regulations).

A. Authority of the Captain

128. The captain has the authority to command and supervise seamen and give orders to persons onboard to the extent necessary to perform their duties (§7 Seamen's Act).

129. In addition, the captain has the authority to discipline seamen who do not observe the onboard rules of conduct, by prohibiting them from going ashore and by issuing warnings (§§22, 23 Seamen's Act). Onboard rules of conduct include the following (§21 Seamen's Act):

- compliance with orders given by their superiors;
- prohibition against neglecting and obstructing duty;
- observation of designated embarkation times;
- prohibition against disembarking without permission;
- prohibition against the unauthorized use of equipment;
- prohibition against misusing food and fresh water;
- prohibition against the unauthorized use of electricity and fire;

- observation of prohibited smoking areas; and
- prohibition against any other acts that disturb order onboard the ship.

130. The captain is also granted certain compulsory powers, such as (a) the right to take custody of and disposing weapons and other dangerous objects possessed by sailors and other persons onboard (§25 Seamen's Act), (b) the right to take preventative measures against persons attempting to commit dangerous acts against the ship or persons onboard, and (c) the right to forcibly remove sailors who refuse to disembark from the ship after being notified of the termination of their employment contracts (§§26, 27, 28 Seamen's Act). Abuse of these compulsory powers is punishable by imprisonment of up to two years (§122 Seamen's Act).

131. The captain also performs the duties of a judicial police officer for crimes onboard the ship (§190 Code of Criminal Procedure, §6 Act for Emergency Measures on the Appointment of Judicial Police Officers Etc. Imperial Edict No. 528 of 1923). In addition, they are responsible for reporting births and deaths taking place onboard the ship (§§55, 93 Family Register Act).

B. Duties of the Captain

132. The Seamen's Act also imposes public law obligations on the captain to ensure onboard safety. These include the following:

- The obligation to carry out pre-departure inspections of the ship (§8 Seamen's Act). Violation is punishable by a maximum fine of JPY 300,000 (§126 Seamen's Act).
- The obligation to depart without delay and sail to the port of arrival without altering the scheduled course unless necessary (§9 Seamen's Act). Violation is punishable by a maximum fine of JPY 300,000 (§126 Seamen's Act).
- The obligation to take command on deck when entering or leaving a port or when passing through a narrow waterway (§10 Seamen's Act). Violation is punishable by a maximum fine of JPY 300,000 (§126 Seamen's Act).
- The obligation to remain onboard the ship from cargo loading or passenger embarkment up to discharge or disembarkation unless a substitute is left in charge or there are compelling circumstances (§11 Seamen's Act). Violation is punishable by a maximum fine of JPY 300,000 (§126 Seamen's Act).
- The obligation to take all necessary measures to protect life and rescue the ship and her cargo against imminent danger (§12 Seamen's Act). Violation is punishable by a maximum of five years imprisonment (§123 Seamen's Act).
- The obligation to carry out rescue operations and declare the ship's name, shipowner, port of registry, last departed port and destination port in the event of a ship collision, unless the ship under command faces imminent danger (§13 Seamen's Act). Violation of the duty to perform rescue operations is punishable by a maximum of three years imprisonment or a maximum fine of JPY 1 million, and failure to declare the required information is punishable by a maximum fine of JPY 300,000 (§§124, 126 Seamen's Act).

- The obligation to take necessary measures to rescue lives onboard other ships and aeroplanes in distress unless the ship under their command faces imminent danger (§14 Seamen's Act). Violation is punishable by a maximum of two years imprisonment or a maximum fine of JPY 500,000 (§125 Seamen's Act).
- The obligation to report extreme weather conditions and other navigational hazards to the coast guard or other equivalent agency if the ship has radio equipment (§14-2 Seamen's Act).
- The obligation to prepare and post a muster list if the ship does not fall under certain exclusions (§14-3 Seamen's Act). Violation is punishable by a maximum fine of JPY 300,000 (§126 Seamen's Act).
- The obligation to conduct training drills and to inform any passengers of evacuation procedures, etc. (§§14-3(2), 14-4 Seamen's Act, §3-10 Seamen's Act Enforcement Regulations).
- The obligation to implement duty hours and a patrol system (§14-4 Seamen's Act, §§3-5, 3-6 Seamen's Act Enforcement Regulations).
- The obligation to maintain the ship's watertightness (§14-4 Seamen's Act, §3-7 Seamen's Act Enforcement Regulations).
- The obligation to inspect and maintain emergency passageways and life-saving equipment (§3-9(1) Seamen's Act Enforcement Regulations).
- The obligation to implement onboard education for the seamen regarding the use of rescue, firefighting, and life-saving equipment as well as survival on the seas (§§3-11–3-12, 11.2.6, 3-13 Seamen's Act Enforcement Regulations).
- The obligation to operate multiple steering equipment appropriately in hazardous waters if available on the ship (§3-14 Seamen's Act Enforcement Regulations).
- The obligation to exercise care when using automatic steering equipment (§3-15 Seamen's Act Enforcement Regulations).
- The obligation to take proper custody of goods left onboard by a person deceased or gone missing in the ship (§16 Seamen's Act). Violation is punishable by a maximum fine of JPY 300,000 (§126 Seamen's Act).
- The obligation to perform repatriation of overseas citizens when ordered by the Japanese consulate in a foreign nation (§17 Seamen's Act). Violation is punishable by a maximum fine of JPY 300,000 (§126 Seamen's Act).
- The obligation to maintain the ship's documents such as her certificate of nationality, crew list, logbook, and passenger list (§18 Seamen's Act). Failure to keep such documents and enter required information or entering false information is punishable by a maximum fine of JPY 300,000 (§126 Seamen's Act). In addition, the Com. Code also requires the captain to keep an inventory list (§710 Com. Code).
- The obligation to report marine casualties, salvage and rescue operations, distressed ships, dead and missing persons onboard, alterations in the scheduled course, detention, capture, or other significant event regarding the ship to the minister of the MLIT (§19 Seamen's Act). Failure to report or false reporting is punishable by a maximum fine of JPY 300,000 (§126 Seamen's Act).

III. The Legal Status of a Ship's Captain under Maritime Law

A. *The Appointment of a Captain*

133. Generally, the shipowner appoints the captain. However, in a ship lease (bareboat charter), the lessee (bareboat charterer) appoints the captain (§703 Com. Code). In a ship co-ownership, the ship's husband appoints the captain on behalf of the co-owners (§698(1) Com. Code).

B. *The Substitute Captain and Acting Captain*

134. When the captain becomes unable to command the ship due to unavoidable circumstances, they may appoint a substitute captain to perform their duties. When this happens, the captain is liable to their employer only regarding the substitute captain's appointment and not for their supervision (§709 Com. Code). If the captain becomes deceased, leaves the ship, or otherwise becomes unable to take command without appointing a substitute captain, the sailors engaged in the ship's operation must perform the captain's duties by their order of rank, as acting captains (§20 Seamen's Act).

C. *The Captain's Authority of Representation*

135. Outside the port of registry, the captain has the authority to take all actions in and out of court on behalf of the shipowner to the extent necessary for the voyage, except to mortgage the ship or borrow monies (§708(1) Com. Code). 'Port of registry' in this context is the commercial home port (*see* paragraph 61). 'Voyage' refers to the entire period from the ship's departure from the commercial home port to the ship's return, and not to individual voyages between the various ports of call (Supreme Court Judgment of 27 February 1912). Actions 'necessary for the voyage' include fitting out and repairing the ship, hiring, and releasing seamen, purchasing consumables, and contracting for rescue and salvage. Since the provision is not mandatory, the above-mentioned powers may be contracted out. A captain acting beyond their power of representation is liable to the shipowner for breach of contract. Restrictions on the captain's power of representation have no effect against a third party in good faith (§708(2) Com. Code).

136. Within the commercial home port, the captain does not have the above-mentioned rights of representation, unless specifically empowered by contract.

137. The captain also has the authority to issue Bs/L, combined Bs/L, and sea waybills (SWBs) (§§757, 769, 770 Com. Code).

D. The Captain's Right to Dispose of and Use Carried Goods

138. If it becomes necessary during a voyage to dispose of the carried goods for the benefit of the interested parties, the captain must carry out such disposal on behalf of the interested parties in a manner consistent with their best interests (§711(1) Com. Code). 'Interested parties' refers to shippers and consignees, and 'during a voyage' is understood to mean the period from receipt to delivery. An example of 'disposal' is when the goods are wetted, or packing is damaged due to a casualty and the captain lands and warehouses the goods to prevent further damage. The interested parties bear the consequences of disposal because the captain acts on their behalf. If the interested parties become liable to third parties as a result of the disposal, they may be exempted by transferring their rights in the goods to that third party. In effect, this limits the liabilities arising from the captain's disposal to the value of the goods. However, the interested parties may not be exempted if their fault necessitated the disposal (§711(2) Com. Code).

139. The captain may also use the carried goods if necessary to continue the voyage (§712(1) Com. Code). An example of 'use' is consumption as fuel or food. Since such use is for the shipowner's benefit, the shipowner becomes liable to reimburse the owner of the goods. The amount of reimbursement is determined based on the market value of the goods at their destination on the expected date of delivery, and costs saved using the goods are deducted from the reimbursed amount (§§576(1), (2), 712(2) Com. Code). Use of the goods for the voyage does not affect the freight payable to the carrier (§746, Com. Code).

E. The Captain's Liability for the Acts of Seamen

140. The captain is liable to compensate for damage caused to a third party by an intentional or negligent act of a sailor in the course of their duties. The captain may be released from this liability if they prove that they were not negligent in their supervision of the sailor (§713 Com. Code).

F. Dismissal and Termination of the Captain

141. The shipowner may dismiss the captain at any time (§715(1) Com. Code). However, the captain may claim damages if the dismissal lacked valid grounds (§715(2) Com. Code). If the captain was one of the ship's co-owners and the dismissal was decided against their will, the captain may demand that the other co-owners buy out their shares (§715(3) Com. Code). The captain's contract may also be terminated by expiration of the employment term, resignation, or death.

§2. SEAMEN

I. General Remarks

142. The Seamen's Act defines 'seamen' as captains, sailors and reserve seamen who embark on ships to which the act applies (§1 Seamen's Act; *see also* paragraph 127). A 'sailor' is a member of the ship's crew who is not the captain, and a 'reserve seaman' is a sailor employed to work on a ship but who is not currently working onboard (§2 Seamen's Act).

143. The Seamen's Act provides that reserve seamen are 'employed', while captains and sailors engaged to work onboard a particular ship are 'hired' (§31 Seamen's Act et seq.). There are various academic theories on the relationship between being employed and being hired, but a court precedent held their relationship as follows (Nagasaki D.C. Judgment of 14 October 1955): In companies which retain reserve seamen, a hiring contract for working onboard a particular ship exists separately from the general employment contract, and the two contracts co-exist when a seaman is engaged to work onboard a specific ship. Meanwhile, in companies that do not retain reserve seamen, the employment contract and the hiring contract are fused into one contract, wherein seamen are only employed and hired while working onboard.

144. Contracts of employment are subject to general regulations concerning ordinary employment contracts. Japan has also been a party to the Maritime Labour Convention 2006 since 2013, but has not ratified the Work in Fishing Convention, 2007 (No. 188). The following paragraphs outline the protective provisions within the Seamen's Act applying to hiring contracts and contracts of employment.

II. The Hiring Contract

A. The Parties

145. The shipowner and the seaman (including captains) are the parties to a hiring contract. Minors whose legal representatives have granted permission to become seamen have the same capacity to act as adults regarding hiring contracts (§84 Seamen's Act). However, persons under the age of 16 (or, for fishing boats, before the first 31 of March after they turn 15) and women who are pregnant or have not yet gone eight weeks after giving birth may not, in principle, be employed onboard (§§85, 87 Seamen's Act).

B. Conditions

146. When entering into a hiring contract, the shipowner must provide the seaman with a written explanation of the wages, working hours, period of employment and other working conditions. The same applies when making any amendment to an existing hiring contract (§32(1) Seamen's Act, §16(1) Seamen's Act Enforcement Regulations). When a hiring contract is concluded, the shipowner must deliver a document stating the contractual conditions to the seaman while keeping a copy onboard (§36 Seamen's Act). A shipowner who fails to comply with this obligation is liable for a maximum fine of JPY 300,000 (§131 Seamen's Act). Furthermore, a hiring contract may not contain a liquidated damage clause or require the seaman to make a compulsory deposit (§§33, 34(1) Seamen's Act). In addition, the shipowner may not set off a claim against a seaman's wages unless the amount of the set off is one-third of their wages or less, or unless the shipowner's claim arose from a criminal act by the seaman (§35 Seamen's Act).

C. Termination

147. Hiring contracts are automatically terminated if the ship sinks, is destroyed, or becomes unfit for service (§39(1) Seamen's Act). Furthermore, if the ship's whereabouts are not known for one month, the ship is presumed to have been destroyed and the hiring contract is terminated (§39(2) Seamen's Act). A change in the shipowner also terminates the existing hiring contract unless such change is caused by a total succession such as inheritance or company mergers. In such a case, a new hiring contract is deemed concluded between the seaman and the new shipowner on the same conditions as the previous contract. The seaman is entitled to request termination of the new hiring contract with a minimum of twenty-four hours written notice (§§42, 43 Seamen's Act).

148. In addition, the shipowner may terminate the hiring contract when the seaman (a) is extremely unfit for duty, (b) is exceptionally lax or shows gross negligence in the performance of their duties, (c) does not embark onboard the ship by the time specified by the captain, (d) is highly disruptive to onboard rules of conduct (*see* paragraph 129), (e) is unable to perform their duties due to injury or illness, or (f) due to other unavoidable reasons (§40 Seamen's Act). On the other hand, a seaman may terminate a hiring contract when (a) the ship loses her nationality as of the time the hiring contract was concluded, (b) the working conditions described in the hiring contract are significantly different from the actual conditions, (c) the seaman becomes unable to perform their duties due to injury or illness, (d) the seaman intends to receive education at a school, maritime academy, sailor's school or fisheries college, or (e) the seaman finds a substitute who is deemed suitable by the captain (§41 Seamen's Act). In hiring contracts without a term, either party may terminate the contract without cause with twenty-four hours' written notice (§42 Seamen's Act).

D. Statutory Compensation and Allowance for Termination

149. When the hiring contract is terminated due to the sinking or total loss of a ship, the seaman must be given monthly unemployment allowances for a maximum of two months from the day following the termination of the contract of employment, pro rata to their wages (§45 Seamen's Act). If the hiring contract is terminated by no fault of the seaman or due to a change of shipowner, a termination allowance equal to one month's wages must be paid (§46 Seamen's Act). A shipowner failing to pay these allowances is punishable by imprisonment for a period not exceeding six months or a fine not exceeding JPY 300,000 (§130 Seamen's Act). In addition, when a hiring contract is terminated without gross negligence on the part of the seaman, or when a hiring contract reaches the end of its term outside the seaman's home nation, the shipowner must repatriate the seaman or pay the costs of repatriation (§47 Seamen's Act). Repatriation costs include freight, lodging and board during actual repatriation, and the cost of lodging and board from termination to departure for repatriation, provided that the departure was made without delay (§48 Seamen's Act). The shipowner must also pay a repatriation allowance pro rata to the seaman's wages for each day of repatriation, regardless of whether the shipowner repatriates the seaman or merely pays the cost of repatriation (§49 Seamen's Act). If the shipowner breaches their obligations concerning repatriation, they are punishable by imprisonment for a period not exceeding six months or a fine not exceeding JPY 300,000 (§130 Seamen's Act).

E. Obligation of the Captain to Give Notice Regarding the Contract

150. When a hiring contract is concluded, terminated, renewed, or modified, the captain must notify the minister of the MLIT if in Japan (§37(1) Seamen's Act), or, if outside Japan, a Japanese consular officer (§103 Seamen's Act), without delay. Upon receiving notification of a hiring contract, the notified authority confirms whether the employment contract complies with the laws and regulations relating to the safety of navigation or labour conditions and whether the agreement was made under satisfactory circumstances. If deemed necessary, the authority may issue corrective orders or take other necessary measures (§38, §101(1) Seamen's Act).

III. Provisions for the Protection of Reserve Seamen under Employment Contracts

151. The shipowner's obligation to explain working conditions, the ban on liquidated damages, and the prohibition of compulsory deposits (*see* paragraph 146) also apply to employment contracts for reserve seamen (§31 Seamen's Act).

152. A shipowner may not dismiss a reserve seaman (a) during absence due to injury or illness suffered during employment, (b) until eight weeks after the seaman's childbirth or pregnancy, or (c) during the thirty days following the preceding periods. However, the restriction does not apply when a seaman has been absent from work for over three years to recuperate, or when the minister of the MLIT provides certification that the shipowner is unable to continue their business due to a natural disaster or other unavoidable cause (§44-2 Seamen's Act).

153. When dismissing a reserve seaman, the shipowner must give thirty days' notice of dismissal or pay an allowance equivalent to one month's wages. When the notice period is shorter than thirty days, the shipowner must pay an allowance corresponding to the shortened number of days. These requirements do not apply when the dismissal is (a) caused by the shipowner's inability to continue their business due to natural disaster or other unavoidable circumstances or (b) when the dismissal is based on reasons attributable to the reserve seaman and has been approved by the minister of the MLIT (Seamen's Act §44-3).

IV. Rights and Duties of Seamen, Etc.

154. Sailors hired on a ship must comply with the general onboard rules of conduct (*see* paragraph 129).

155. Other rights and duties of the seamen etc. are determined by the contract. However, the Seamen's Act contains detailed provisions on the method and timing of remuneration (§53 Seamen's Act), the right to claim wages and allowances during sickness and injury (§57 Seamen's Act), the application of the Minimum Wages Act (§59 Seamen's Act), working hours and holidays (§§60, 61, 62 Seamen's Act), overtime work (§64 Seamen's Act), etc.

Chapter 4. Contracts for the Carriage of Cargo by Sea

§1. Contract for the Carriage of Goods by Sea

I. Relevant Statutes

156. Japanese law classifies contracts for the carriage of goods as contracts for work, which is one of the thirteen typical contracts stipulated in Chapter II 'Contracts' of the Civ. Code. In a 'contract for work', one party undertakes to complete certain work and the counterparty undertakes to pay remuneration for the result of the work (§632 Civ. Code). Due to the peculiarities of maritime trade, the Com. Code, and the International Carriage of Goods by Sea Act ('COGSA') have detailed special provisions which supersede the general rules in the Civ. Code. As such, the Civ. Code provisions regarding contracts for work are seldom applied to the carriage of goods by sea.

157. The Com. Code places provisions common to land transportation, sea transportation and maritime transportation in its Part II 'Commercial Transactions', Chapter VIII 'Transportation Business' (§§569–594). It then dedicates its entire Part III 'Maritime Commerce' (§§684–850) to maritime law. Part III, Chapter III 'Special Provisions for the Carriage of Goods by Sea' consists of four sections titled 'Carriage of Individual Goods' (§§737–747), 'Voyage Charters' (§§748–756), 'Bills of Lading Etc.' (§§757–769) and 'Sea Waybills' (§§770–787). It is the first two of these sections which deal with contracts for the carriage of goods by sea. This structure was implemented by the 2018 revision of the Com. Code, prior to which only Part III 'Maritime Commerce' Chapter III 'Carriage', section 1 'Carriage of Goods' applied to the carriage of goods by sea, while the provisions regarding general carriage in Part II Chapter VIII applied only to carriage over land.

158. In addition to the Com. Code, COGSA sets forth special provisions for the carriage of goods by sea where either the loading port or discharging port is outside Japan (§1 COGSA). COGSA is a domestic law enacted to implement the 1924 International Convention for the Unification of Certain Rules on Bills of Lading (Hague Rules, 'H.R.') and its 1968 and 1979 Protocols (the amended rules specifically referred to as 'H.V.R.'). However, unlike the H.R., which applies only to contracts of carriage covered by a bill of lading ('B/L', plural 'Bs/L') or similar document of title (Article I(b) H.R.), COGSA applies to all types of international carriage by sea, including voyage charters. Also, the period of the carrier's liability under COGSA is from receipt until delivery by default (§3(1) COGSA), whereas under the H.R. it is from loading until discharge (Article II H.R.). Prior to the 2018 revision of the Com. Code, rules concerning Bs/L were not uniform between domestic and international carriage, and the Com. Code and COGSA each contained slightly differing provisions relating thereto. The 2018 revision amended the domestic rules to match those in COGSA, and the B/L provisions were moved from the COGSA to the Com. Code, which is the base law governing maritime trade.

II. Overview and Definitions

159. The Com. Code defines 'carriage by sea' as the carriage of goods or passengers by a ship (§569(iii) Com. Code). A 'contract for the carriage of goods' is defined as a contract whereby a carrier undertakes to receive, carry, and deliver the goods while the shipper undertakes to pay freight for the resultant carriage (§570 Com. Code). 'Ship' includes both ocean-going ships and ships navigating only in waters other than the sea, such as a lakes, rivers, or harbours (§§684, 747 Com. Code). 'Goods' must be tangible objects, and while they need not necessarily be within the ship (e.g., towed cargo), they must be in the custody of the carrier.

160. The parties to a contract for the carriage of goods by sea are the carrier and the consignor of the goods. 'Carrier' means a person who is engaged in the business of accepting carriage by land, sea, or air (§569(1) Com. Code). The 'consignor' is the party who consigns the goods to the carrier for carriage. In the Com. Code, the consignor is called a 'shipper' in a carriage of individual goods (§737(1) Com. Code) and 'charterer' in a voyage charter (§748(1) Com. Code). When COGSA applies, however, 'shipper' refers to the consignor in both types of carriage (§2(3) COGSA). The 'consignee' is the person to whom the goods are to be delivered under the contract of carriage. Although they are not party to the contract, the consignee acquires the rights and obligations of the consignor upon arrival of the goods at the destination (§581 Com. Code). Rights so acquired include the right to demand delivery, claim damages, or pay freight.

161. Of the two categories of contracts for the carriage of goods by sea, the Com. Code first provides a section regarding the carriage of individual goods (§§737–747 Com. Code). It then provides a section specific to voyage charters (§§748–755 Com. Code), to which some of the provisions related to the carriage of individual goods are applied *mutatis mutandis* (§756(1) Com. Code). Keeping to the structure of the Com. Code, the present chapter will focus on the carriage of individual goods while touching on the position under voyage charters, as necessary. Voyage charters will be discussed in more detail in the chapter on charter parties (*see* paragraphs 266 et seq.).

§2. The Carrier

I. The Obligations of the Carrier

162. In all contracts for the carriage of goods by sea, the carrier must carry by ship the goods received from the shipper (or charterer) and deliver them to the consignee (§570 Com. Code, §15 COGSA). In performing the carriage, the carrier is subject to the following obligations.

A. Warranty of Seaworthiness

163. First, the carrier must provide a seaworthy ship (§§739, 756(1) Com. Code, §5 COGSA).

164. The elements of seaworthiness are as follows: (a) the ship must be in a condition to withstand the voyage (seaworthiness in the narrow sense), (b) the ship must be properly manned, rigged and supplied with provisions and equipment (operational capability), and (c) the holds, refrigerated compartments and other places where goods are loaded must be in a condition suitable for receiving, carrying and storing the goods (cargo-worthiness) (§§739(1), 756(1) Com. Code, §5 COGSA). Lack of seaworthiness in the narrow sense may involve internal factors such as hull strength or equipment failure, as well as external factors such as poor loading (Tokyo D.C. Judgment of 15 July 2011). Operational capability includes the maintenance of documents necessary for the voyage, such as the ship's certificate of nationality.

165. The ship must be seaworthy 'at the time of departure' (§§739(1), 756(1) Com. Code, §5 COGSA). 'Time of departure' means the time when the ship departs from the loading port in respect to each carried good. Therefore, the time at which the ship must be seaworthy may differ between multiple goods loaded at multiple ports.

166. Special provisions exempting or reducing the carrier's obligation of seaworthiness are null and void with regard to contracts for the carriage of individual goods (§739(2) Com. Code, §§5, 11(1) COGSA). The prohibition does not apply however to voyage charters (*see* paragraph 269).

B. Obligations Related to the Loading of Goods

167. Next, the carrier has certain obligations related to loading. In a carriage of individual goods, the carrier must load and stow the goods received from the shipper (§737(1) Com. Code, §15 COGSA). Thus, the carrier is responsible for damage to the goods during loading and stowage. On the other hand, in a voyage charter, it is the charterer who is in principle responsible for loading, although in practice the responsible party would be set out in the contract (*see* paragraph 271).

C. Obligation to Perform the Voyage

168. The carrier must set sail after loading and carry the cargo from the loading port to the discharging port. The carrier must follow the scheduled route without unnecessary deviation.

D. Obligation to Keep Custody of the Goods with Due Care

169. The carrier must keep custody of the goods with due care between the receipt and delivery of the goods (§575 Com. Code, §3(1) COGSA). The content and standard of the duty of due care would vary depending on the specific circumstances. For example, in the event of an accident which damages the goods during the voyage, the carrier must either take appropriate mitigatory measures or seek instructions from the shipper (or charterer) to satisfy this obligation.

E. Obligation to Comply with the Instructions of the Shipper or Charterer

170. The carrier must comply with any instructions given by the shipper (or charterer or the B/L holder if a B/L has been issued) to suspend carriage, to change the consignee or to take other measures regarding the disposal of the goods (§580, 768 Com. Code, §15 COGSA). 'Other measures regarding disposal' is understood to include various measures concerning carriage, such as a change of route. The shipper/charterer's right of disposal does not however extend to such actions which would confer a further obligation to the carrier than was originally agreed within the contract of carriage. Accordingly, the shipper (or charterer or B/L holder) cannot instruct the carrier to return goods already in transit to the loading port or instruct the carrier to commence a judicial sale of the goods (Nagasaki C.A. Judgment of 2 May 1932). This provision does not automatically confer a right of stoppage in transit, where a seller who has shipped the goods may stop transit and resume possession if the buyer becomes insolvent. Such right may only be exercised in the capacity of a creditor against an insolvent buyer in formal insolvency proceedings (§63 Bankruptcy Act, §52(2) Civil Rehabilitation Act, §64(2) Corporate Reorganization Act), and not in the capacity of a shipper (or charterer).

F. Obligation to Discharge and Deliver the Goods

171. When the ship arrives at the discharge port, the carrier must discharge the goods and deliver them to the consignee. Responsibility for discharge lies with the same parties responsible for loading, whereby the carrier is responsible for discharge in a carriage of individual goods, while in principle the charterer would be responsible in a voyage charter (*see* paragraph 275). Where no B/L is issued, the goods must be delivered to the consignee designated in the contract of carriage. If the consignee cannot be identified, or if the consignee refuses to or is unable to receive the goods, the carrier may deposit the goods with an official depository (§§582(1), 583 Com. Code, §15 COGSA; *see* paragraph 210). The carrier also has the option under such circumstances to give reasonable notice to the shipper (or charterer) and put the goods up for auction (§582(2), §583 Com. Code, §15 COGSA; *see* paragraph 211). However, this right of auction does not arise if a B/L has been issued (§768 Com. Code, §15 COGSA).

II. The Liability of the Carrier

A. Liability for Want of Due Care

172. If the goods are lost, damaged, or delayed by the fault of the carrier during the period of their responsibility, it would constitute a breach of the contract of carriage. The carrier is liable to compensate such loss, damage or delay and may not be released from liability unless they prove that they were not negligent (§575 Com. Code, §§3(1), 4(1) COGSA). The contents of the carrier's liability are understood to be uniform between international carriage and domestic carriage, but they are provided for separately in the Com. Code and COGSA due to the way the H.V. exclusions for errors in navigation or management, fire, and the excepted causes (which only apply to international carriage) are structured in the COGSA wording (*see* paragraphs 345 et seq.).

173. The period of carrier's responsibility is from the time of receipt to the time of delivery, regardless of whether the carriage is domestic or international (§575 Com. Code, §3(1) COGSA). In international carriage, it is possible to exclude the period before loading and after unloading from the period of liability by special agreement, effectively matching the period of carrier's responsibility to that of the H.R. (Article II H.R., §11(3) COGSA). However, such exclusion is not effective against a third-party B/L holder unless the exclusion is expressly stated on the B/L (§11(4) COGSA).

B. Liability for Unseaworthiness

174. The carrier is also liable for damages for loss, damage, or delay in arrival of the goods arising from breach of the obligation of seaworthiness (§§739(1), 756(1) Com. Code, §5 COGSA). However, the carrier can be exempted from their liability if they establish that they exercised due diligence regarding seaworthiness (§§739(1) proviso, 756(1) Com. Code, §5 proviso COGSA).

C. Loss, Damage or Delay

175. 'Loss' of the goods is not limited to physical loss and includes cases where the carrier is unable to regain lost possession by law or fact, including theft, misplacement, or good faith acquisition by a third party. 'Damage' is any condition that reduces the value of the goods, and includes damage, alteration, and the misplacement of some constituent parts. 'Delay' means that the goods do not arrive at the agreed date and time or, if there is no agreed date and time, at the date and time when they should have arrived under normal circumstances.

D. Title to Sue

176. If no B/L is issued, then the shipper (or charterer) as the contracting counterparty has the primary right to claim compensation against the carrier. However, if the goods have already arrived at the destination or become a total loss, the consignee obtains the same rights as the shipper (or charterer) to claim compensation (§581(1) Com. Code, §15 COGSA). Although these rights of the shipper (or charterer) and consignee may co-exist, the shipper (or charterer) may no longer exercise their right after the consignee exercises their right to either demand delivery or claim compensation (§581(2) Com. Code, §15 COGSA). If a B/L has been issued, however, only the rightful holder of the B/L has title to claim compensation (cf. Supreme Court Judgment of 4 May 1908).

E. Exclusions of the Carrier in International Carriage

177. COGSA provides that the carrier is exempted from liability if the damage to the goods was caused by an act of the captain, sailors, pilots, or other servants of the carrier in the navigation or management of the ship or caused by a fire onboard the ship without the personal intent or negligence of the carrier (§3(2) COGSA). COGSA also lists eleven excepted causes and provides that the carrier may be excluded from liability if it is proven that a cause existed, and that the loss would ordinarily result from such cause (§4 COGSA). These exclusions are derived from the corresponding rules in the H.R. (Article IV Rule 2) and only apply to international carriage. The exclusions shall be discussed in Chapter 7 (*see* paragraphs 347, 349–350).

F. Valuation of Claim

178. In domestic carriage, the amount of losses for loss of or damage to goods is determined by the market or quoted price of the goods at the place and time when they are to be delivered. However, if there is no market or quoted price, the amount of compensation is determined according to the normal value of goods of the same kind and of the same quality at the place and time of delivery. Freight and other expenses which are no longer payable because of the loss or damage are deducted from the compensated amount. However, this method of valuation does not apply where loss or damage was caused by the intention or gross negligence of the carrier (§576 Com. Code).

179. In international carriage, the amount of compensation for loss or damage as well as for delay in arrival is determined by the same standards as domestic carriage but at the place and time of discharge (§8 COGSA). As with domestic carriage, expenses no longer required payment are deducted from the amount of compensation. The valuation method becomes inapplicable in an international carriage when the loss, damage or delay was caused by wilful intent or a reckless act with knowledge of the possibility of causing damage on the part of the carrier (§10 COGSA).

180. Precedents have varied in the method of determining the 'normal value' of equivalent goods when there is no applicable market price, and have variedly (a) applied the insured value calculated at 110% of the cost insurance freight (CIF) value (Osaka C.A. Judgment of 28 February 1979), (b) applied the insured value calculated at CIF value plus customs duties, import duties, bank charges, and other costs (Kobe D.C. Judgment of 30 March 1983 and Kobe D.C. Judgment of 14 April 1970), or (c) applied the going prices in other markets (Tokyo D.C. Judgment of 10 February 1982).

G. High Value Goods

181. The carrier is not liable for loss of, damage to or delay in delivery of cash, negotiable instruments, or other valuables unless the shipper declared their type and value at the time of consignment. This exclusion does not apply however if (a) the carrier knew when entering into the contract that the goods were valuables, or (b) the loss, damage or delay in arrival was caused by the intention or gross negligence of the carrier (§577 Com. Code, §15 COGSA). 'Valuables' are understood to mean goods which are expensive in relation to their volume or weight, and large and weighty machinery may not fall under valuable goods even if they have a high trading value (Supreme Court Judgment of 21 April 1970).

H. Limitation of Liability in International Carriage

182. COGSA also provides for a limitation of liability pursuant to the corresponding provisions in the H.V.R. (§9 COGSA, Article IV Rule 5 H.V.R.). As with the exclusion for error in navigation or management and fire onboard the ship, the limitation only applies to international carriage, and does not apply to domestic carriage. The limitation shall be discussed in Chapter 7 (*see* paragraphs 354 et seq.).

I. Objection Against Damage or Partial Loss

183. In domestic carriage, the liability of the carrier for damage to or partial loss of the goods is extinguished when the consignee receives the goods without immediate objection. However, if the damage or partial loss cannot be immediately detected, the consignee is given two weeks from the date of delivery to raise objection (§584(1) Com. Code). To raise objection, the consignee must state that damage or partial loss occurred and provide a summary of their contents. There is no requirement under domestic carriage to bring the objection in writing.

184. In international carriage, the consignee must upon receipt of the goods give written notice to the carrier regarding partial loss or damage. However, if the loss or damage cannot be immediately detected, the consignee is given three days from the date of receipt to give written notice (§7(1) COGSA). In the absence of such notice, the goods are presumed to have been delivered without loss or damage (§7(2) COGSA), but the presumption does not apply if the condition of the goods was confirmed in the joint presence of the parties at the time of delivery (§7(3) COGSA). Even if the presumption applies, it can be overturned by counterproof, unlike with the case of domestic carriage where failure to raise objection leads to the claim being extinguished (*see* paragraph 359).

J. Time Bar

185. Unless a judicial claim is raised, the liability of a carrier for loss or damage to the goods is extinguished upon the passing of one year from the date when the goods were delivered (or, when the goods are a total loss, from the date when the goods should have been delivered) (§585 Com. Code, §15 COGSA). In a delay, the one-year period is understood to commence on the date on which delivery was actually made. A 'judicial claim' may be raised by (a) commencing litigation, (b) sending a notice and demand for the appointment of an arbitrator, (c) applying for civil mediation, (d) filing claims in a shipowners' limitation of liability proceedings or (e) filing a third-party application for insolvency. The one-year period can be extended by agreement, but only after the loss or damage has occurred, and not beforehand (§585(2) Com. Code, §15 COGSA).

186. If the carrier further consigns the carriage to a third party and the carrier compensates the damage or receives a judicial claim within the one-year period, the limitation period for the third party's liability to the carrier is extended until the expiration of three months from the date on which the carrier compensates the damage or receives a judicial claim (§585(3) Com. Code, §15 COGSA). For example, if a contractual carrier subcontracts the carriage to an actual ocean carrier and the actual shipper files a judicial claim against the contracting carrier ten months after the date of delivery, the time limit for the contractual carrier to bring a recourse action against the actual ocean carrier is deemed to have been extended to thirteen months after the date of delivery. However, if the actual shipper agreed to a one-year time extension with the contractual carrier before filing a judicial claim two years after the date of delivery, the contracting carrier's recourse claim against the actual ocean carrier would have already expired, since the judicial claim was not raised within the one-year time limit and the three months' statutory extension would not apply. For the contractual carrier to preserve their rights in such situation, they must agree to a back-to-back time extension with both the actual shipper and the actual ocean carrier.

K. Prohibition of Certain Special Agreements

187. In domestic carriage, it is prohibited to conclude a special agreement exempting the carrier from liability for damage caused by unseaworthiness in a carriage of individual goods (§739(2) Com. Code). Such special provision may be agreed to regarding voyage charters, but the exemption does not have effect against a third-party holder of a B/L (§756(2) Com. Code).

188. In international carriage, any special agreement regarding the provisions of the COGSA relating to the carrier's liability, valuation of claim, limitation of liability, the one-year limitation period and written notice that is disadvantageous to the shipper, consignee or holder of a B/L is null and void (§11(1) COGSA; *see* paragraph 365). Special agreements disadvantageous to the carrier are valid. However, there are several exceptions to the general prohibition against special agreements in the case of voyage charters, period of carrier's liability, goods with a special nature or characteristic and voyages under special circumstances, and livestock and deck cargoes (*see* paragraph 366).

L. Application to Liabilities in Tort

189. Under Japanese law, liabilities in contract and tort arising from the same cause may co-exist at the same time. In domestic carriage, the provisions regarding valuation of claim (*see* paragraph 178), high value goods (*see* paragraph 181), objection against damage or partial loss (*see* paragraph 183) and the one-year time bar (*see* paragraph 185) are applied *mutatis mutandis* to claims in tort by the shipper, consignee, or third-party B/L holder against the carrier for loss, damage or delay (§587 Com. Code). In international carriage, the exclusions and limitations for error in navigation or management or fire defence (*see* paragraph 347), neutralization of dangerous goods (*see* paragraph 363), valuation of claim (*see* paragraphs 179, 353), high value goods (*see* paragraphs 181, 357), limits of liability (*see* paragraph 354) and the one-year time bar (*see* paragraphs 185, 186, 360, and 361) are applied *mutatis mutandis* to claims in tort by the shipper, consignee or third-party B/L holder against the carrier for loss, damage or delay (§16(1) COGSA).

190. The exclusions and limitations do not apply to a consignee's claim in tort if the consignee had refused the shipper's consignment of the goods in advance (§587 proviso Com. Code, §16(2) COGSA). When the carrier's liability in tort is limited or excluded by virtue of the above, claims in tort against the carrier's servants for the same cause are also limited or excluded to the same extent, provided that the servant's act was not intentional or grossly negligent (§588 Com. Code, §16(3), (5) COGSA).

III. Rights of the Carrier

A. Rights Related to the Carriage of Illegal or Dangerous Goods

191. The carrier may at any time unload any good that has been loaded in violation of laws and regulations (illegal goods) or not in accordance with the contract for carriage, and may abandon such goods if there is a risk of harm to the ship or to others (§§740(1), 756(1) Com. Code, §15 COGSA). Undeclared dangerous goods (*see* paragraphs 198 et seq.) would fall under this category. If the carrier completes the carriage of said items, then the carrier may claim the maximum amount of freight applicable to the same type of good at the time and place of loading, and may also claim damages against the shipper (or charterer) for loading such goods (§§740(2), (3), 756(1) Com. Code, §15 COGSA).

B. Right of Retention and Time Bar for Claims by the Carrier

192. The carrier may also obtain various claims against the shipper (or charterer) or consignee for unpaid freight, charges, or other cause. The carrier has a right of retention over the carried goods until the related freight and other costs are paid. They may also put the goods up for judicial auction to recover their claim (§§574, 741, 742 Com. Code, §15 COGSA; *see* paragraph 125).

193. The time limit for claims by the carrier against the shipper (or charterer) or consignee is one year, after which the claim would be extinguished by prescription (§586, Com. Code). Expiry of the prescription period may be postponed by commencement of legal procedures (§147 Civ. Code), compulsory execution (§148 Civ. Code), provisional seizure (§149 Civ. Code), demand (§150 Civ. Code), or an agreement to negotiate the claim (§151 Civ. Code).

§3. The Shipper

194. Under the ML, the shipper is the party who consigns the goods to the carrier for carriage by sea (§570 Com. Code, §2(2) COGSA). As discussed earlier, the concept of a shipper in Japanese law includes both (a) the shipper in a carriage of individual goods in domestic carriage, and (b) the shipper or charterer in an international carriage (*see* paragraph 160).

I. Obligations of the Shipper

A. Obligation to Pay Freight

195. The shipper (or charterer) is under obligation to pay freight (§570 Com. Code, §15 COGSA). According to statute, freight becomes payable when the goods are delivered at the destination (§573(1) Com. Code, §15 COGSA). However, because the provision is not mandatory, it is frequent practice to agree to prepayment of freight and non-refund of received freight, which practice has been confirmed valid by court precedents (Supreme Court Judgment of 5 November 1906, Supreme Court Judgment of 2 December 1937). The shipper (or charterer) may not refuse to pay freight by reason of the goods becoming lost or damaged due to their nature or inherent defect (§573(2) Com. Code). On the other hand, if the goods are lost or damaged by force majeure, the shipper (or charterer) is released from their obligation to pay freight and may demand a refund if it is prepaid (§536(1) Civ. Code). This again is a non-mandatory provision and agreements to the contrary, such as those making freight earned on loading, are valid.

B. Obligation to Deliver Documents

196. The shipper (or charterer) must deliver any documents necessary for carriage to the ship's captain within the loading laytime (§§738, 756(1) Com. Code, §15 COGSA). 'Documents necessary for carriage' may include myriad items such as customs clearance documents.

C. Obligation to Deliver a Shipping Label

197. Upon request by the carrier, the shipper (or charterer) must deliver a shipping label to the carrier (§571(1) Com. Code). The shipping label must state the type of goods, the volume or weight of the goods, or the number of packages or individual items, the marks of the goods, the type of packing, the names of the shipper and consignee, and the origin and destination. With the carrier's consent, the shipping label may be delivered by email or facsimile (§571(2) Com. Code). Since this is a voluntary provision, it can be contracted out of by special agreement.

D. Obligations Related to Dangerous Goods

198. If the goods are flammable, explosive or otherwise dangerous, the shipper (or charterer) must, before consigning them to the carrier, notify such danger and provide the name, nature, and other information necessary for their safe carriage (§572 Com. Code, §15 COGSA). Notice may be given orally or in writing. 'Dangerous' goods are goods that are physically dangerous, and do not include contraband or other goods which have a legal danger of causing delays in carriage due to stoppages and seizures. Whether a good is dangerous is determined in accordance with the list of dangerous goods in the Regulations for the Carriage and Storage of Dangerous Goods by Ships which is the domestic adaptation of the International Maritime Dangerous Goods Code, and in accordance with other public law regulations such as the Fire Services Act and the Civ. A.A. Enforcement Regulations. The shipper's liability arising from their failure to provide notice is not strict liability, and thus they may be released if it is established that they were not at fault (§415 Civ. Code). For example, in a scenario where the actual shipper failed to notify the existence of dangerous goods when consigning the carriage of a container to a non-vessel owing common carrier (NVOCC) and the NVOCC subcontracted the carriage to an ocean carrier, the NVOCC may be exempted from their liability towards the actual carrier if it is established that the NVOCC could not have been expected to know that the container contained dangerous goods. In practice, contracts for international carriage often contain special provisions imposing strict liability on the shipper for failure to notify dangerous goods, which is allowed under Japanese law.

199. In international carriage, the carrier is given additional rights to dispose of the dangerous goods, which shall be discussed in Chapter 7 (*see* paragraph 363).

200. Further, a shipper consigning dangerous goods specified in the Regulations for the Carriage and Storage of Dangerous Goods in Ships must submit a written declaration of the contents and quantity of the dangerous goods to the shipowner or captain (§§17, 30, 35 Regulations for the Carriage and Storage of Dangerous Goods in Ships). Failure to declare dangerous goods or submission of a false declaration is subject to a fine of up to JPY 200,000 (§§394, 395 Regulations for the Carriage and Storage of Dangerous Goods in Ships).

II. Rights of the Shipper

A. *Right to Dispose of the Goods*

201. Where no B/L has been issued, the shipper (or charterer) may instruct the carrier to suspend carriage, change the consignee, or take other measures (*see* paragraph 170). However, when the goods arrive at the destination or become a total loss, these rights become simultaneously exercisable by the consignee. When the consignee requests delivery of the goods or claims compensation for damages, these rights may no longer be exercised by the shipper (§581 Com. Code, §15 COGSA; *see also* paragraph 176). When a B/L has been issued, the right to dispose the goods must be exercised by the B/L holder (*see* paragraph 311).

B. *Right to Cancel the Carriage*

202. In the carriage of individual goods, the shipper may cancel the contract before the carrying ship sets sail by paying the lesser of the (a) full amount of freight or (b) damages suffered by the carrier due to such cancellation prior to the departure of the carrying ship (§743(1) Com. Code, §15 COGSA). If a part or whole of the goods were already loaded, the shipper must obtain the consent of all the other shippers and charterers to cancel the contract and bear the costs of loading and unloading the goods (§743(2) Com. Code, §15 COGSA). Even after cancellation, the shipper remains liable to pay any ancillary costs and monies paid on its behalf (§744 Com. Code, §15 COGSA).

203. For the shipper to cancel the contract for carriage of individual goods after the carrying ship sets sail, the shipper must obtain the consent of all other shippers and charterers as well as either (a) paying compensation for all losses arising from the loading and unloading of the goods or (b) providing adequate security (§745 Com. Code, §15 COGSA).

204. The charterer's right of cancellation will be discussed in the section regarding voyage charters (*see* paragraph 276).

§4. The Consignee

I. Identifying the Consignee

205. The consignee is the person who is to receive the goods from the carrier under the contract for the carriage of goods (§570 Com. Code, §15 COGSA). Where no B/L has been issued, the consignee is the person who is designated as such in the contract of carriage between the carrier and shipper/charterer (§570 Com. Code).

206. Where a B/L has been issued, the consignee is the rightful holder of the B/L (§764 Com. Code). In a to-order B/L, which is transferable by endorsement, the consignee is the last endorsee. Since Japanese law allows a B/L to be transferred even if the consignee is named (§762 Com. Code), a straight B/L operates in principle the same way as a to-order B/L unless it is specifically stated that the bill is non-negotiable. In a non-negotiable straight B/L, the consignee is the person stated as such on the instrument. In a holder B/L (under Japanese law, a bill specifying the holder as the consignee or a bill that is not a to-order B/L but does not name the consignee), the person who actually holds or brings the bill is the consignee (*see also* paragraphs 315 et seq.).

II. Obligations of the Consignee

A. Obligation to Pay Freight and Other Costs

207. The consignee acquires the same rights and obligations as the shipper when either (a) the goods arrive at the place of destination or (b) when the goods suffer a total loss (§581(1) Com. Code, §15 COGSA). The obligation to pay freight, ancillary costs and monies paid on the shipper's or their behalf to the carrier is also acquired by the consignee upon arrival or loss of the goods (§§574, 581(3) Com. Code). In addition, the consignee must pay any other amounts due in respect of the goods for general average contributions or salvage (§741(1) (ii) Com. Code).

208. The charterer's obligations acquired from the shipper co-exist with the shipper's original obligations as a type of joint and several liability. Therefore, even after the consignee becomes liable to pay, the carrier may still claim against the shipper (or charterer). If under such circumstances the shipper pays part of the freight, the common obligation is extinguished to the extent paid, and the shipper may claim recourse against the consignee if it was agreed by contract that the consignee should pay.

B. Lack of Obligation to Take Receipt of the Goods and Carrier's Remedy

209. Under Japanese law, a creditor is not under obligation to receive performance unless not doing so under the specific circumstances would violate the general principle of good faith. According to this view, a consignee is not always under obligation to receive the goods, and refusal to do so would not immediately constitute a default.

210. One of the carrier's remedies against a consignee's refusal to take receipt of the goods is to deposit the goods with a depository (§§583, 582(1) Com. Code). However, depositing goods is impractical under Japanese law. Under the Deposit Act, items such as carried goods can only be deposited with only about twenty warehouses designated by the Minister of Justice (§5(1) Deposit Act). Warehouses are only under obligation to receive deposited goods of a kind it usually deals in, and in quantities within their capacity, and may refuse acceptance of any other goods (§5(2) Deposit Act). For these reasons official deposits are seldom if ever used for carried goods. Private warehouses can be used, but only if there is a specific agreement or provision allowing this in the contract of carriage or B/L. Costs for private warehousing are borne by the consignee (§413(2) Civ. Code), meaning that if the consignee continues refusing delivery it will only lead to accumulated costs for the carrier.

211. Another option is to put the goods up for auction, in which case the carrier must give reasonable notice to the shipper (or charterer), start proceedings for a judicial sale, and appropriate all or part of the proceeds to the freight, etc. (§§583, 582 Com. Code). The right of auction does not arise if a B/L has been issued (§768 Com. Code, §15 COGSA; *see also* paragraph 171). A voluntary sale bypassing the judicial sale would be impractical, because as the seller of a good not belonging to them, the carrier would have to buy the goods from the owner of the goods and pass it on to the end buyer (§561 Civ. Code).

III. Right of the Consignee to Demand Delivery and Claim Compensation

212. If no B/L has been issued, the consignee may demand delivery when the goods arrive at the destination. The consignee may also claim damages for the goods if the goods have arrived damaged, or if the goods have been lost or destroyed. This by virtue of the consignee acquiring the rights of the shipper upon arrival or total loss of the goods (§581(1) Com. Code, §15 COGSA; *see also* paragraphs 176, 207).

Chapter 5. Shipowners' Limitation of Liability

§1. General Remarks

I. Japan as a Party to the Limitation Conventions

213. Japan ratified the 1957 International Convention relating to the Limitation of the Liability of Owners of Sea-Going Ships ('LLMC 1957'). The Limit. Act was enacted in 1975 as the domestic law giving effect to the LLMC 1957. Since then, the Limit. Act has been amended successively to incorporate the Convention on Limitation of Liability for Maritime Claims, 1976 ('LLMC 1976') and the Protocol 1996 ('1996 Protocol'), to which Japan is a party. Japan has abandoned the 1957 LLMC with its signing of LLMC 1976.

II. The Limitation Conventions and Japanese Law

214. The Japanese regime for shipowner's limitation of liability is generally the same as that provided by LLMC 1976 as amended by the 1996 Protocol and the amendment of 2012. However, it has several notable features in comparison with the Convention.

215. First, the Convention does not require a shipowner to establish a limitation fund in order to invoke limitation, but permits a party state to make the constitution of a limitation fund a precondition for the limitation of liability (Article 10(1) LLMC 1976). The Limit. Act adopts this option and requires a shipowner to constitute a limitation fund to limit its liability (§33 Limit. Act).

216. The Convention provides that the rules relating to the constitution and distribution of the limitation fund, and all rules of procedure in connection therewith will be governed by the laws of the State Party in which the fund is constituted (Article 14 LLMC 1976). The Limit. Act modelled its procedure on insolvency procedures, in which the insolvent estate is distributed to the claimants in proportion to their claims. Due to the similarity in procedural structure, the Japanese courts assign limitation procedures to their divisions dealing with insolvencies. Specifically, the Tokyo D.C. assigns limitation procedures to their division handling corporate reorganization proceedings, and the Osaka D.C. assigns them to their division handling bankruptcy and insolvency proceedings.

217. The Convention allows State Parties to reserve the right to exclude the application of §2-1(d) and (e) thereof (Article 18(1) LLMC 1976) at the time of their signature, ratification, acceptance, approval, or accession. Japan made both reservations, and thus 'claims in respect of the removal, destruction or the rendering harmless of the ship which is sunk, wrecked, stranded or abandoned, including anything that is or has been on board such ship' and 'claims in respect of the removal, destruction or the rendering harmless of the cargo of the ship' cannot be limited in Japan. However, this does not apply if these claims are claimed in recourse by third-party payors. For example, if a voluntary salvor or the local government carries out wreck removal work for a ship sunken by a collision, the shipowner may not limit the claims brought forth by the salvor or local government. However, when the shipowner seeks to claim recourse of the salvage or wreck removal fees against the owner of the opponent ship, the opponent shipowner may limit their liability (*see* paragraph 240).

218. Paragraph 3*bis* in Article 15 of the Convention, added by Article 6 of the 1996 Protocol, allows State Parties to regulate the system of liabilities to be applied to claims for loss of life or personal injury to passengers of a ship, provided that the limit is not lower than that prescribed in the convention. Pursuant to this provision, the 2005 revision of the Limit. Act removed the limits on claims for death and personal injury to the passengers of the ship (§3(4) Limit. Act).

§2. Parties Entitled to Limit Liability

219. The persons who can limit their liability are the shipowner, etc., the salvor or their servants, etc. (§§3(1), (2) Limit. Act). Any of them may become an applicant for the commencement of limitation proceedings, or become beneficiaries entitled to limit their liabilities within those proceedings (§2(1)(viii) Limit. Act).

I. Shipowner, Etc.

220. 'Shipowner, etc.' includes in principle the shipowner, ship lessee (bareboat charterer), charterers, and, if these entities are corporations, any of their members with unlimited liability (§2(1) (ii) Limit. Act). 'Shipowner' includes both sole owners and co-owners. 'Charterer' includes time charterers, voyage charterers, and slot charterers.

221. In addition to the above, the manager and operator of a ship and their members with unlimited liability are treated in the same manner as shipowners (§98(1) Limit. Act). Further, the insurer of a claim subject to limitation is granted equivalent status as the insured, and as a result the insurer of a shipowner is also entitled to limit their liability (§98(2) Limit. Act).

II. Salvor

222. 'Salvor' means a person rendering services in direct connection with salvage operations (§2(1)(ii)-2 Limit. Act). 'Salvage operations' include measures for raising, removing, destroying, or rendering harmless a sunken, wrecked, stranded, or abandoned ship or anything aboard such a ship; measures for removing, destroying, or rendering harmless cargo; and other measures which are taken in order to prevent or mitigate damages that would give rise to a claim subject to limitation. It does not however include salvage operations performed as a public service (§2(2) Limit. Act). The insurer of a salvor is also entitled to limit their liability (§98(2) Limit. Act).

III. Servants, Etc.

223. 'Servants etc.' means (a) the servant of a shipowner etc. or salvor, or (b) any other person for whose actions the shipowner, etc. or salvor is responsible for (§2(1) (iii) Limit. Act). This includes the ship's captain and sailors, as well as persons who are not servants of the shipowner or salvor but for whose acts the shipowner or salvor may be liable. Examples of the last category of persons are contractors such as onboard stevedores who are under the command and supervision of the captain.

§3. Limitation of Liability

224. A shipowner etc., salvor or their servants etc. must limit their liability through a formal limitation of liability procedure and cannot invoke limitation as a defence in individual actions (*see* paragraph 215).

225. The limitation of liability by the shipowner, etc. or their servants, etc. applies to the aggregate of all claims against them arising from the same occasion in respect of the ship (§6(1) Limit. Act). Therefore, the limit of liability is unchanged even if there are multiple responsible parties for the same ship.

226. Similarly, limitation of liability by either (a) a salvor based on a salvage ship, (b) a shipowner of a salvage ship or (c) their servants, etc. applies to the aggregate of all claims against them arising from the same occasion in respect of the salvage ship (§6(2) Limitation of Shipowner 's Liability Act). The limitation of liability by a salvor who is not based on a salvage ship or by their servants, etc. applies to all claims arising from the same occasion in respect of each salvor (§6(3) Limit. Act).

§4. Ships for Which Liability May Be Limited

227. Limitation of liability is available to private ships used for sea voyages. Ships steered mainly by oars or paddles and ships used for public purpose are excluded from limitation (§2(1) (i) Limit. Act).

228. Air-cushion vehicles and floating platforms may limit their liability under the Limit. Act, despite being excluded from limitation under the convention (Article 15(5) LLMC 1976).

§5. CLAIMS SUBJECT TO LIMITATION

I. Claims Against the Shipowner, Etc.or Their Servants, Etc.

229. Under the Limit. Act, there are five types of claims for which the liability of a shipowner, etc. or its servants, etc. can be limited. If a claim falls under one of these categories, it is subject to limitation regardless of whether it is contractual or in tort, or whether it is based on strict liability or fault.

230. First, there are claims for personal injury and property damage. Personal injury claims are claims for damages resulting from a loss of life or injury. Property damage claims are claims for damages resulting from loss of or damage to property other than the ship in question. Both types of claims must arise onboard the ship or in direct connection with the operation of the ship (§3 1(1) Limit. Act). Causes of claim occurring onboard the ship would include death or injury to cargo handlers and loss or damage to cargo, luggage, or cargo handling equipment. Causes of claim directly related to the operation of the ship would include personal injury and property damage on the opponent ship of a collision, as well as damage to port facilities and fishing facilities in an allision.

231. Second, there are claims for damages resulting from a delay in the ship's carriage of cargo, passengers, or their luggage (§3(1) (ii) Limit. Act). This category of claim would include a claim for delay in transhipment.

232. Third, there are claims for damages resulting from an infringement of rights other than damage or loss to the ship and contract rights, which occurred in direct connection with the operation of the ship (§3(1) (iii) Limit. Act). Examples of this would be claims for the infringement of fishing rights and right to operate a souvenir shop on a passenger ship.

233. Fourth, there are claims for secondary damages suffered as a result of measures to avert or minimize loss, other than claims belonging to the shipowner, etc. or their servant, etc. thereof (§3(1) (iv) Limit. Act). This would include claims for damage to another ship's hull or to the cargo during mitigation measures, damage to fishing nets during the deployment of an oil fence, and damage to fisheries caused by the use of oil treatment chemicals. Aversion or mitigation measures must be reasonable, taking into account the effectiveness of the measure in preventing the primary damage and the magnitude of the resulting risk of secondary damage. Measures to avert or minimize loss may have been carried out by a third party or by the shipowner, etc. of the ship.

234. Fifth, there are claims arising in connection with measures taken to avert or minimize loss, other than (a) claims belonging to the shipowner, etc. or the servant etc. thereof, and (b) claims for remuneration and expenses under a contract concluded with the party carrying out such measures (§3(1) (v) Limit. Act). Typical claims would include claims in tort or unjust enrichment by third parties who voluntarily towed a damaged ship, deployed an oil fence, or sprayed oil dispersant.

II. Claims Against the Salvor or Their Servants, Etc.

235. In addition to the above, the Limit. Act provides four statutory categories of claims for which the salvor or their servants, etc. may limit their liability.

236. First, there are claims for personal injury and property damage. Property damage does not include damage to the salvage ship operated by the salvor. Both types of claims must arise in direct connection with salvage operations (§3(2) (i) Limit. Act). For example, if a mishap during the salvage operation causes personal injury to the passengers or crew of the salvaged ship or damage to the salvaged ship's cargo or fishing facilities, claims arising thereby would fall under this category.

237. Second, there are claims for damages resulting from an infringement of rights other than damage or loss to the salvage ship operated by the salvor and contract rights, which occurs in direct connection with salvage operations (§3(2) (ii) Limit. Act).

238. Third and fourth, there are claims based on secondary damages suffered as a result of measures to avert or minimize loss, and claims arising in connection with such measures but excluding claims belonging to the salvor or servant, etc. thereof and excluding claims for remuneration and expenses under a contract concluded with a party who voluntarily carried out such measures (§§3(2) (iii), (iv) Limit. Act). Measures to avert or minimize loss in this context means measures to prevent damage from further occurrences caused by the salvage operation.

III. Claims for Bunker Oil Pollution

239. In addition to the above, claims for oil pollution caused by the bunker oils of general ships and tankers are subject to limitation of liability under the Limit. Act (§§39, 40 OPDA; *see* Chapter 13).

§6. Claims Which Cannot Be Limited

I. Claims for Wreck Removal, Etc.

240. When Japan acceded to the LLMC 1976, she reserved right to exclude the application of the articles providing the right to limit 'claims in respect of the raising, removal, destruction or the rendering harmless of a ship which is sunk, wrecked, stranded or abandoned, including anything that is or has been on board such ship' and 'claims in respect of the removal, destruction or the rendering harmless of the cargo of the ship' (Article 2(1)(d), (e) LLMC 1976; *see* paragraph 217). As such, these claims are not subject to limitation under Japanese law. An example of a claim falling under this category would be one brought by an administrative body which carried out wreck removal work due to public obligation under the Act on Port Regulations ('APR') or Act on Prevention of Marine Pollution and Maritime Disaster ('APMPMD') (§25 APR, §39(3) APMPMD). However, if the shipowner pays these costs and then claims recourse against the opponent ship of the collision which caused the wreck, such recourse claim is subject to limitation as a claim based on damages resulting from an infringement of rights that occurs in direct connection with the operation of a ship (*see* paragraph 232).

II. Claims for Loss of Life or Personal Injury to Passengers

241. A shipowner, etc. or their servants, etc. may not limit their liability for claims for loss of life or personal injury to passengers on the ship (§3(4) Limit. Act; *see* paragraph 218).

III. Claims Based on Salvage or General Average Contributions and Claims by the Servants of the Ship or Salvage Ship and Their Heirs, Etc.

242. In addition, a shipowner, etc. or salvor may not limit their liability for (a) claims based on salvage or contribution in general average, (b) claims by servants of the shipowner, etc. or salvor whose duties are connected with the ship or the salvage operations, and (c) claims held by third parties which arose from the loss of life or personal injury to such servants (§§4(i), (ii) Limit. Act). 'Third parties' would include heirs, dependants, and families.

IV. Claims for Tanker Oil Pollution

243. As shall be discussed in Chapter 13, claims against tanker owners based on oil pollution damage caused by crude oils, etc. loaded in the hold of a tanker cannot be limitation under the Limit. Act because these claims are subject to a separate limitation of liability under the OPDA (§5 OPDA). However, oil pollution caused by the bunker oils of general ships and tankers is still subject to limitation of liability under the Limit. Act (§40 OPDA; *see* paragraph 239).

V. Claims for Nuclear Damage

244. Further, the provisions of the Limit. Act do not apply to claims for nuclear damage (§4(3) Act on Compensation for Nuclear Damage). 'Nuclear damage' includes damage occurring during the carriage of nuclear fuel materials or materials contaminated thereby

§7. COUNTERCLAIMS

245. If a shipowner, etc., a salvor or their servants, etc. has a counterclaim against the claimant of a claim subject to limitation which arose from the same occurrence, their respective claims are set off against each other and the provisions of the Limit. Act apply only to the balance (§5 Limit. Act). The set-off is carried out automatically regardless of whether one or both parties have limited their liability, and without need for the parties to manifest their intent to set off. For example, if ship X and ship Y collide due to mutual fault and limitation proceedings are only commenced for ship X, shipowner Y's claim would be set off against shipowner X's claim after which only the balance would be subject to ship X's limitation of liability. If both ships commence limitation proceedings, the balance would be subject to the owing ship's procedure only.

§8. BREAKING LIMITATION

246. Even if a claim is eligible for limitation, the right to limitation is barred when the loss resulted from the personal act or omission of the shipowner, etc., salvor, or their servants, etc., committed with the intent to cause such loss or recklessly and with knowledge that there was risk of such loss (§3(3) Limit. Act).

247. The act or omission must be 'personal' to the shipowner, etc., salvor or their servants, etc. wishing to limit their liability. Therefore, a captain's intention or knowing recklessness would not bar the shipowner from limiting their liability.

§9. LIMIT OF LIABILITY

248. Japan has is a State Party to the 1996 Protocol, and the current limit of liability is the same as the amount under the amendment in 2012.

I. Limits of Liability for Property Damage Only

249. If a person seeks to limit liability on in respect of property damage claims, the limit for a wooden ship with a gross tonnage of less than 100 tons is 507,360 Special Drawing Right (SDR); a ship of 2,000 tons or less is limited at 1,510,000 SDR; a ship of more than 2,000 tons but not more than 30,000 tons is limited at the previous amount plus 604 SDR per ton in excess of 2,000 tons; a ship of more than 30,000 tons but not more than 70,000 tons is limited at the previous amount plus 453 SDR per ton in excess of 30,000 tons; and a ship of more than 70,000 tons is limited at the previous amount plus 302 SDR per ton in excess of 70,000 tons (§7(1)(i) Limit. Act).

II. Limits of Liability for Claims including Personal Injury

250. If a person seeks to limit personal injury claims in addition (either when only personal injury claims are limited and when both personal injury claims and property damage claims are limited), the limit for a ship with a gross tonnage of 2,000 tons or less is limited at 4,530,000 SDR; a ship with a gross tonnage of more than 2,000 tons but less than 30,000 tons is limited at the preceding amount plus 1,812 SDR per ton in excess of 2,000 tons; a ship with a gross tonnage of more than 30,000 tons but less than 70,000 tons is limited at the preceding amount plus 1,359 SDR per ton in excess of 30,000 tons; and a ship with a gross tonnage of more than 70,000 tons is limited at the preceding amount plus 906 SDR per ton in excess of 70,000 tons (§7(1)(ii) Limit. Act).

III. Apportionment of Dividends when Both Types of Claims Are Limited

251. If both property damage and personal injury claims are limited:

- Compensation for property claims will be paid out of: ((the limit for property claims only) / (the limit for property and personal injury claims)) * (the portion of the fund used for payment to creditors).
- Compensation for personal injury claims will be paid out of the remainder of the fund used for payment.
- If the remainder is insufficient to settle the personal injury claims, the amount originally allocated to pay for property damage will be re-allocated between the two categories of claim based on the ratio of their unpaid balance (§7(2) Limit. Act).

252. For example, if the ship was 2,000 tons, and assuming that no interest has been incurred and the full amount of the fund is being used for payment, 1,510,000 SDR ((1,510,000 SDR/4,530,000 SDR) × 4,530,000 SDR) will be allocated for property damage, and the remaining 3,020,000 SDR will be allocated to personal injury. However, if the claim for personal injury is equivalent to 4,020,000 SDR and there is a shortage of 1,000,000 SDR while the property claim is also equivalent to 1,000,000 SDR, the 1,510,000 SDR originally allocated to property loss will be re-allocated so that 755,000 SDR will be used to pay property claims while 755,000 SDR plus the originally allocated 3,020,000 SDR will be used to pay personal injury claims.

§10. Limitation of Liability Proceedings and the Limitation Fund

253. The Japanese procedure for limitation of liability is based on insolvency proceedings (*see* paragraph 216). The proceedings may be summarized as follows.

I. Jurisdiction

254. The district court having jurisdiction over the port of registry has jurisdiction over the limitation of liability proceedings of a ship or salvage ship of Japanese nationality.

255. If the ship or salvage ship does not have Japanese nationality, the district court having jurisdiction over any one of the following has jurisdiction: (a) the location of the general venue (the domicile or address) of the applicant, (b) the place of the occurrence, (c) the first place where the ship arrived after the occurrence, or (d) the place where the applicant's property was seized or subjected to execution of a provisional seizure based on a claim subject to limitation.

256. If salvors or their servants not based on a salvage ship seek to limit liability, the district court having jurisdiction over the domicile of the applicant, the place of the occurrence or the place where the applicant's property was seized or subjected to execution has jurisdiction (§9 Limit. Act).

II. Application and Deposit

257. An applicant must make prima facie showing of the facts identifying the occurrence giving rise to claims which are subject to limitation. The applicant must also make prima facie showing that the amount of the claims subject to limitation exceeds the applicable limits of liability and set out the names and addresses of the known claimholders (§18 Limit. Act).

258. If the court finds the application to be in order, the applicant is ordered to make a deposit of money within a period not exceeding one month. The deposit must be made in Japanese yen, in an equivalent to the limit of liability plus interest accrued thereon at the statutory interest rate (as of this writing, 3% p.a.) from the time of the occurrence up to the time of the deposit (§19(1) Limit. Act). In lieu of such deposit, the applicant may, with the court's permission, file a deposit entrustment contract ('DEC'), where the entrusted party (usually banks and insurers) undertakes to make a deposit with the official depository in the amount of the limit of liability plus statutory interest accruing thereon from the time of the occurrence up to the time when the DEC is filed with the court, plus further interest on the preceding sums accruing thereon at the rate of the statutory deposit interest (as of this writing, 0.0012% p.a.) from the time of the commencement order up to the time when the actual deposit is made. When a DEC is filed with the court, the entrusted party does not have to make an actual deposit until ordered by the court to do so, which usually happens at the final stages prior to the actual distribution of dividends (§20(1) Limit. Act). Only certain entities are allowed to become an entrusted party in a DEC, and foreign insurers must have established a branch office etc. in Japan and have received a licence from the Prime Minister to be eligible (item 7 Limit. Act Enforcement Order, §§2(vii), 185 Insurance Business Act).

III. Commencement of Proceedings

259. The limitation proceedings take effect at the time of the commencement order (§26 Limit. Act). With the order, the court appoints an administrator and specifies a filing deadline for claims subject to limitation, which must be between one to four months from the commencement order. It also schedules a date for the investigation of claims subject to limitation within one week to two months from the end of the filing period (§27 Limit. Act). The administrator's fees and other expenses must be prepaid by the applicant separate from the limitation amount, and upon accruing further fees and expenses the court may order further prepayment from the applicant (§91 Limit. Act). After the commencement order, the court issues public notice of the limitation proceedings through the official gazette and serves a document outlining the particulars of the limitation proceedings to the administrator, the applicant, known holders of claims subject to limitation, and the beneficiaries (§28(2) Limit. Act).

260. Once proceedings are commenced, the claimant of a claim subject to limitation may no longer exercise their rights against the property of the applicant or beneficiaries unless against than the limitation fund (§33 Limit. Act). Individual lawsuits and individual executions that have commenced prior to the limitation proceedings are not automatically stayed, suspended, or dismissed, however, and the applicant or beneficiaries must file individual defences and objections within the respective procedures which refer to the limitation proceedings (§§35, 36 Limit. Act).

IV. Filing and Investigation of Claims

261. Claimants may participate in the limitation proceedings by filing their claims subject to limitation (§47(1) Limit. Act). In addition, a person who is not the original holder of a limited claim but who is expected to subrogate on the same claim in the future (e.g., a cargo underwriter), a person who will have a right of recourse against the applicant or beneficiary with respect to the same claim (e.g., an NVOCC who may pay the primary cargo claimant and claim recourse against the ocean carrier), or a person who is likely to be subject to compulsory execution in a foreign country based on the same occurrence (which typically occurs in jurisdictions which are not party to the LLMC regime or which refuse to recognize the commencement of Japanese limitation proceedings) may also participate in the proceedings in the same position as the original holder of the claim (§47(3), (4) Limit. Act).

262. On the date for investigating claims, the court investigates whether the filed claims are subject to limitation, the contents of the claim, and distinguishes whether it is a claim for property damage or personal injury (§57 Limit. Act). If the investigation is not completed during a single court date, it may be extended and continued for multiple dates. If the administrator and the other parties do not raise any objections against the filed claims, they become final (§60 Limit. Act). In practice, the administrator would first investigate and issue a report stating their opinion against each filing, after which the other participants would raise objections against the administrator's report. If objections are raised against a claim, the proceedings in respect of that claim shift to an assessment procedure whereby the court must determine the issues in dispute (§61 Limit. Act). If there is a further objection to the court's assessment, the proceedings are further shifted to litigation, where the merits of the court's assessment are determined in an ordinary three-tier litigation (§63 Limit. Act).

V. Distribution and Close of Proceedings

263. The administrator effects distribution of the fund without delay after either (a) the final court date for investigations is finished without any objections, or (b) the expiration of the time for filing an objection against the court's assessment (§§68, 69 Limit. Act). Distribution is carried out in accordance with a schedule prepared by the administrator and approved by the court (§70 Limit. Act). The entrusted party in a DEC would usually be ordered to deposit the funds at this time. After the administrator directs the depository to pay dividends and the claimants become entitled to receive actual payment of dividends, the applicant and beneficiaries are fully discharged from the respective claims directed at them (§76 Limit. Act). Upon conclusion of distribution, the court issues an order for the conclusion of the limitation of liability proceedings and issues public notice to that effect (§80 Limit. Act).

Chapter 6. Charter Parties

§1. Definition and Types of Charter Parties

264. A charter party is a contract between a shipowner and a charterer for the use of a specific ship. In practice, charter parties are usually classified into voyage charters, time charters and bareboat charters. In a voyage charter, the carrier undertakes one or more voyages for the charterer, and the charterer is entitled to the use of the ship during the voyage(s). A time charter is a contract whereby the charterer is granted the use of a ship fitted and manned by the owner, and the charterer is entitled to the use of the ship during an agreed span of time. A bareboat charter is a contract where the charterer obtains possession of and fits and mans a ship supplied by the owner.

265. Prior to the 2018 amendment, the Com. Code equated charter parties with voyage charters, referred to bareboat charters as ship leases, and lacked any mention of time charters. The amended Com. Code has separate provisions for voyage charters and time charters in addition to ship leases (bareboat charters). However, as the legal nature of the three types of charter parties were deemed too different, they are provided for in separate sections of the Com. Code.

§2. Voyage Charters

I. Definition

266. Under the Com. Code, a voyage charter is defined as 'a contract of carriage involving all or part of a ship' (§748 Com. Code). It is categorized as one of two types of contracts for the carriage of goods by sea, alongside the carriage of individual goods (§737 Com. Code; *see* paragraph 157).

II. Carriage of Goods under a Voyage Charter

267. A broad restatement of the laws relating to carriage of goods by sea with particular focus on voyage charters is as follows.

A. The Parties

268. The parties to a voyage charter are the called the 'carrier' and 'charterer' in domestic carriage (§748 Com. Code), and the 'carrier' and 'shipper' in international carriage (§2(3) COGSA). To avoid confusion, the shipper in an international voyage charter will also be referred to as 'charterer' in this section.

B. Warranty of Seaworthiness

269. A carrier in a voyage charter must provide a seaworthy ship (§§739(1), 756(1) Com. Code, §5 COGSA). The contents of this warranty are the same as those discussed for the carriage of individual goods (*see* paragraphs 163 et seq.). The carrier is liable for damages for loss, damage, or delay in arrival of goods due to breach of the seaworthiness obligation (§§739(1), 756(1) Com. Code, §5 COGSA; *see* paragraph 174). Unlike the carriage of individual goods (*see* paragraph 166), special agreements exempting or reducing the carrier's obligation of seaworthiness are valid in a voyage charter (§§739(2), 756(1) Com. Code, §12 COGSA). However, if a B/L is issued under a voyage charter, the carrier cannot assert such special agreement to a third-party B/L holder (§756(2) Com. Code, §12 proviso COGSA).

C. Loading and Laytime

270. When the necessary preparations for loading have been completed, the captain must issue a notice of readiness to the charterer without delay (§748(1) Com. Code, §15 COGSA). If the voyage charter does not state when laytime for loading should commence, time is counted from the issuance of the notice of readiness (§748(1) Com. Code, §15 COGSA).

271. Unlike in the carriage of individual goods (*see* paragraph 167), the charterer is in principle responsible for loading in a voyage charter (§748(3) Com. Code, §15 COGSA). In practice, however, the charter party would provide for the responsible party. The charterer (unless agreed otherwise) must load the cargo within the laytime for loading, during which time the carrier must wait. If the charterer is unable to load due to force majeure, such period of inability is not counted in laytime for loading (§748(2) proviso Com. Code, §15 COGSA). When the charterer continues loading for periods in excess of the laytime for loading, the carrier may claim reasonable demurrage even where demurrage is not expressly agreed to (§748(2) Com. Code, §15 COGSA). In the absence of an agreement, the amount of demurrage is determined according to fairness and equity, taking into consideration the ship's tonnage. If goods for loading are to be received from a third party other than the charterer but the third party cannot be identified or does not load the goods, the ship's captain must immediately give notice to the charterer, upon which the charterer must load the goods themselves within the laytime for loading (§749 Com. Code, §15 COGSA).

D. Departure and Voyage

272. After the laytime for loading has elapsed, the ship's captain may immediately set sail even if all the goods have not yet been loaded (§751 Com. Code, §15 COGSA). The charterer also may request the captain to set sail even if all the goods have not yet been loaded (§750(1) Com. Code, §15 COGSA). In both cases, the charterer must pay the carrier the full amount of freight, and in the latter case must also pay any extra expenses incurred by not loading the full cargo and provide reasonable security (§§750(2), 751 Com. Code, §15 COGSA).

273. The carrier is under obligation to set sail and carry the goods from the loading port to the discharging port. As with the carriage of individual goods, the carrier must follow the scheduled route without making any unnecessary deviation (*see* paragraph 168). The carrier is under obligation to keep custody of the goods with due care, from their receipt until delivery (§575 Com. Code, §3(1) COGSA; *see also* paragraph 169).

E. Disposal of the Goods

274. The carrier is under obligation to comply with any instructions given by the charterer or B/L holder (if a B/L is issued) to suspend carriage, change the consignee or to take other action to dispose of the goods (§§580, 768 Com. Code, §15 COGSA; *see* paragraph 170).

F. Discharge

275. When the carrier has completed the necessary preparations for discharge, the ship's captain must issue a notice of readiness to the consignee without delay (§752(1) Com. Code, §15 COGSA). Unless agreed otherwise in the contract, it is the charterer who must carry out discharge, which is contrary to the default position for the carriage of individual goods (*see* paragraph 171). As was the case with loading, issuance of a notice of readiness marks the commencement of laytime for discharge unless otherwise agreed. If discharging continues after the expiry of laytime for discharge, reasonable demurrage may be claimed even when there is no specific agreement for demurrage within the contract (§§752(2), (3) Com. Code, §15 COGSA).

G. Cancellation of the Charter

276. In a voyage charter involving the entire ship, the charterer may cancel the charter party prior to the ship's departure by paying the lesser of either (a) the full amount of freight and demurrage or (b) the amount of damage suffered by the carrier as a result of the cancellation (§753(1) Com. Code, §15 COGSA). If the cancellation takes place after all or part of the goods have been loaded, the charterer must also bear the costs of loading and unloading the goods (§753(2) Com. Code, §15 COGSA). On the other hand, if the charterer wishes to cancel after the ship has already sailed, the charterer must pay freight, ancillary costs, monies paid on its behalf, and any other amount that it must bear in terms of general average contributions or salvage costs in proportion to the value of the goods, and indemnify any loss arising from the unloading of the goods or provide security (§§741, 745, 754 Com. Code, §15 COGSA).

277. In a voyage charter involving part of the ship, the charterer may cancel the charter party prior to the ship's departure by paying the same base amount as the cancellation of a charter for the entire ship (§§753(1), 755 Com. Code, §15 COGSA). However, if a part or whole of the goods were already loaded, the charterer must obtain the consent of all other shippers and charterers to cancel the contract and must bear the costs of loading and unloading the goods (§§743(2), 755 Com. Code, §15 COGSA). When cancelling after the ship has already sailed, the charterer must obtain the consent of all other shippers and charterers and either (a) pay compensation for all losses arising from the loading and unloading of the goods or (b) provide adequate security (§§745, 755 Com. Code, §15 COGSA).

278. Regardless of whether the voyage charter is for the entire ship or part of the ship, the carrier may deem the charterer to have cancelled the voyage charter if the charterer fails to load the goods within the loading laytime (§§753(3), 755 Com. Code, §15 COGSA).

§3. Bareboat Charters

I. Overview

279. Bareboat charters are equivalent to ship leases under the Com. Code. A 'ship lease' is a type of lease contract involving ships. 'Lease contracts' are one of the thirteen typical contracts stipulated in Chapter II 'Contracts' of the Civ. Code, where one party undertakes to allow the other party to use and gain profit from a certain property, and the counterparty undertakes to pay rent and return that property upon conclusion of the contractual term (§601 Civ. Code).

280. The relationship between the shipowner and lessee in a ship lease is governed primarily by the terms of the lease contract. This is usually agreed based on standard forms such as BIMCO's BARECON form and the Bareboat Charter Party Form of the Japan Shipping Exchange. If there is no agreement or contractual provision concerning a specific issue, the Com. Code would apply, although it has only three provisions regarding ship leases, only one of which concerns the contractual relationship. In the absence of a specific provision within the Com. Code, maritime commercial custom would apply (cf. §1(2) Com. Code). It is only when the relationship between the parties cannot be determined by these methods that the general provisions of the Civ. Code regarding lease contracts apply.

II. Effect Against Third Parties

281. If a ship is subject to registration (*see* paragraph 60), a lease of that ship can be registered with the ship registry (§3(1) (iii) Ship Registration Order). After registration, the ship lease has effect against a person who later acquired ownership or a mortgage over the ship (§701 Com. Com. Code). If the lease is not registered, it does not have effect against a new shipowner or mortgagee, and the lessee will have to return the ship without remedy. Such leases are seldom registered in practice, however, and instead a provision that the shipowner shall not sell or mortgage the ship without the consent of the lessee is often inserted in the lease contract.

III. Responsibility for Repairs

282. If a ship lessee uses the ship for a voyage at sea for the purpose of conducting a commercial activity, and the ship suffers damage after delivery and requires repairs, the lessee is responsible to carry out repairs at their own cost. The exception is when the damage was caused by reasons attributable to the lessor (§702 Com. Code). This is a new provision introduced by the 2018 revision to the Com. Code to reflect general practice in ship leases. Prior to the revision, it was the lessor who was principally responsible to repair the ship in such circumstances, if the general provisions of the Civ. Code were to be applied (§606 Civ. Code). If the ship lessee does not engage in maritime activities (e. g., when the lessee merely on-leases the ship to a third party), then the lessor remains responsible for repairs per the Civ. Code.

IV. Liability to Third Parties

283. A ship lessee engaging in maritime activities has the same rights and obligations towards third parties as the shipowner (§703(1) Com. Code). The scope of such rights and obligations are not limited by whether they relate to seamanship or not. For example, if the captain enters into a ship repair contract with a third party outside the port of registry, the ship lessee is responsible to pay for the repairs (Tokushima D.C. Judgment of 18 May 1953). If a collision caused by the negligence of the captain or other seaman causes damage to a third party, the ship lessee is liable to pay for such damage (§§703(1), 690 Com. Code; *see also* paragraph 77). When this provision applies, the ship lessee alone is liable to pay to third parties, while the shipowner is not.

284. An exception is liens arising from the lessee's use of the ship, which are also effective against the shipowner, unless the lienholder knew that such use was contrary to the terms of the ship lease agreement (§703(2) Com. Code). Liens in this context are not limited to maritime liens and includes for example general liens for the preservation of movable properties, which may arise by reason of repair costs on a ship (§320 Civ. Code, Supreme Court Judgment of 5 February 2002).

§4. Time Charters

I. Overview

285. Prior to the 2018 amendment, the Com. Code did not contain any express provisions regarding time charters. Precedents and academic theories construed time charters in many ways, for example (a) as hybrid contracts between a ship lease and a contract for the supply of crew labour, (b) as another variant of a contract of carriage (alongside the carriage of individual goods and voyage charters), or (c) as a contract for the lease of a single organic maritime enterprise comprised by the ship and her crew, etc.

286. The 2018 Amendment defined a time charter as a contract where 'one party undertakes to man and fit out a ship and make her available to the other party for use during a certain period of time, and the other party undertakes to pay hire therefor' (§704 Com. Code). The 'certain period' may be defined by a specific number of days, months, or years, or by the duration of a certain event such as a voyage. Trip charters therefore may qualify as time charters. The prescription period for the extinction of charter hire is normally five years after becoming claimable, in line with that of general claims under the Civ. Code (§166(1) (i) Civ. Code).

287. As with bareboat charters, time charters are also concluded using industry standard forms with detailed amendments and addenda. Accordingly, the Com. Code sets out only four express provisions on the subject, including the definition clause in the previous paragraph. The contents of the remaining provisions are as follows.

II. Right to Give Instructions and Collision Liability

A. Time Charterer's Right to Give Instructions

288. First, 'a time charterer may give instructions to the captain regarding the determination of route and other matters necessary for the use of the ship' (§705 Com. Code). This provision is understood to embody the essence of a time charter in allowing the charterer to use the ship during the charter period. However, 'pre-departure inspections and other matters relating to the safety of the voyage are excluded' from the scope of allowed instructions (§705 proviso Com. Code). Thus, the time charterer cannot instruct the ship's captain to omit safety checks before departure or take other dangerous measures, and if a casualty ensues because the captain followed such order, it is the captain and shipowner (§690 Com. Code) who will be held responsible.

B. Precedents on Time Charterer's Collision Liability

289. In connection to this, the question often arises as to whether a time charterer can be held liable for ship collisions caused by the crew's negligence. There have been three widely publicized precedents decided under the Com. Code before the 2018 revision, all of which found the time charterer liable for a collision.

290. In the *Full Moon* case (Tokyo D.C. Judgment of 17 June 1974), a cargo ship time chartered on the BALTIME form collided with a fishing boat, sinking the fishing boat and killing two fishermen onboard. The plaintiffs sued the time charterer, (a) arguing that a time charter had the elements of a ship lease and (b) relying on the provision in the pre-revision Com. Code which provided that a ship lessee engaging in maritime activities has the same rights and obligations towards third parties as the shipowner (§704(1) Pre-revision Com. Code, equivalent to §703(1) after 2018 revision; *see* paragraph 284). The court held that although the time charterer did not employ the captain and their authority to instruct the captain did not extend to matters of seamanship, the charterer's authority 'was in substance comparable to that of an employer', since the captain was under obligation to 'prosecute all voyages with the utmost dispatch' and the time charterer had certain rights over the captain such as the right to demand a change of crew under certain circumstances. The court then drew attention to the fact that the registered shipowner was a Liberian special purpose vehicle without substance and could not have had any substantive authority over the captain and crew, in contrast to the time charterer which was an active corporation. The court concluded that, that under the specific circumstances, the time charterer's position in relation to third parties was similar to that of a ship lessee, and thus liable for the collision by application *mutatis mutandis* of the aforementioned provision concerning ship leases.

291. In the *Shinko Maru* case (Osaka D.C. Judgment of 12 August 1983), a cargo ship collided with a fishing boat and one fisherman went missing, later declared dead. In this case, the plaintiffs sued the shipowner, the captain, and the time charterer. The court found the time charterer liable by directly applying §704(1) of the pre-revision Com. Code by simply relying on the legal theory that a time charter was a hybrid contract with the features of a ship lease (*see* paragraph 285), without going into the details of the contractual relationship.

292. In the *Takami/Iou* case (Supreme Court Judgment of 28 April 1992), a barge under tow collided with two moored minesweepers owned by the Japanese State. Since the tugs towing the barge were time chartered, the State sought to hold the time charterers liable under the aforementioned provision regarding ship leases. The Supreme Court held that, because there was no statutory provision regarding the collision liability of a time charterer, such issue must be determined 'in accordance with the contractual provisions and the substance of the contractual relationship'. After noting that: (a) the relevant time charter parties were extremely brief and contained only very short statements such as 'the authority to give all orders and instructions regarding the use of the ship belongs to [the time charterer]', (b) both tugs were exclusively engaged in the time charterer's business, (c) both tugs were marked with the funnel marks of the time charterer, and (d) the time charterer routinely issued specific instructions and orders relating to the operation of the tugs, the Supreme Court affirmed the judgment of the original instance court finding the time charterer liable for collision by applying §704(1), of the pre-revision Com. Code *mutatis mutandis*.

C. Discussion

293. There is some variation between the precedents on whether the relevant provision regarding ship leases applies directly (as in the *Shinko Maru*) or *mutatis* mutandis (as in the *Full Moon* and *Takami/Iou*). There is also a difference in the depth of inquiry on the facts forming the basis for the ship lease provision to be applied. Notwithstanding these reservations, all three judgments concur that time charterers could be held liable for a collision.

294. As discussed earlier (*see* paragraph 288), the revised Com. Code expressly excludes matters relating to the ship's safety from the time charterer's authority to give instructions to the captain (§705 proviso Com. Code). It also refuses to apply the provision regarding a ship lessee's third-party liabilities (§703(1) Com. Code) to time charters, despite applying the adjacent provision regarding a lien arising from the ship lessee's use of the ship (§§703(2), 707 Com. Code; *see also* paragraph 301). These provisions imply that the revised Com. Code takes the position that a time charterer cannot in principle be held liable for the negligence of the captain and crew.

295. However, these implicative provisions in the revised Com. Code only apply to contracts concluded after the revisions came into force on 1 April 2019 (§§9, 10 Com. Code Supplementary Provisions). Further, the draftsman's commentary for the 2018 revision expressly states that a time charterer may still be found liable for a ship collision, under circumstances similar to precedents where the ship was part of the time charterer's corporate organization and the charterer had daily command and control over the ship. Thus, it can be said that the collision liability of a time charterer is not totally denied under the revised law, and the issue would be determined on a case-by-case basis, taking into consideration the scope of command, control, and supervision the time charterer had over the ship.

III. Responsibility to Pay Costs

296. Bunkers, pilotage, port charges and other 'regular costs relating to the use of the ship' are borne by the time charterer (§706 Com. Code). This is understood to also include terminal and cargo yard charges. On the other hand, fixed costs such as taxes, insurance, ship's equipment costs and salaries, as well as special costs such as repair fees are borne by the owner. This is understood to follow industry practice where the owner usually bears costs related to the maintenance of the ship and crew while the time charterer bears voyage expenses.

IV. Application of Provisions Relating to Carriage of Goods and Ship Leases

297. Several provisions within the Com. Code concerning carriage and ship leases are applied *mutatis mutandis* to time charters.

298. First, when intending to carry dangerous goods, the time charterer must provide advance notice to the owner regarding information necessary for safe carriage (§§572, 707 Com. Code; *see also* paragraph 198). In practice, time charterers would be under obligation to provide notice to the owner after they receive notice from the actual shipper.

299. Second, the owner is under obligation to guarantee the seaworthiness of the ship at the time of departure for each voyage under the time charter (§§707, 739(1) Com. Code; *see* paragraphs 163 et seq.).

300. Third, the owner may at any time unload any goods that have been loaded in violation of laws and regulations and may abandon the goods if there is a risk of harm to the ship or others (§§707, 740(1) Com. Code; *see also* paragraph 191).

301. Fourth, a lien arising from the use of a ship by a time charterer is also effective against the owner, unless the lienholder knew that the relevant use was not allowed under the time charter (§§707, 703(2) Com. Code; *see also* paragraph 284). Thus, a maritime lien held against a ship by a bunker supplier who supplied fuel under an order by the time charterer will also have effect against the owner.

Chapter 7. Transport under a Bill of Lading

§1. Definition and Function of a Bill of Lading

I. Definition

302. A B/L is a document of title whereby the carrier agrees to carry and deliver the goods to its rightful holder, and which serves as evidence that the carrier received or loaded the goods. Prior to the 2018 revision of the Com. Code, there were separate provisions concerning Bs/L in the Com. Code (applying to domestic carriage) and COGSA (applying to international carriage). The revision unified the B/L provisions for domestic and international carriage for the most part, and the provisions of the COGSA relating to Bs/L were transferred to the Com. Code (*see* paragraph 158).

II. Three Functions of a Bill of Lading

303. A B/L is considered to have three functions.

304. First, the B/L functions as document evidence of receipt or loading by the carrier; the former in a received B/L and the latter in a shipped B/L (§757(1) Com. Code, §15 COGSA).

305. Second, a B/L is document proof of the contents of the contract of carriage: The terms and conditions of the contract of carriage are usually pre-printed on the front and back of the B/L by the carrier, and contracts of carriage are often concluded as adhesion contracts. Such terms and conditions stated in the B/L are, in principle, also binding on the transferee.

306. Third, a B/L is a document of title which represents the right to demand delivery of the goods.

III. Characteristics of a Bill of Lading

307. A B/L has the following characteristics under Japanese law:

308. A B/L is said to be a 'formal document', requiring certain statutory entries in order for the document to be valid (§758 Com. Code, §15 COGSA; *see* paragraph 330). Compared to other negotiable instruments and cheques, the formality required of a B/L is often described as being 'loose', as missing entries do not immediately render the document null and void (*see* paragraph 331).

309. A B/L is a 'causal document' (from the German *kausale Wertpapier*), which must be based on a certain underlying transaction and requires actual receipt or loading of the goods to become valid. Although there is academic debate on the relationship between the B/L's causal nature and the fact that the contents of the B/L bind the carrier, the courts appear to adhere to the view that a B/L requires an underlying cause (Tokyo C.A. Judgment of 24 February 1993).

310. A B/L is a 'literal document', whose wording is binding between the carrier and a third-party B/L holder. The carrier is under obligation to abide by the wording of the B/L in relation to third-party B/L holders in good faith (§760 Com. Code, §15 COGSA; *see* paragraph 333).

311. A B/L is considered a 'document of disposal', whereby any disposal of the goods must be made by means of the B/L where one is issued (§761 Com. Code). 'Disposal' would include return of the goods to the loading port, cancellation of carriage, change of destination, transfer of the goods and establishing a pledge on the goods (*see* paragraph 170).

312. When a B/L is lawfully delivered to a transferee, the delivery of the bill has the same effect as the delivery of the goods with regard to the transfer of rights over the goods (§763 Com. Code). Transfer of movables becomes effective against third parties upon delivery of the movable (§178 Civ. Code), but this provision makes it possible to substitute delivery of the goods with the delivery of the B/L.

313. When a B/L is issued, a person may request delivery of the goods only against the presentation of and in exchange for the B/L (§764 Com. Code).

§2. Types of Bills of Lading and Similar Transport Documents

314. There are many types of B/L depending on the method of classification, but the main ones are as follows.

I. To-Order, Straight, and Bearer Bills of Lading

315. The first method is to classify Bs/L according to how the person having title is determined. Under Japanese law, documents of title are generally classified into four categories: (a) order papers (from the German *Orderpapier*) (§520-2 et seq. Civ. Code), (b) named papers with a holder clause (from the German *Namenspapier mit Inhaberklausel*) (§520-13 et seq. Civ. Code), (c) other named papers (from the German *Namenspapier*) (§520-19 Civ. Code) and (d) non-named papers (equivalent to the German *Inhaberpapier*) (§520-20 Civ. Code). In the context of Bs/L, they take the following forms.

316. 'To-order Bs/L' are bills in which the consignee is not named, and the goods are to be delivered according to orders given by the shipper (or a person specified by the shipper such as the buyer or the bank issuing the letter of credit). To-order Bs/L are a type of 'order paper' under Japanese law. This type of bill must be endorsed and delivered for a transfer to take effect (§520-2 Civ. Code). The holder of a to-order B/L is presumed as the rightful holder if the endorsements (including blank endorsements) can be traced to the shipper or other initial ordering party (§§520-3, 520-4 Civ. Code, §§13(2), 14(2) Negotiable Instrument Act). To-order Bs/L are subject to good faith acquisition (*see* paragraph 73) by an acquirer who proves the link of endorsements, unless the acquirer had knowledge of or was grossly negligent regarding theft or loss (§520-5 Civ. Code). The carrier may not raise defences against a third-party B/L holder unless those defences are stated in the bill or arise from the nature of the bill, even if such defences could have been raised against the shipper (§520-6 Civ. Code). An example of defences arising from the nature of the bill would be cases where there was no underlying carriage of contract or where the goods were never received or loaded by the carrier (*see* paragraph 309). A carrier is not under obligation to investigate the identity of the presenter of the bill nor the authenticity of the endorsements, and only becomes liable for failure to do so if they had knowledge or were grossly negligent regarding false identity or inauthenticity (§520-10 Civ. Code). All types of Bs/L may be nullified (e. g., in cases of loss or theft) by a non-contentious proceedings involving two months' public notice and a court decision (§520-11 Civ. Code), and in such case the holder may demand the carrier to either deliver the goods to an official depository or to deliver the goods against reasonable security (§520-12 Civ. Code).

317. 'Straight Bs/L' are bills in which a specific person is named as the consignee. A peculiarity of Japanese law is that a straight B/L is in principle negotiable by endorsement in the same way as to-order Bs/L, unless there is a specific agreement prohibiting negotiation (§762 Com. Code, §15 COGSA). Therefore, a straight B/L without an express prohibition of negotiation would function the same way as a to-order B/L. Non-negotiable Straight Bs/L are classified as 'other named papers' under the Civ. Code. They may only be transferred by way of assignment of claim (§520-19(1) Civ. Code), where the right to receive delivery of the goods from the carrier is the object of transfer. Although seldom seen in practice, assignment is accomplished by agreement but becomes effective against third parties only after the assignor issues notice of the assignment to the carrier (§§466, 467 Civ. Code). The procedure for nullifying a straight B/L and demanding delivery under such circumstances are common between all types of Bs/L (§520-19(2) Civ. Code).

318. A 'bearer B/L' is a bill which either (a) indicates the 'bearer' or actual holder as the consignee or (b) does not name anyone as the consignee but is not a to-order B/L. Depending on which they fall under, they may be classified as either 'named papers with a holder clause' or 'non-named papers'. Physical possession of a bearer B/L is sufficient for the holder to qualify as the rightful holder, and there is no need to trace the endorsements. A bearer B/L may only be transferred together with delivery of the bill itself (§§520-13, 520-20 Civ. Code). A person who possesses a bearer B/L is presumed to be the rightful holder of the rights represented thereon (§§520-14, 520-20 Civ. Code). As with to-order Bs/L, bearer Bs/L are subject to good faith acquisition (§§520-15, 520-20 Civ. Code), the carrier is barred from raising defences not stated in the bill or arising from the nature of the bill against third-party transferees (§§520-16, 520-20 Civ. Code), and the carrier is not under obligation to investigate the identity of the presenter (§§520-10, 520-18, 520-20 Civ. Code). The procedure for nullifying a straight B/L and demanding delivery under such circumstances are common between all types of Bs/L (§§520-11, 520-12, 520-18, 520-20 Civ. Code).

II. Received and Shipped Bills of Lading

319. Next, there is the statutory distinction between a 'received B/L' and a 'shipped B/L'. A 'received B/L' is a bill stating that the goods have been received for shipment. Upon request by the shipper or charterer, the carrier or ship's captain must issue a received B/L after receiving the goods (757(1) Com. Code, §15 COGSA). A 'shipped B/L' is a bill stating that the goods have been loaded on a specific ship. Upon request by the shipper or charterer, the carrier or captain must issue a shipped B/L without delay after the goods have been loaded (§757(1) Com. Code, §15 COGSA). If received Bs/L were already issued, the shipper may only request shipped bills in exchange for all copies of the received bills (§757(2) Com. Code, §15 COGSA). In lieu of issuing shipped Bs/L anew, the carrier may simply state on the received bills that the shipments have been shipped, together with a signature or seal (§758(2) Com. Code, §15 COGSA).

III. Clean and Foul Bills of Lading

320. There is also the distinction between a 'clean B/L' and a 'foul B/L'. The carrier is under obligation to state the type, volume or quantity, and marks of goods (in accordance with the shipper's or charterer's notice if given) and their externally recognizable condition on the B/L (§759(1), 758(1) (ii), (iii) Com. Code, §15 COGSA; *see* paragraph 330). However, if there is reasonable cause to believe that the notice is inaccurate, the carrier is released from this obligation. In this case the B/L should contain a remark regarding issues such as inconsistent type, insufficient quantity, or defect in the cargo, in order to avoid potential liability to third-party holders pursuant to the wording of the bill (§§759(2), 760 Com. Code, §15 COGSA; *see also* paragraph 310). Bills with these remarks are considered 'foul', while those without are considered 'clean'. Foul Bs/L are usually unacceptable for letter of credit purposes, so it is widespread practice for the shipper to request the issuance of a clean B/L in exchange for a letter of indemnity. There is no published Japanese precedent on whether such letters of indemnities can be enforced, but they are understood to be enforceable if there was no fraudulent intent or blatant misrepresentation on the part of the carrier. In connection to the issue of clean and foul Bs/L, when the carrier is unable to check whether the shipper's statement regarding the cargo is accurate (e.g., in respect of containerized goods), the carrier would usually issue a clean B/L while printing or otherwise including 'said to contain' wording to the effect that the carrier has no knowledge of the contents of the shipper's statement and is not responsible for them. The Japanese courts have held that such clauses are valid (Tokyo D.C. Judgment of 13 October 1998).

IV. Master and House Bills of Lading

321. The distinction between a 'master B/L' issued by the actual ocean carrier and a 'house B/L' issued by an NVOCC is also generally recognized. When an NVOCC receives goods from the actual shipper, it would issue a house B/L which indicates the NVOCC as the carrier and the actual shipper as the shipper. The NVOCC would then consign the goods to the actual ocean carrier, who would issue a master B/L indicating the actual ocean carrier as the carrier and (usually) the NVOCC as the shipper.

V. Surrendered and Other Bills of Lading

322. There are also cases where, at the request of the shipper, the carrier (a) issues and immediately collects (or simply purports to issue and collect) the original B/L at the place of export (origin), (b) affixes a 'surrendered' stamp on the B/L, (c) sends a copy of the B/L to the shipper by email or facsimile, and (d) allows the consignee stated on the emailed or facsimiled copy to receive the goods at the place of import (destination) without presentation of the original bill. This arrangement or the bill itself is called a 'surrendered B/L' and is often seen in East Asia. A court precedent held that a surrendered bill does not qualify as a B/L in the context of COGSA because it was never meant to be delivered to the consignee for presentation to the carrier, and determined that an arbitration clause on the reverse side of the surrendered B/L did not bind the consignee (Tokyo D.C. Judgment of 26 March 2008). According to this precedent, carriage by a surrendered B/L would be equivalent to carriage without a B/L under Japanese law.

323. In addition to the above, categories such as 'direct Bs/L', 'through Bs/L', 'combined Bs/L', 'local Bs/L', etc. are also widely recognized depending on the number of carriers or means of transportation.

VI. Sea Waybills

324. A document similar to the B/L is the SWB, which is a document issued by the carrier to the shipper (or charterer) in lieu of a B/L and serves as proof of the receipt or loading of the goods and as proof of the contents of the contract of carriage. SWBs are not negotiable instruments, and thus they cannot be used to dispose of or transfer the goods, and they do not need to be presented in exchange for delivery of the goods. Many SWBs incorporate the Comite Maritime International Uniform Rules for Sea Waybills into their terms and conditions, but the Com. Code also has several provisions applying thereto.

325. First, an SWB (either received or shipped) is issued upon request by the shipper or charterer. The information to be stated in an SWB is effectively the same as the statutory entries of a B/L (§§770(1), (2) Com. Code; *see also* paragraph 330). The carrier may issue an SWB by electromagnetic means with the consent of the shipper or charterer (§770(3) Com. Code). The methods of electromagnetic issuance permitted by law are (a) electronic files sent by telecommunication, (b) electronic data displayed on the receiver's terminal by telecommunication, (c) electronic files delivered on electronic storage media, etc., and (d) facsimile transmission (§12 Com. Code Enforcement Regulations). When a B/L has already been issued, the carrier is not under obligation to issue an SWB even upon request by the shipper or charterer (§770(4) Com. Code).

VII. Electronic Bills of Lading

326. The provision allowing for the issuance of SWBs by electromagnetic means does not apply to Bs/L. Although electronic services provided by Bolero International Ltd and essDOCS Exchange Ltd have recently seen some use in the Japanese market mainly due to demand from shippers, their legal position is unclear as there are no provisions in the Com. Code or publicized court precedents dealing with the subject. A study group consisting of academics, legal practitioners, industry representatives and delegates from the Ministry of Justice held sessions from April 2021 to March 2022 to prepare a report for submission to the national legislative council, which is expected to hold sessions regarding new legislation concerning electronic Bs/L from April 2022.

VIII. Charter Parties and Bills of Lading

327. A B/L may be issued based on a contract of carriage in the form of a voyage charter (§757(1) Com. Code).

328. There is no published Japanese precedent on whether the B/L or charter party takes priority when there is an inconsistency between them. The academic literature appears to take the position that the voyage charter takes precedence when the B/L is held by the charterer, but the B/L takes precedence when the bill is transferred to a third-party holder.

329. The terms and conditions on a B/L may provide for the incorporation of the provisions of a charter party. There is a precedent where the court held that the transferee of a B/L was bound by an arbitration clause in the charter party which was incorporated by reference into the B/L (Osaka D.C. Judgment of 11 May 1959). According to the facts, the B/L provided to the effect that 'all the terms and conditions and disclaimers in the charter party, including the arbitration clause, shall be deemed to be merged into this bill' while the charter party provided that 'any dispute arising out of this Charter Agreement shall be settled by arbitration in London'. The court did not expressly indicate the legal requirements for such incorporation to take valid effect.

§3. The Contents of a Bill of Lading

330. After the 2018 revision of the Com. Code, the statutory entries that must be stated in a B/L were unified between international and domestic carriage (§15 COGSA, §§758, 759(1) Com. Code). They are as follows:

- the type of goods;
- either (a) the volume or weight of goods or (b) the number of packages or individual units, and (c) the markings on the goods;
- the condition of the goods as recognizable from the outside;
- the name of the shipper or charterer;
- the name of the consignee;
- the name of the carrier;
- the name of the ship (only for shipped Bs/L);
- the loading port and date of loading (only for shipped Bs/L);
- the discharging port;
- the amount of freight;
- the number of Bs/L issued when there are multiple copies;
- the place and date of their preparation; and
- the signature or printed name and seal of the carrier or the captain.

331. Even if some of these entries are missing, it does not immediately render the B/L invalid. Precedent holds that a B/L missing some of the statutory entries may still be valid if the essence of the B/L is not prejudiced (Supreme Court Judgment of 13 May 1932). In this respect, it is said under Japanese law that a B/L is a formal document but subject to a 'loose formality' (*see* paragraph 308). The type of goods, the condition of the goods as recognizable from the outside, the name of the carrier, the discharging port, and the signature etc. of the carrier or the captain of the ship are considered mandatory and essential entries that cannot be omitted. Missing or incomplete entries for the remaining items do not immediately affect the validity of a B/L.

332. The carrier is under obligation to state the type, volume or quantity, and marks of goods on the B/L in accordance with the shipper's or charterer's notice (§§759(1), 758(1) (ii), (iii) Com. Code, §15 COGSA). However, the shipper or charterer are liable to the carrier for any damage caused by their notice being inaccurate (§759(3) Com. Code, §15 COGSA).

333. A carrier has the obligation to abide by the wording of the B/L in relation to third-party B/L holders in good faith (§15 COGSA, §760 Com. Code). The said to contain clauses and letters of indemnity in exchange for issuance of clean Bs/L have been discussed above (*see* paragraph 320).

§4. CARRIAGE UNDER A BILL OF LADING

I. Overview

334. Japan ratified the H.R. (International Convention for the Unification of Certain Rules on Bills of Lading, 1924) in 1957 and incorporated it in her domestic law by enacting COGSA the same year. COGSA was amended in 1992 to incorporate the changes introduced by the Protocols of 1968 and 1979. Japan has not adopted the Hamburg Rules or Rotterdam Rules as of the time of this writing.

335. There are two major differences between the H.R. and COGSA. The first is that COGSA applies to all types of international carriage by sea, including voyage charters (§1 COGSA), whereas the H.R. applies only to contracts of carriage covered by a B/L or similar document of title (Article I(b) H.R.). The second is that the period of the carrier's liability under COGSA extends by default from receipt until delivery (§3(1) COGSA), whereas under the H.R. it is from loading until discharge (Article II H.R.).

336. Prior to the 2018 revision of the Com. Code, the rules for Bs/L regarding domestic carriage and those regarding international carriage were provided for in the Com. Code and COGSA respectively, and the contents of the H.V.R. were stated in the COGSA. After the revision, many of the provisions were unified between domestic and international carriage, resulting in most of the COGSA provisions regarding Bs/L being merged into the Com. Code, the latter being the base law (*see* paragraph 158). As such, the contents of the H.V.R. are now interspersed among the Com. Code and the COGSA.

337. Since Bs/L are seldom used in domestic carriage, the following paragraphs in this section shall deal mainly with international contracts of carriage under a B/L.

II. Choice of Governing law and Jurisdiction

A. *Choice of Governing Law*

338. Under the Japanese conflict of laws, parties to a contract are at liberty to agree to a governing law (§7 Act on General Rules for the Application of Laws). There is no requirement for the agreement to be in writing, and the courts will heed a valid agreement absent exceptional circumstances where the results of applying the different law were so drastically severe as to be deemed contrary to public policy (§42 Act on General Rules for Application of Laws).

339. There has been academic discussion whether COGSA should be interpreted to apply regardless of governing law so as to prevent circumvention of certain semi-mandatory provisions (*see* paragraphs 365 et seq.) by choice of law. However, judicial precedents take the position that COGSA is a substantive law which is applied after the governing law is determined (Tokyo D.C. Judgment of 20

April 1963), and thus choosing a different law to avoid COGSA causes no issues unless the results are deemed to go against public policy.

B. Jurisdiction Agreements

340. Japanese procedural law recognizes jurisdiction agreements regarding specific legal relationships when they are in writing or recorded in electronic form (§3-7 CCP). The agreement need not be signed by both parties and may be included in the B/L terms and conditions prepared by the carrier. 'Electronic form' means all 'electronic, magnetic or other form of recording used for information processing by computers and not directly readable by the senses', and is understood to include emails, data files, instant text messages and possibly voice recording data. A jurisdiction agreement within a B/L would be construed according to the law governing the bill.

341. Jurisdiction agreements submitting to the jurisdiction of a Japanese court are generally recognized if it meets the above requirements.

342. Jurisdiction agreements submitting to the exclusive jurisdiction of a non-Japanese court are generally recognized if: (a) the agreement is in writing, (b) the case does not belong to the exclusive jurisdiction of the Japanese courts, (c) the agreement designates the court of a specific country which according to that country's law has jurisdiction over the case, and (d) there is nothing preventing that court from exercising its jurisdiction under law or fact (§3-7(4) CCP, Supreme Court Judgment of 28 November 1975).

343. Notwithstanding the above, a Japanese court may refuse to recognize a jurisdiction agreement when it is found to violate the public order. In a precedent where a Cypriot carrier with an all-Japanese board of directors sought to rely on an exclusive jurisdiction clause on its B/L submitting to the courts of Malaysia, the court refused to recognize the clause because: (a) the terms and conditions printed on the B/L, including the jurisdiction clause, were only copied from the terms and conditions of an unrelated company, (b) neither the dispute nor involved parties had any relation to Malaysia and bringing the case there would bring no benefit while resulting in undue delay and imposing a unilateral disadvantage on the claimant, and thus (c) the agreement was so grossly unreasonable that enforcing it would be in violation of the public order (Tokyo D.C. Interim Judgment of 13 September 1999).

C. Arbitration Agreements

344. The Japanese Arbitration Act ('AA') requires arbitration agreements to be made in writing with respect to a civil dispute that can be settled (§13(1), (2) AA). Arbitration agreements in a B/L are considered valid both in relation to the shipper, consignee, and B/L holder. If the defendant in a Japanese litigation proves the existence of a valid arbitration agreement, it will result in the case being dismissed without prejudice (§14 AA).

III. Liabilities of the Carrier, Exclusions and Burden of Proof

345. The following paragraphs outline the liabilities of the carrier for lost, damaged or delayed goods according to the burden of proof borne by each party.

A. First Cause of Claim: Carrier's Liability for Want of Due Care

346. The carrier is liable for loss, damage, or delay in delivery of the goods caused by want of due care on the part of the carrier or their servants in 'receiving, loading, stowing, carrying, storing, unloading and delivering the goods' (§3(1) COGSA). Because the burden of proof for exercising due care lies with the carrier, it suffices for the claimant to prove that the loss, damage, or delay occurred during the period of the carrier's responsibility. In the case of loss or damage, this is usually established by production of a clean B/L and a survey report at the place of discharge or delivery. Delay in delivery is established by the passage of a fixed or guaranteed delivery date.

B. Defence for Error in Navigation or Management, or Fire

347. The carrier may defend against the first cause of claim by invoking (a) the error in navigation or management defence or (b) the fire defence. COGSA provides that the carrier is exempted from their liability for want of due care on the goods when the loss was caused by an act of the captain, sailors, pilot or other servants of the carrier in the navigation or management of the ship or when caused by a fire onboard the ship, provided that the fire was not caused by the personal intent or negligence of the carrier (§3(2) COGSA). The carrier must establish the grounds of this defence, including the fact that the fire was not caused by their personal intent or negligence. 'Acts relating to navigation' include acts (and omissions) relating to the choice of course or anchorage, reading of charts, heeding weather reports and signal lights, steering and other acts relating to seamanship. 'Acts relating to the management of the ship' refer to acts (and omissions) other than those relating to her navigation but directed towards the ship for the safety of the voyage. Such acts may be either intentional or negligent. 'Acts of other servants of the carrier' include the acts of stevedores and ship repair workers. There is dispute whether 'fire onboard the ship' includes cases where an external fire spreads to the ship. 'Personal intent or negligence' means that the carrier themself must have caused the fire by intention or negligence, and it is not sufficient for their servants such as the captain or crew to be at fault. This defence only arises in international carriage and does not apply to domestic carriage.

C. Defence for Exercise of Due Care

348. In the absence of the error in navigation or management defence or the fire defence, a carrier cannot escape their liability unless they prove that they or their servants exercised due care in respect of the goods during their period of responsibility (§4(1) COGSA). The degree of care to be exercised by the carrier varies according to the individual goods, but it is considered sufficient if the carrier acts in accordance with industry standards for the actual goods, and that they are not required to give independent consideration to all of the vulnerabilities and peculiarities of each individual cargo, unless otherwise notified by the shipper. The contents of this defence are the same as that in domestic carriage (*see* paragraphs 169, 172).

D. Defence for Excepted Causes

349. Further, the carrier may be released from liability if they prove that (a) the damage, loss, or delay in delivery of the goods arose from one of the following causes and (b) such cause would ordinarily result in the damages in question (§4(2) COGSA):

– Dangers that are peculiar to the sea or other navigable waters: This includes risks inherent in the sea, such as storms, collisions, and groundings. Dangers which can be foreseen and prevented by the carrier and its servants or severe weather which can be anticipated in the relevant sea area and season are not included.
– Natural disasters: This includes disasters caused by natural forces, such as typhoons and lightning strikes, for which the carrier has no possibility to avoid the consequences.
– War, civil war, or insurrection.
– Piracy and other similar actions: This would include hijackings and robberies.
– Judicial seizure, quarantine restriction or other disposition by a public authority: This would not include cases where the carrier is responsible, such as when the ship is arrested due to the carrier's failure to pay taxes.
– The acts of the shipper, owner of the goods or their servants: This includes cases where the shipper has given insufficient notice regarding the dangerous nature of the carried goods.
– Strike, sabotage, lockout, and other labour disputes: This is not limited to strikes etc. by the carrier's servants and includes strikes etc. by stevedores.
– Activities for the rescue of life or property at sea, or deviation therefor or any other lawful reason.
– Special characteristics or latent defect in the goods: 'Special characteristics' are properties such as the perishable nature of foodstuffs, the proneness of livestock to suffer injury or death, and the possibility of liquids to evaporate. Latent defects include for example insufficient drying of grains.
– Imperfect packing or markings of the goods.

- Hidden defects in cranes and other similar facilities: This refers to defects in the berth, shore cranes and other cargo handling equipment outside the ship and does not include latent defects in the ship herself (which would be covered by the seaworthiness warranty).

350. When the carrier proves any of the above causes, the burden of proof regarding the carrier's exercise of due care is transferred to the cargo claimant, who must now prove that the damage was avoidable if the carrier had exercised due care but failed to do so (§4(2) COGSA). As with the errors in navigation or management and the fire defence, this defence does not apply to domestic carriage as there are no equivalent provisions in the Com. Code.

E. Second Cause of Claim: Unseaworthiness

351. Separately and independently from the carrier's liability for want of due care over the goods, the carrier is also liable to compensate damage caused by loss, damage, or delay in delivery of the goods caused by the lack of seaworthiness at the time of departure (§5 COGSA). To establish this cause of claim, the cargo claimant needs to prove that (a) the ship was not seaworthy at the time of her departure and (b) there was a causal connection between unseaworthiness and the loss, damage, or delay. The contents of seaworthiness are the same as in domestic carriage, consisting of (a) seaworthiness in the narrow sense, (b) operational capability and (c) cargo-worthiness (*see* paragraphs 164 et seq.).

F. Defence for Exercise of Due Diligence

352. To counter the unseaworthiness claim, the carrier must prove that they and their servants exercised due diligence with regard to seaworthiness at the time of her departure (§5 proviso COGSA). As evident from the structuring of the provisions, liability for unseaworthiness cannot be discharged by reason of fire, error in navigation/management or by reason of the excepted causes.

IV. Amount of Compensation

A. Method of Valuation

353. In international carriage, the amount of compensation in respect of the goods is determined by their market price or by their quoted price on an exchange, at the place and time of discharge. If there is no market price or quoted price, the amount of compensation is determined according to the normal value of goods of the same kind and quality at the place and time of discharge (§8 COGSA; *see also* paragraphs 179, 180). The position is the same as domestic carriage save that under the Com. Code the valuation is made at the place and time of delivery (§576 Com.

Code). Freight and other expenses which no longer need to be paid due to the loss or damage of the goods are deducted from the amount of damages (§8(2) COGSA, §576(2) Com. Code).

B. Limits of Liability

354. The limits of a carrier's liability in international carriage are derived from the convention (Article IV Rule 5 H.V.R.). Specifically, the carrier's liability for loss, damage or delay in delivery of the goods is limited to the greater of (a) the amount obtained by multiplying the number of packages or units of the goods involved in the loss, damage or delay by 666.67 times one unit of account and (b) the amount obtained by multiplying the total weight of the goods by two times one unit of account per kilogram (§9(1) COGSA). Where goods are transported in containers, pallets or other article of transport, the number of such articles is deemed to be the number of packages or units for the purpose of calculating the limit, unless the number of packages or individual goods, the volume, or weight of the goods is stated on the B/L or SWB (§9(3) COGSA). The 'articles of transport' must be packed by the shipper for their number to be deemed as the number of packages or units. It is also understood that, when the 'number of individual goods, or the volume or weight' of the goods stated on the transport document do not assist in determining the number of units, the number of transport articles would be deemed as the number of units. The limit of liability applies to the aggregate of the amounts recoverable from the carrier and its servants (§§9(4)).

355. Although rare in practice, if the type and value of the goods are declared by the shipper at the time of consignment and a B/L is issued with such type and value written thereon, the limits of liability do not apply (§9(5) COGSA). The carrier is totally exempted from their liability if the shipper intentionally declares a value significantly in excess of the actual value (§9(6) COGSA), and if the shipper intentionally declares a value significantly below the actual value, then such lower value is deemed to be the amount of loss (§9(7) COGSA). However, if the carrier had knowledge that the value declared by the shipper was grossly inaccurate, they will neither be released from liability nor entitled to enjoy the grossly lower value declared by the shipper (§9(8) COGSA).

356. The method of valuation and limits of liability can be broken if is proven that the loss, damage, or delay in delivery of the goods was caused by a personal act or omission of the carrier done with the intent to cause such loss etc. or recklessly with knowledge of the possibility of such loss etc. occurring (§10 COGSA). Because the intentional or reckless conduct must be personal to the carrier, acts and omissions of the captain, crew or other servants of the carrier do not bar the carrier's rights.

C. High Value Goods

357. Further to the above, the carrier is not liable for loss of, damage to or delay in delivery of cash, negotiable instruments, or other valuables unless the shipper declared their type and value at the time of consignment. This exclusion does not apply if (a) the carrier knew when entering into the contract that the goods were valuables, or (b) the loss, damage or delay in arrival was caused by the intention or gross negligence of the carrier (§577 Com. Code, §15 COGSA; *see* paragraph 181).

V. Title to Sue, Notice, Time Bar

A. Title to Sue

358. Title to sue rests with the same parties in both international carriage and domestic carriage (*see* paragraph 176). Where a B/L is issued, only its rightful holder has title to claim damages for loss, damage, or delay in arrival of the goods (cf. Supreme Court Judgment of 4 May 1908). If no B/L is issued, title belongs primarily to the shipper, who is the carrier's counterparty in the contract of carriage. However, when the goods arrive at the destination or all the goods are lost, the consignee acquires the same title to claim as the shipper. Once the consignee has requested delivery or exercised its right to claim for damages, the shipper is no longer able to exercise their title to sue over the goods (§15 COGSA, §§581(1), (2) Com. Code).

B. Notice

359. In international carriage, the consignee or B/L holder must upon receipt of the goods give written notice to the carrier regarding partial loss or damage to the goods The notice must set out the general nature of the loss or damage, but does not need to be accurate or detailed because the purpose of such notice is to provide opportunity for the carrier to investigate the accident and preserve evidence. If the loss or damage cannot be immediately detected, the consignee is given three days from the date of receipt to give written notice (§7(1) COGSA). In the absence of such notice, the goods are presumed to have been delivered without loss or damage (§7(2) COGSA), but the presumption does not apply if the condition of the goods was confirmed in the joint presence of the parties at the time of delivery. If there is cause to suspect that the goods have been lost or damaged, the carrier, consignee and/or B/L holder must provide mutual necessary assistance for the inspection of the goods, and when the condition of the goods are confirmed during such inspection in the attendance of the parties, the consignee or B/L holder is released from their obligation to give the above notice (§§7(3), (4) COGSA). This requirement regarding notice does not apply to total loss.

C. Time Bar

360. The time bar for claims for loss, damage, or delay in delivery of the goods is the same as in domestic carriage: (a) one year from the date when the goods were delivered in case of partial loss, damage or delay in delivery, and (b) one year from the date when the goods should have been delivered in case of total loss. Claims are extinguished if judicial claims are not commenced by the one-year limit (§585 Com. Code, §15 COGSA; *see also* paragraph 185). Judicial claims include litigation, arbitration, mediation, filings in shipowners' limitation of liability proceedings and third-party applications for insolvency of the carrier. The one-year limit may be extended by agreement, but only after the loss, damage or delay has occurred (§15 COGSA, §585(2) Com. Code).

361. If the carrier has further subcontracted the carriage to a third party and the carrier compensates the cargo claimant or receives a judicial claim within the one-year period, the time limit for carrier to claim against the third-party subcontractor is deemed to be extended until the expiration of three months from the date on which the carrier compensates the cargo claimant or receives a judicial claim (§15 COGSA, §585(3) Com. Code).

VI. Dangerous and Illegal goods

362. A shipper of dangerous goods (or charterer) must notify the carrier and provide their name, nature, and other information necessary for their safe carriage (§572 Com. Code, §15 COGSA). This obligation is common between domestic and international carriage (*see* paragraph 198).

363. COGSA contains additional provisions regarding the disposal of dangerous goods. Specifically, goods which are flammable, explosive or otherwise dangerous may be unloaded, destroyed, or rendered harmless at any time if their dangers were not known to the carrier, ship's captain or agent of the carrier at the time of loading (§6(1) COGSA). In addition to these rights of disposal, the carrier has the right to claim against the shipper for any damages arising from such dangerous goods (§6(2), COGSA). If the carrier, ship's captain, or the carrier's agent were aware of the dangerous nature of the goods at the time of loading, the goods may be unloaded, destroyed, or rendered harmless whenever they pose risk of damage to the ship or cargo (§6(3), COGSA). The carrier is not liable for any damage caused to the goods by their unloading, destruction or rendering harmless by reason of the above provisions (§6(4), COGSA).

364. Provisions regarding illegal goods are common between domestic and international carriage and have already been discussed in Chapter 4 (*see* paragraph 191).

VII. Semi-mandatory Provisions and Exceptions

A. Semi-mandatory Provisions

365. In international carriage, the following COGSA and Com. Code provisions are semi-mandatory, and special agreements regarding the provisions which are disadvantageous to the shipper, consignee or B/L holder are prohibited (§11(1) COGSA):

- the carrier's liability for loss, damage, or delay in delivery of the goods due to negligence of the carrier during their period of responsibility (§§3(1), 4(1) COGSA, *see also* paragraphs 346, 348);
- the carrier's liability for loss, damage, or delay in delivery of the goods due to failure to exercise due diligence regarding seaworthiness (§5 COGSA, *see also* paragraph 351);
- the grounds and conditions of the carrier's exclusions for fire, errors in navigation or management, or for the excepted causes (§§3(2), 4(2) COGSA, *see also* paragraph 347);
- the period during which the consignee must give notice to the carrier regarding loss or damage and the effects of failing do so, etc. (§7 COGSA, *see also* paragraph 359);
- method of claim valuation and the limitation of liability (§§8–10 COGSA, *see also* paragraphs 353–356);
- the one-year limitation period applicable to claims for loss, damage, or delay in delivery of the goods (§585 Com. Code, *see also* paragraphs 360 and 361);
- the carrier's obligation to state (a) the type of the goods, either (b) the volume or weight of the goods or (c) the number of packages or number of units, and (d) marks of the goods on the B/L according to the shipper's notification (§759 Com. Code, *see also* paragraphs 320, 330)
- the carrier's obligation to abide by the wording of the B/L in relation to third-party B/L holders in good faith (§760 Com. Code, *see also* paragraph 310); and
- the prohibition of covenants that assign the rights arising from the cargo insurance to the carrier (§11(1) COGSA).

B. Exceptions

366. Notwithstanding the above, the following are exceptions to the general prohibition against special agreements

367. The prohibition of special agreements does not apply to voyage charters. However, special agreements between the voyage charterer and a third-party B/L which are contrary to the semi-mandatory provisions has no effect against a third-party B/L holder (§12 COGSA).

368. Special agreements to shorten the period of carrier's liability from receipt until delivery to loading until discharge are permitted (§11(3) COGSA). For this type of agreement to have effect against a third-party B/L holder, it must be expressly stated in the bill (§11(4) COGSA, *see also* paragraph 173). In practice, many Japanese carriers incorporate such special provision into their B/L terms, rendering their period of liability identical with that under the H.R.

369. When a special nature or characteristic of the goods of the special circumstances in which the carriage takes place justify the exemption or reduction of the carrier's liability, special agreements for such exemption or reduction are allowed (§13 COGSA). 'Special nature or characteristic of the goods' include the test carriage of goods which may be unsuitable for carriage, and the transhipment of goods which have become wetted due to a marine accident. 'Special circumstances in which the carriage takes place' includes adventurous carriages agreed to despite a real risk of detention, etc. However, such exemption or reduction has no effect against a third-party B/L holder regardless of whether it is stated on the B/L.

370. Special agreements may also be made in the carriage of livestock and deck cargo. In the carriage of livestock, the special agreement may be effective against a third-party B/L holder only if it is expressly stated in the B/L. In the carriage of deck cargo, the special agreement is effective against a third-party B/L holder only if both the special agreement and the fact that the goods were loaded on deck are expressly stated on the B/L (§14 COGSA). It is generally understood that loading cargo on deck is prohibited unless allowed by agreement or custom. Under this position, a carrier relying on a special agreement with respect to deck cargoes must also establish that loading goods on deck was permitted under the circumstances.

VIII. Application to Liabilities in Tort

371. In international carriage, the exclusions and limitation for error in navigation or management and fire onboard the ship (*see* paragraph 346), valuation of claim (*see* paragraph 353), high value goods (*see* paragraph 357), limits of liability (*see* paragraphs 354 et seq.), requirement to give notice regarding damage or partial loss (*see* paragraph 359) and the one-year time bar (*see* paragraphs 360 and 361) are applied *mutatis mutandis* to claims in tort by the shipper, consignee, or third-party B/L holder against the carrier (§16(1) COGSA).

372. The exclusions and limitations do not apply to a consignee's claim in tort if the consignee had refused the shipper's consignment of the goods in advance (§587 proviso Com. Code, §16(2) COGSA). When the carrier's liability in tort is limited or excluded by virtue of the above, claims in tort against the carrier's servants for the same cause are also limited or excluded to the same extent, provided that the servant's act was not intentional or grossly negligent (§588 Com. Code, §16(3), (5) COGSA).

Chapter 8. Pilotage

§1. General Remarks

373. Modern pilotage in Japan is said to have begun when the 200-year isolation policy taken by the Tokugawa shogunate was abandoned in the mid-nineteenth century and western steamships began to call port in Japan. The Pilotage Licence Rules for Western Ships were enacted in 1876 and 1878 to ensure the safety of marine navigation. In 1899, the Old Pilotage Act was enacted to require compulsory membership in a pilotage union and to provide licensed pilots a monopoly on pilotage services. The current Pilotage Act was enacted in 1949, after the end of World War II.

§2. Legal Provisions Regarding Pilotage

374. Japanese law defines ‘pilotage’ as the act of boarding and guiding a ship in a pilotage area. A ‘pilot’ is defined as a person licensed to pilot a certain pilotage zone (§2(1), (2) Pilotage Act).

375. There are three levels of pilot licences, depending on the maximum size of the piloted ship (§4(3) Pilotage Act). In order to qualify for a licence, a pilot must (a) be a Japanese citizen (§6(1) Pilotage Act), (b) have a maritime officer certificate and a certain number of years’ experience onboard a ship (§5(1) (i) Pilotage Act), and (c) complete a training course in the relevant pilotage zone and pass an examination administered by the minister of the MLIT (§5(1) (ii), (iii) Pilotage Act). Pilots must undergo an annual physical examination to ensure their physical and mental fitness (§13(1) Pilotage Act).

376. As of 2020, there were thirty-four pilotage zones within Japan (§33 Pilotage Act, §3, Appendix 1 Pilotage Act Enforcement Order). Ten of these are mandatory pilotage zones (§35 Pilotage Act, §4, Appendix 2 Pilotage Act Enforcement Order).

377. Pilots may demand a pilotage fee from the shipowner or captain of a ship after providing pilotage services. The maximum amounts of their fees must be determined and approved beforehand by the minister of the MLIT (§46 Pilotage Act). The terms and conditions of pilotage must also be filed with the same minister (§47(1) Pilotage Act). A pilotage tariff and the terms and conditions must be posted in the pilot’s office in a manner that is easily visible to users (§§46(6), §47(3) Pilotage Act).

378. When a pilot is approached by a ship’s captain requesting pilotage services, the pilot is under obligation to visit the ship unless there is justifiable cause to refuse. If upon visiting the pilot is requested to provide pilotage services, the pilot must comply (§§40, 42 Pilotage Act). The captain is also under obligation to allow a visiting pilot to perform pilotage services unless there is justifiable cause not to do so (§41(1) Pilotage Act). The captain must take appropriate measures to ensure that the pilot can embark on and disembark from the ship safely (§43 Pilotage Act).

§3. The Relationship Between the Pilot and Captain

379. Legally, the pilot is an advisor to the ship's captain who provides knowledge about a particular pilotage zone. After receiving the pilot's advice, it is the captain who is responsible to determine the ship's actual course and method of manoeuvre. The statute confirms this by stating that the captain is not discharged from their responsibility for the safe operation of the ship even when a pilot is engaged to provide pilotage services (§41(2) Pilotage Act). A court precedent has held both the captain and the pilot liable for a collision caused by the pilot's negligence, by reason of the pilot being a servant of the captain (Supreme Court Judgment of 3 June 1935).

380. Standard forms of pilotage agreements currently used in Japan provide that the pilot is not liable for any loss or damage sustained by the ship, its captain, crew or any third parties by reason of the pilot's negligence, and that the captain or shipowner must indemnify the pilot against any claim by a third party. The exclusion and indemnity are broken when the liability arose from intentional acts, reckless acts carried out with knowledge of the risk of loss or damage, or other grossly negligent acts equivalent to intentional acts (§21 Tokyo Bay Licensed Pilots' Association's Standard Pilotage Agreement amended 2019). In practice, it is difficult to break this exclusion and indemnity. In a case where a pilot mistook a hazard buoy for a waterway sign and gave instructions which resulted in a grounding, the first instance court found the pilot liable for gross negligence, but the appeal court overturned this, finding that the pilot was not in breach of 'the minimum level of care required of ordinary pilots' under the circumstances (Osaka C.A. Judgment of 14 October 2016, Kobe D.C. Judgment of 3 September 2015).

§4. The Relationship Between the Pilot and the Shipowner

381. The relationship between the pilot and the shipowner is considered to be that of a contract of employment (§623 Civ. Code), and the shipowner (or ship lessee in a ship lease) is liable for any damage caused to a third party by the pilot's negligence (§690 Com. Code).

Chapter 9. Tug and Tow

§1. General Remarks

382. A towage contract is a contract in which the owner of the towing ship ('Tug') promises to either complete towage work or provide towage services for the owner of the towed ship ('Tow'), and the tow owner promises to pay remuneration. There are two types of towage contracts:

(1) 'contracts for towage work' (§632 Civ. Code), where remuneration is paid for the completion of work; and
(2) 'employment-type tow contracts' (§623 Civ. Code), where remuneration is paid for the provision of labour.

383. Contracts for towage work are further subdivided into two subcategories:

(1-a) 'carriage-type tow contracts', where the Tow is under the custody of the Tug (which occurs when there are few or no sailors onboard the Tow), and
(1-b) 'towage contracts in the narrow sense', where the Tow ship is only under the command of the Tug (which occurs when there are sufficient sailors manning the Tow).

384. Right of command over the tug and tow rests with the Tow in employment-type tow contracts. In contracts for towage work, the right of command over the tug and tow belongs to the tug, although there is some academic dispute regarding towage contracts in the narrow sense.

§2. Legal Provisions Regarding Towage

385. There are almost no statutory provisions dealing with towage in Japanese law. One provision in the Com. Code states that towage fees give rise to maritime liens (§842(iii) Com. Code; *see* paragraph 93). The Act on Preventing Collision at Sea also has several provisions concerning ships engaged in towage. However, these limited provisions are vastly insufficient to paint the whole picture. As such, the legal relations arising under towage contracts must be construed according to the general provisions of the Civ. Code and the Com. Code.

§3. Internal Relationships of a Towage Contract

386. In a carriage-type tow contract, the Tug owner must provide a seaworthy Tug (§739 Com. Code). In an employment-type tow contract or a towage contract in the narrow sense, it is sufficient for the Tug owner to exercise a general duty of care to make necessary preparations for towage.

387. In an employment-type tow contract where the Tow has command over the tug and tow, the Tug is under obligation to follow the orders of the Tow except when it is clear that Tow's orders are wrong. Upon receiving such wrong orders, the Tug must take immediate actions necessary for the safety of the ship (Supreme Court Judgment of 20 October 1917). In carriage-type tow contracts and towage contracts in the narrow sense where the Tug has command, the Tow must follow the Tug's orders and manoeuvre accordingly.

388. Regardless of the type of towage contract, if the Tow suffers damage caused by the fault of the Tug's crew, the Tug owner is liable to the Tow owner in both contract (under §575 Com. Code in a carriage-type tow and §690 Com. Code in employment-type tow contracts and towage contracts in the narrow sense) and in tort (§690 Com. Code).

389. The Tug owner has a right to claim remuneration for their services. In a carriage-type tow contract or a towage contract in the narrow sense, remuneration becomes payable when towage is completed (§573 Com. Code, §633 Civ. Code). In an employment-type tow contract, remuneration becomes payable at the conclusion of the agreed provision of labour or at the agreed due dates (§624 Civ. Code). The Tug owner has a maritime lien over the Tow and her equipment with respect to the remuneration claim (§842(iii) Com. Code; *see* paragraph 93).

390. A collision between a Tug and a Tow would in principle constitute a breach of the towage contract. In such case, the negligence of both ships may be compared against each other to determine apportionment, and where the respective degrees of negligence cannot be determined, the damages are apportioned equally between the two parties (§788 Com. Code).

§4. External Relationships of a Towage Contract

391. The main question that arises in relation to the external relations of a towage contract is whether the Tug or the Tow is liable to third parties in the event of a collision or allision caused by the negligence of their respective crew.

392. There is an old precedent which held that 'under Maritime Law, a towed tender is not an independent ship but forms a single integral unit with the towing ship in a ship collision' (Supreme Court Judgment of 10 September 1938). The issue in the case was whether the Com. Code provisions relating to collisions were applicable to a ship's tender if it was being towed by another ship (*see* paragraph 52), but since both the Tug and the towed tender were public ships, the court concluded that the Com. Code could not apply (*see* paragraph 53), and so the holding was made in obiter. It has been said that this precedent recognized the 'unit theory' in English law, under which the tug and tow formed one unit and liability to third parties would principally fall upon the owners of the Tow. However, the academic majority rejects this notion of unity, and instead takes a position close to the 'control theory', whereby the owner of the ship in actual command of the tug and tow should bear liability.

393. In a carriage-type tow contract, the Tow is placed in the custody of the Tug which has command over the tug and tow, meaning that the Tug owner would be liable in principle. In an employment-type tow contract, the Tow has command over the tug and tow so it would be the Tow owner who would be primarily liable. Although there is dispute regarding who has command in a towage contract in the narrow sense, in any case the owner of the ship having actual command over the tug and tow would bear primary liability. If the crew of both the Tug and the Tow were liable, both owners would be held jointly and severally liable to third parties (§690 Com. Code, §719(1) Civ. Code) while having the right to claim recourse against each other for amounts paid in excess of their actual proportion of liability (§§702, 703 Civ. Code).

Chapter 10. Salvage and Assistance

§1. Definition

I. The 1910 Convention

394. Japan has not ratified the International Convention on Salvage, 1989. However, Japan has ratified the Convention for the Unification of Certain Rules of Law respecting Assistance and Salvage at Sea, 1910.

395. The 1910 Convention does not clarify the definition of 'assistance' and 'salvage' in Article 1. Japanese academic theories interpret 'assistance' as cooperation with the crew of a vessel in danger, and 'salvage' as being done after the crew has given up trying to overcome the danger.

396. The 1910 Convention does not provide a definition of 'in danger' in Article 1. The Japanese academic view is that the term 'in danger' means the danger that the crew cannot prevent by themselves, or in other words with the assistance of a third party, the loss of or damage to the vessel or to the cargo or other property onboard, or the death or injury of any person onboard.

II. Commercial Code

397. The Com. Code of Japan has provisions relating to marine salvage (Articles 792 to 807 of the Com. Code). However, Article 792 paragraph 1 of the Com. Code only stipulates that 'involved in a marine accident' and 'has salvaged' and does not define 'marine accident' and 'salvage'. According to the academic views, 'salvage' means 'the rescue of a vessel or cargo, in whole or in part, from a marine accident and its consequences'. The definition of 'maritime casualty' is the same as that of 'in danger' in the 1910 Convention. Salvage includes assistance.

398. It is said that there are two types of marine salvage cases: (1) a case where the salvor and the salved person conclude a contract about the salvage and the salvor performs the salvage based on the contract, and (2) a case where there is no contract about the salvage and the salvor performs the salvage without obligation. The Com. Code is applicable to both salvage by contract and salvage without contract (Article 792 paragraph 1 of the Com. Code).

399. In what follows, non-contractual salvage is described in §§2-3, and contractual salvage is described in §7.

§2. STATUTORY PROVISIONS

I. Governing Law

400. When a trial is held in Japan, first of all, it is judged whether the 1910 Salvage Convention is not directly applicable. There is a dispute about the application of the 1910 Salvage Convention in academic theory, and there are two theories: the majority theory that the flag of the salvage vessel and the flag of the vessel to be salved must be the Contracting Party of the 1910 Salvage Convention, and the influential theory that the flag of the salvage vessel or the flag of the vessel to be salved must be the Contracting Party of the 1910 Salvage Convention. However, if all interested parties are Japanese person or Japanese corporations, Japanese law is applied and the Convention does not apply (Article 15 paragraph 2 of the Convention).

401. Second, in salvage cases to which the 1910 Salvage Convention does not apply, the governing law of claims and obligations is determined in accordance with the Act on General Rules for the Application of Laws. If the salvage takes place in Japanese territorial waters, Japanese law is the governing law. There is a dispute about the governing law when the salvage takes place on the high seas. The majority of academic views hold that the law of the flag of the salvage vessel and the law of the flag of the vessel to be salved should be superimposed, but another academic view hold that *lex fori* should be applied, and therefore views are divided.

II. 1910 Salvage Convention

402. For the Convention to apply, a vessel, any things onboard, or freight must be in danger. 'Sea-going vessels' is divided into sea navigating vessels and inland waterways vessels, and the Convention applies to the salvage and/or the assistance of sea navigating vessels, no matter from which vessel or from land the work is done. On the other hand, the Convention applies to inland waterways vessels only when the inland waterways vessel salvage and/or assist the sea navigating vessel, or when the sea navigating vessel salvage and/or assist the inland waterways vessel. In addition, the Convention does not apply to salvage by public authorities (Article 13). The Convention also does not apply to vessels of war or to government vessels appropriated exclusively to a public service by the State (Article 14). The term 'any things onboard' includes not only cargo but also all other things. The meaning of 'in danger' has been interpreted as synonymous with 'marine accident' in the Com. Code. Salvors of human life, who have taken part in the services rendered on the occasion of the accident giving rise to salvage or assistance, are entitled to a fair share of the remuneration awarded to the salvors of the vessel, her cargo, and accessories (Article 9 paragraph 2 of the Convention).

403. In order for there to have been a salvage at sea, the salvage must have been successful (Article 2 paragraphs 1 and 2 of the Convention). The circumstances in which a salvage may be said to have been successful are determined on a case-by-case basis. The act of salvage need not be the direct cause of the success of the salvage. If the salvage is not successful, 'remuneration' cannot be claimed. It is understood that this 'remuneration' includes not only the bonus for the salvage act but also the damages and expenses that the salvor suffered during the salvage act. As for salvage of human life, it is necessary to succeed in rescuing property, but not in rescuing human life. However, if it is not successful in the human life salvage, the amount of the remuneration will be calculated lower.

404. The act of salvage must be done 'without obligation'. This is not expressly stated in the Convention. However, Article 4 of the Convention provides that a tug shall have the right to demand remuneration only when the tug has performed special services in excess of the obligations under the tug contract. It is constructed that this is a special provision to avoid disputes about the act of towing, which causes the most problems, and that the act of salvage must have been voluntarily performed.

405. The Supreme Court Judgment dated 26 September 1974, held, in summary, that (i) in order for the right to claim the remuneration to arise under the 1910 Salvage Convention, it is necessary that the salvage and/or assistance act be performed without obligation, (ii) the owner of the towing vessel is obliged in principle to take appropriate measures against the danger of the towed vessel, even if the towing work itself requires more labour and expense than expected, as long as there is no imminent danger to the vessel and (iii) the salvage action in this case is within the scope of the obligation.

406. Remuneration shall be paid even if there is a salvage and/or assistance between vessels belonging to the same owner (Article 5 of the Convention).

407. Even if an act of salvage is carried out without obligation and is successful, a claim for the remuneration may not be allowed. A person who has performed a salvage action in spite of an express and reasonable refusal by the vessel to be salved cannot claim the remuneration (Article 3 of the Convention). In addition, if the salvors have by their fault rendered the salvage or assistance necessary or have been guilty of theft, fraudulent concealment, or other acts of fraud, the court may not allow the claim for the remuneration (Article 8 paragraph 3 of the Convention).

III. Japanese Law

408. Article 800 of the Com. Code prior to the amendment in 2018 provided that where all or part of a vessel or its cargo encountered a marine accident, a person who salvaged it without obligation could claim a reasonable remuneration for the result. However, Article 792 paragraph 1 of the Com. Code after the amendment in 2018 stipulates that when all or part of a vessel or cargo or other things in a vessel (hereinafter the 'Cargo, etc.' in this chapter) encounters a marine accident, the salvor may demand payment of a remuneration for the result even if the salvor salvaged it without a contract. The following two points have been changed regarding the requirements for the establishment of marine salvage as stipulated by the Com. Code: (1) both salvage not based on a contract and salvage based on a contract fall under marine salvage, and (2) the scope of salvage is expanded to include objects on the vessel other than cargo, such as bunker oil.

409. The requirements for marine salvage without a contract are (i) a vessel or Cargo, etc. encounters a marine accident, (ii) the act of salvage was performed without private law obligations, and (iii) the salvage of all or part of the vessel or Cargo, etc. was successful. However, (iv) in exceptional cases, even if these are satisfied, the salvor may not have the right to claim the remuneration.

410. With respect to the (i) above, 'vessel' refers to both sea navigating vessels and non-sea navigating vessels (Articles 684 and 807 of the Com. Code and Article 35 paragraphs 1 and 2 of the Vessel Act). It does not include official vessels (proviso to Article 35 paragraph 1 of the Vessel Act). Salvage of human life does not constitute a marine salvage, but if a vessel or Cargo, etc. is successfully salvaged, the person who was engaged in the salvage of human life, if any, may also receive payment of the remuneration (Article 796 paragraph 2 of the Com. Code). A 'marine accident' is understood to be a danger related to navigation to a degree that the vessel cannot overcome by itself. According to the academic view, a marine salvage does not apply to a vessel on land or in a dock.

411. With regard to the (ii) above, the dominant theory is that it is sufficient to perform a salvage act without a private law obligation, and that the absence of a public law rescue obligation is not a requirement. It is also understood that even if the salvor has a private law duty, if the rescue is made to an extent that transcends that duty, a marine salvage without a contract is established. Since the effect of salvage extends to a person other than the vessel owner, a marine salvage is established even when the salvage vessel and the salved vessel belong to the same owner.

412. With respect to the (iii) above, the principle of No Cure No Pay is adopted. In order to be able to say that the salvage was successful, it is necessary that the vessel or Cargo, etc. is spared from marine accident and placed in a relatively safe condition due to the salvage act. However, it is not necessary that the act of salvage is the direct cause of the successful salvage. As a modification of the No Cure No Pay principle, there is a special compensation fee system. *See below* paragraphs 440–447.

413. With respect to the (iv) above, the Com. Code prior to the amendment in 2018 provided that (a) a marine accident was caused intentionally or negligently, (b) a salvage was carried out even though the salvage was refused for justifiable reasons, or (c) a salved article was concealed or disposed of in an unreasonable manner (Article 809). However, after the amendment, it was changed to (a) when a marine accident was intentionally caused or (b) when a salvage was carried out even though the salvage is refused for justifiable reasons (Article 801 of the Com. Code). The remaining grounds are included in the circumstances that the court considers when determining the amount of the remuneration (Article 793 of the Com. Code).

§3. Salvage Remuneration

I. 1910 Salvage Convention

A. *Outline*

414. When the aforementioned requirements for the establishment of a marine salvage are fulfilled (*see* the paragraphs 402–407 above), a claim for remuneration arises (Article 2 paragraph 1 of the Convention).

415. The creditor and debtor of the claim for the remuneration are not explicitly stated in the Convention. However, the salved person of human life is not a debtor (Article 9 paragraph 1 of the Convention).

416. There is no provision in the 1910 Salvage Convention for security for a claim for remuneration. Under the academic views, it is understood that this is a cession of the enactment of the provision to the Convention on Maritime Liens and Mortgages. However, Japan has not ratified the Maritime Lien Convention, and it is an open question whether the right to claim the remuneration under the 1910 Salvage Convention is secured by a lien under Japanese law.

417. The right to claim the remuneration is extinguished by the statute of limitations in two years from the date when the work of salvage and/or assistance is completed (Article 10 paragraph 1 of the Convention).

B. *Amount of Remuneration*

418. If there is a special agreement on the remuneration, it is a salvage by contract. *See* §7.

419. In the absence of a special agreement on the remuneration, the court shall determine the remuneration based on the following matters, taking into account the circumstances of each case (Articles 6 and 8 paragraph 1 of the Convention). The circumstances that the court should take into consideration in the first place are: measure of success obtained, the efforts and deserts of the salvors, the danger run by the salved vessel, by her passengers, crew and cargo, by the salvors, and by the salving vessel, the time expended, the expenses incurred and losses suffered by the salvors, the risks of liability and other risks run by the salvors, and the value of the property exposed to such risks, due regard being had to the special appropriation (if any) of the salvors' vessel for salvage purposes; secondly, the value of the property salved. The reason why the Convention ranks them in this way is explained that, although the purpose of the remuneration is to encourage maritime salvage and the calculation of the amount of the remuneration should first focus on the skills, labour and risks involved in the rescue, judges, when calculating the remuneration, focus on the size of the value of the property salved and may neglect the above points. It is also explained that such a situation may approve the bad wind of occupation of the salved property to some extent.

420. The amount of the remuneration may not, at any time, exceed the value of the property salved (Article 2 paragraph 2 of the Convention).

C. Proportion of Remuneration (Distribution)

421. In the case of a joint salvage by independent salvors, the court shall determine the proportion of the remuneration to be distributed (Article 6 paragraph 2 of the Convention). The circumstances to be taken into account by the court in determining the proportion are the same as those to be taken into account in determining the amount of the remuneration (Article 8 paragraph 2 of the Convention).

422. When there are persons who are jointly engaged in salvage, there may be persons who are engaged in property salvage and persons who are engaged in life salvage. The life salvor has the right to receive a reasonable share of the remuneration (Article 9 paragraph 2), but the amount of the share is understood to be determined at the discretion of the judge. Also, the influential theory constructs that the life salvor cannot directly demand the remuneration from the salvaged person.

II. Japanese Law

A. Outline

423. When the requirements for a marine salvage are met, the right to claim remuneration arises (Article 792 paragraph 1 of the Com. Code).

424. The creditor of the claim for the remuneration is the owner of the vessel and the crew who engaged in the salvage (Article 797 paragraph 1 of the Com. Code). It is understood that a life salvor can claim the remuneration directly against the debtor, same as a property salvor's claim for the remuneration.

425. The debtor of the claim for the remuneration is the owner of the salved vessel and the owner of the salved Cargo, etc. (Article 804 of the Com. Code). The salved person of human life is not the debtor.

426. The claim for remuneration may be secured by a statutory lien or a possessory lien. Under the General Rules for the Application of the Law in Japan, there is a dispute as to how to interpret the governing law for the establishment and effect of the statutory lien or the possessory lien. If the governing law is Japanese law, the claim for the remuneration is secured by maritime lien over the salved vessel (Article 842 item 2 of the Com. Code). For more information about maritime lien in general, please refer to Chapter 2. In addition, the claim for the remuneration is secured by a statutory lien over the salved Cargo, etc. (Article 802 paragraph 1 of the Com. Code). This lien has priority over other liens, but it is extinguished when one year has passed since it was created (Article 802 paragraph 2, Article 844 and Article 846 of the Com. Code). If the salvor is in possession of the Cargo, etc., it has the possessory lien over it (Article 295 paragraph 1 of the Civ. Code).

427. The claim for remuneration is extinguished by the statute of limitations in two years from the time when the salvage work is completed (Article 806 of the Com. Code). Before the amendment in 2018, it was one year from the time of salvage, but it has been amended to be consistent with the 1910 Salvage convention.

428. As for the claim for the remuneration, the owner of the salved vessel cannot limit the liability under the Japanese Vessel Owners' Liability Limitation Act (Article 4 item 1 of the same law).

B. Amount of Remuneration

429. If there is a special agreement on the remuneration, it is a rescue by contract. *See* §7.

430. If there is no special agreement on the remuneration, the court shall determine the remuneration by taking into consideration the degree of danger, the result of salvage, the labour and expenses required for salvage (including those for prevention and/or mitigation of marine pollution) and all other circumstances (Article 793 of the Com. Code). According to the amendment of the Com. Code in 2018, the labour and expenses for the prevention and/or mitigation of marine pollution has been added as one of the elements to be considered. The purpose of this is to promote the salvage of vessels that cause marine pollution, which is the same as the 1989 Salvage Convention.

431. The amount of the salvage cannot exceed the total amount of the value of the salved items (including the amount of the freight of the salved cargo) if there is no special agreement (Article 795 of the Com. Code). According to the amendment of the Com. Code in 2018, it is clearly stated that the maximum amount of the remuneration includes the amount of the salved freight. This is to make the rule the same as the 1910 Salvage convention in consideration of the fact that the cargo was rescued and the extinction of the freight was avoided.

432. Before the amendment in 2018, there was a provision that the amount of the remuneration could not exceed the amount obtained by deducting the amount of the claim of the priority statutory lien holder from the value of the salved object

(Article 803 paragraph 2 of the Com. Code before amendment). However, this provision has been deleted. The reason for deletion is that this rule does not exist in the 1910 Salvage Convention or the form of salvage contract used in practice.

433. It is sufficient that the owner of the Cargo, etc. be liable for the remuneration obligation with the salved goods (Article 804 of the Com. Code). This liability is interpreted as limited liability.

434. With respect to a judicial decision to determine the remuneration, the Master of the salved vessel has the authority to take all judicial and extrajudicial actions concerning the payment of the remuneration on behalf of the debtor of the remuneration (Article 801 paragraph 1 of the Com. Code). The Master may also act as a plaintiff or a defendant for the remuneration debtor in relation to the remuneration debt (Article 803 paragraph 2 of the Com. Code). On the other hand, the Master of the vessel engaged in the salvage can be a Plaintiff or a Defendant for the creditor of the remuneration (the owner of the vessel and the seamen of the vessel) (Article 803 paragraph 3 of the Com. Code). Article 803 paragraph 3 of the Com. Code has been added by the amendment of the Com. Code in 2018. The provisions of Article 803 paragraphs 1 through 3 of the Com. Code do not apply to contract salvage (Article 803 paragraph 4 of the Com. Code).

C. Proportion of Remuneration (Distribution)

435. In the case of a joint salvage by several salvors, the proportion of the remuneration to be paid to each salvor is determined by the court, taking into consideration the degree of danger, the result of the salvage, the labour and expenses required for the salvage (including those for the prevention and/or mitigation of marine pollution) and all other circumstances (Article 796 paragraph 1 and Article 793 of the Com. Code).

§4. Remuneration of the Crew

I. The 1910 Convention

436. The 1910 Convention leaves the apportionment (distribution) of the remuneration (i) between vessel owners and crews and (ii) between crews to the provisions of the law of the flag of the vessel (Article 6 paragraph 3). There is no independent provision.

II. Japanese Law

A. Proportion of Remuneration Between Vessel Owner and Crew (Distribution)

437. If the salvor is a person whose business is salvage, the full amount of the remuneration must be paid to the salvor (Article 797 paragraph 5 of the Com. Code). Crews receive consideration of providing labour as a salary from the salvor, so they cannot obtain a part of the remuneration. The article has been added in the amendment of the Com. Code in 2018.

438. If the salvor is not in the salvage business, two-thirds of the remuneration for the vessel engaged in the salvage must be paid to the vessel owner and one-third to the crews (Article 797 paragraph 1 of the Com. Code). Any special agreement contrary to this provision that is disadvantageous to the crews is invalid (Article 797 paragraph 2 of the Com. Code). However, if the rate of the remuneration is extremely unreasonable, either the vessel owner or the crew may request the other to increase or decrease it. In this case, the court shall determine the remuneration by taking into consideration the degree of danger, the result of salvage, the labour and expenses required for salvage (including those for prevention and/or mitigation of marine pollution) and all other circumstances (Article 797 paragraph 3 of the Com. Code). Before the amendment of the Com. Code in 2018, the rate was different between steam vessels and sailing vessels, and there was a distinction between the Master and seamen. However, these have been deleted.

B. Proportion (Distribution) Among Crews

439. The proportion of the remuneration to be paid to each seaman shall be determined by the owner of the vessel engaged in the salvage. In such a case, the proportion of the remuneration shall be determined in consideration of the degree of danger, the result of the salvage, the labour and expenses required for the salvage (including those for the prevention and/or mitigation of marine pollution) and all other circumstances (Article 797 paragraph 4 of the Com. Code). In order for the vessel owner to determine the proportion, the vessel owner must prepare a draft of the proportion and present it to the crew before the end of the voyage (Article 798 of the Com. Code). The crew may object to this draft. The objection shall be made to the competent maritime authority of the first port where the objection may be made after the draft has been presented (Article 799 paragraph 1 of the Com. Code). If the competent maritime authority considers that there are grounds for the objection, it may correct the draft (Article 799 paragraph 2 of the Com. Code). The vessel owner may not pay the remuneration to the crew until the competent maritime authority makes a decision (Article 799 paragraph 3 of the Com. Code). If the vessel owner fails to prepare a draft, the competent maritime authority may, at the request of crew, order the vessel owner to prepare the draft (Article 800 paragraph 1 of the Com. Code). If the vessel owner does not comply with this order, the competent maritime authority may decide the proportion of the remuneration by itself (Article 800 paragraph 2 of the Com. Code).

§5. SPECIAL COMPENSATION

I. The 1910 Salvage Convention

440. There is no provision in the Convention.

II. Japanese Law

A. *General Comments*

441. The provision of special compensation has been newly established by the amendment in 2018 (Article 805 of the Com. Code). The purpose is to promote measures to prevent or mitigate marine pollution by making it possible, in light of the 1989 Salvage Convention, for those who have spent a great deal of money to rescue a vessel that may cause environmental damage to be compensated for those expenses by a special compensation fee, even if the salvage is not successful or the remuneration is low.

B. *Requirements and Effects*

442. In the event that the ocean is polluted by oil or other substances discharged from a vessel that has encountered a marine accident, and that such pollution causes a serious disturbance to the preservation of the marine environment in a wide area of coastal waters, or is harmful to human health, or is likely to cause such disturbance, and that a person engaged in the salvage of the said vessel has taken measures to prevent or alleviate the said disturbance, the person (hereinafter the 'Person Engaged in the Salvage of the Vessel to Cope with the Pollution') may demand payment of a special compensation to the vessel owner, except when there is a special agreement (Article 805 paragraph 1 of the Com. Code).

443. The creditor of the claim for the special compensation is the Person Engaged in the Salvage of the Vessel to Cope with the Pollution. The debtor of the claim is the owner of the vessel.

444. The right to claim special compensation is extinguished by the statute of limitations in two years from the time the salvage work is completed (Article 806 of the Com. Code).

C. *Amount of Special Compensation*

445. The amount of the special compensation is the amount equivalent to the expenses that were necessary or beneficial as measures to prevent or alleviate the above-mentioned disturbance (Article 805 paragraph 2 of the Com. Code).

446. If the above-mentioned disturbance is actually prevented or alleviated by the measures taken by the salvor, the amount of the special compensation shall be increased and determined by the court at the request of the parties. The amount determined by the court shall be: (i) in principle, an amount within the range of 100 to 130% of the amount set forth in Article 805 paragraph 2 of the Com. Code. (ii) However, if the amount set forth in Article 805 paragraph 2 of the Com. Code is significantly less than the result of the prevention or alleviation of the disturbance or there are other special circumstances, the amount shall be within the range of 100 to 200% of the amount set forth in Article 805 paragraph 2 of the Com. Code (Article 805 paragraph 3 of the Com. Code). When the court determines the amount, it considers the degree of danger, the result of the salvage, the labour and expenses required for the salvage (including those for the prevention and/or mitigation of marine pollution) and all other circumstances (Articles 805 paragraph 3 and 793 of the Com. Code). In addition, if the above-mentioned disturbance could not be prevented or mitigated due to the negligence of the Person Engaged in the Salvage of the Vessel to Cope with the Pollution, the court may determine the amount of the special compensation in consideration of this (Article 805 paragraph 5 of the Com. Code).

447. If a Person Engaged in the Salvage of the Vessel to Cope with the Pollution has a claim for a salvage remuneration for the same marine disaster, the amount of the special compensation shall be the amount after deducting the amount of the remuneration (Article 805(4) of the Com. Code).

§6. Liability and Limitation of Liability of Salvors

I. Liability of Salvors

448. Where a salvage contract has been entered into, the responsibility of the salvor is determined in accordance with the terms and intent of the salvage contract.

449. If the salvor starts salvage without a salvage contract, it is understood that the salvor bears the duty of care (duty as a manager of benevolent intervention in another's business). Therefore, if there is a breach of duty, the salvor is liable.

II. Limitation of Liability of Salvors

450. Japan has ratified the 1976 LLMC Convention, the 1996 Protocol and the 2015 Protocol. The Limit. Act has been enacted as a law to implement the contents of the Convention.

451. The salvor or its employee, etc. may limit the liability for the following claims; (i) a claim based on damage caused by harm to the life or body of a person directly related to the salvage activities or damage caused by loss or damage to the property other than the salvage vessel pertaining to the said salvor; (ii) a claim based on damage caused by infringement of rights directly related to the salvage activities (excluding a claim based on damage caused by loss or damage to the salvage vessel pertaining to the said salvor and a claim based on damage caused by default of obligations under a contract); (iii) a claim based on damage caused by measures taken to prevent or alleviate damage that should give rise to a claim subject to limitation (excluding a claim held by the salvor and its employee, etc.); (iv) a claim in connection with the measures taken to prevent or mitigate the damage that should give rise to a claim subject to limitation (excluding a claim held by the salvor and its employees, etc. and a claim for remuneration and expenses based on the contract with these persons) (Article 3 paragraph 2 of the Limit. Act). The term 'salvage activities' shall include: (a) measures to salvage, remove, destroy or render harmless a vessel that has sunk, been wrecked, grounded or abandoned or any object on the vessel, (b) measures to remove, destroy or render harmless cargo, and (c) measures taken to prevent or alleviate damage that would give rise to a claim subject to limitation in addition to the measures listed above, but excluding salvage activities conducted in the course of official duties (Article 2 paragraph 2 of the Limit. Act).

452. However, the salvor or its employees, etc. may not limit its liability if these claims relate to damage resulted from its personal act or omission committed with the intent to cause such loss, or recklessly and with knowledge that such loss would probably result (Article 2 paragraph 3 of the Limit. Act).

453. In addition, the salvor may not limit the liability for the following claims; a claim against the employer of the salvor's employee whose duties are related to the salvage activities and a claim held by third parties caused by the harm to the life or body of these persons (Article 2 paragraph 4 of the Limit. Act).

§7. Salvage Contracts

I. Governing Law

454. Under the Japanese academic theory, it is understood that the 1910 Salvage Convention does not apply to salvager based on a contract. However, since Article 7 of the 1910 Salvage Convention is a provision concerning salvage contracts, the following explanation will be given with the application of that Article in mind.

455. When a trial is held in Japan, it is necessary to first determine whether or not the 1910 Salvage Convention is directly applicable. Article 15 paragraph 1 of the Convention provides that if the salving vessel or the salved vessel belongs to a contracting state to the 1910 Salvage Convention, the 1910 Salvage convention applies to all interested parties. The majority of Japanese academic theories hold that it is unjust to impose convention obligations on vessels of non-contracting states, and therefore, the 1910 Convention is applicable only when the salving vessel and the salved vessel are contracting states of the 1910 Salvage convention. However, the prevailing view is that 'or' is sufficient, faithful to the wording. There is a precedent that the 1910 Salvage Convention was applied in a case where the salving vessel and the salved vessel were Japanese flag vessels (the Supreme Court Judgment dated 26 September 1974), but there is no precedent in a case where only one of the salving vessel and the salved vessel is a contracting state. In any case, if all the interested parties are Japanese or Japanese corporations, Japanese law will be applied and the 1910 Salvage Convention will not be applied (Article 15 paragraph 2 of the Convention).

456. Second, in the salvage cases where the 1910 Salvage Convention does not apply directly, the governing law of claims and obligations is determined based on the Act on the General Rules for Application of the Law. Many salvage contracts may include a governing law clause. The Act on General Rules for Application of the Law respects the governing law clause (Article 7 of the Act). If the governing law is Japanese law, the principle of freedom of contract is valid, so basically, the content of claims and obligations is determined according to the content of the salvage contract. If there is no contractual provision, the Com. Code and Civ. Code may be applied.

II. 1910 Salvage Convention

457. The rights and obligations between the parties to a salvage contract are basically governed by the contents of the salvage contract.

458. However, (1) every agreement as to assistance or salvage entered into at the moment and under the influence of danger may, at the request of either party, be annulled or modified by the court, if it considers that the conditions agreed upon are not equitable (Article 7 paragraph 1 of the Convention). (2) In all cases, when it is proved that the consent of one of the parties is vitiated by fraud or concealment, or when the remuneration is, in proportion to the services rendered, in an excessive degree too large or too small, the agreement may be annulled or modified by the court at the request of the party affected (Article 7 paragraph 2 of the Convention).

459. The purpose of (1) above is to achieve equity between the parties. It permits changes in the terms of the contract, not limited to changes in the amount of the rescue fee. It also permits not only changes but also rescission and nullification.

460. The above (2) is not required to be made under the influence at the time of the danger, so it is applicable to the contract concluded after mutual consultation between vessel owners on land. 'Concealment' is the application of the principle of the disclosure obligation in insurance contracts to marine salvage contracts, and it applies to both parties, and it includes the cases of failure to tell the truth and misrepresentation of facts, and it is interpreted to include the cases where the concealment is intentional or negligent. It does not apply to cases where the other party knows the fact of concealment. The 'too large or too small' is judged by comparing the remuneration with the labour, and mere inequality is not enough, but significant inequality is required. The cause of the 'too large or too small' may exist at the time the contract is made or afterwards.

III. Japanese Law

461. The claims and obligations between the parties to a salvage contract are basically governed by the contents of the salvage contract.

462. Article 794 of the Com. Code stipulates that even if a remuneration has been set by contract in the event of a marine accident, if the amount is extremely unreasonable, the parties may request an increase or decrease in the remuneration. The court shall determine the remuneration by taking into consideration the degree of danger, the result of the salvage, the labour and expenses required for the salvage (including those for the prevention and mitigation of marine pollution) and all other circumstances (Articles 794 and 793 of the Com. Code).

463. Unlike the 1910 Salvage Convention, there is no provision in the Com. Code allowing invalidation or modification of contractual clauses other than the remuneration. It is possible that a certain contract clause could be invalidated as a violation of public order and morals (Article 90 of the Civ. Code), but the hurdle is high.

464. With respect to the authority to conclude a salvage contract, the vessel owner and the Master have the authority to conclude a salvage contract on behalf of the owners of the cargo and other items in the vessel (Article 792 paragraph 2 of the Com. Code). It was introduced in the amendment of the Com. Code in 2018, because it is necessary for the vessel owner to conclude the salvage contract promptly in the situation where the owners of the cargo etc. are significantly numerous.

465. If the governing law of the salvage contract is Japanese law, the claim pertaining to the remuneration or special compensation is extinguished by limitation if it is not exercised for two years from the time the salvage work is completed (Article 806 of the Com. Code). Agreeing to a longer period of extinctive limitation is considered invalid.

Chapter 11. General Average

§1. The Concept of General Average

466. General Average means the damage and costs caused by the disposition of a vessel or cargo, etc., in order to avoid the common danger of the vessel and cargo, etc., encountering a maritime disaster. The system to share these damages and costs fairly among the interested parties of the vessels and cargoes, etc. that have benefited is the general average system. For example, the port of refuge expenses when a vessel that encounters a marine disaster needs to make necessary repairs to the vessel in order to complete the voyage safely and the vessel is sent to an port of refuge other than the planned port of call is an example of the general average expenses.

467. General Average is one of the oldest systems in maritime commercial code, and it is said that the *lex Rhodia de jactu* had a system concerning the General Average jettison. In Japan, the Law of the Sea Roads of 1592 contains provisions on the cases where General Average is allowed and on the method of settlement.

468. The basic principle of General Average has been debated in academic theories. The prevailing view in Japan is that a vessel and cargo, etc. constitute an isolated dangerous community at sea, and that when this community encounters a maritime danger, in order to save the community as a whole, the best possible measures should be taken at the partial expense of the vessel or cargo, etc. and if the danger can be overcome by such measures, the damage should be shared fairly by all the interested and concerned parties constituting the community.

469. The legal nature of General Average system is also debated in academic theories. Today's academic theories in Japan consider it to be a special system under the ML.

470. As a source of law on General Average, Japan has the Com. Code. The Com. Code provides five articles on General Average (Articles 808–812 of the Com. Code).

471. Apart from this, efforts have been made to achieve international uniformity in General Average legislation and the York Antwerp Rules have been produced (1890, 1924, 1950, 1974, 1994, 2004, 2016). The York Antwerp Rules are not an international convention, but only have legal effect when the parties include them in their contracts. However, many of the Bs/L and charter parties concluded by Japanese shipping companies stipulate that General Average is governed by the York Antwerp Rules. Therefore, in practice, General Average is dealt with in accordance with the York Antwerp Rules, and the General Average provisions of the Com. Code are only rarely applied.

472. The commentary on the York Antwerp Rules will be left to another book, and the provisions of the Com. Code will be explained below.

§2. Statutory Provisions

I. General

473. With respect to the requirements for the establishment of General Average, Article 808 paragraph 1 of the Com. Code provides that 'When a disposition is made with respect to a vessel or cargo, etc., in order to avoid a common risk to the vessel and cargo, etc., the damage and costs caused by such disposition (hereinafter in this Chapter referred to as a "Common Risk Avoidance Disposition") shall be General Average.'

474. The Com. Code prior to the 2018 amendment stipulated that Common Risk Avoidance Disposition must be made by the Master (Article 788 paragraph 1 of the Com. Code prior to the amendment), but the amended Code has removed that requirement. The reasons for this are: (i) there are cases where a person other than the Master may make a Common Risk Avoidance Disposition, such as when the vessel owner enters into a salvage contract and assumes the obligation to pay the salvage remuneration, and (ii) the York Antwerp Rules also do not limit the subject of Common Risk Avoidance Disposition to the Master.

475. In addition, the Com. Code prior to the amendment in 2018 did not provide for objects in a vessel other than cargo (Article 788 paragraph 1 of the Com. Code prior to the amendment). However, the amended Code have used the concept of 'cargo, etc.', which means 'cargo and other things in the vessel', with respect to the requirements for the establishment of joint marine damage (*see* Article 792 paragraph 1 of the Com. Code). The reason for this is that it was thought to be consistent with the principle of fairness to share the damage, etc. between the vessel owner and the bunker owner when a common danger to the time-chartered vessel and fuel arises, even if the disposition is made to avoid it.

II. Requirements

476. The requirements for the establishment of General Average are divided into the following elements: (i) the existence of a common danger to the vessel and cargo, etc.; (ii) the existence of a disposition to avoid the common danger; (iii) the occurrence of damage or expense to the vessel, cargo, etc. or both; and (iv) the preservation of the vessel or cargo, etc.

477. With respect to the (i) above, since a 'common' danger is required, General Average cannot be established if there is danger only to the vessel or only to the cargo. In addition, the danger must be imminent. Regardless of the cause of the danger, General Average is established even if the danger is caused by force majeure, the negligence of a third party or the negligence of the parties concerned. Where the danger to the vessel and cargo, etc. is caused by negligence, the exercise of the right of recourse by the interested party against the negligent party is not precluded (Article 808 paragraph 2 of the Com. Code).

478. With regard to the (ii) above, it is understood that the disposition referred to herein (Common Risk Avoidance Disposition) must be intentional and extraordinary. For example, jettison, cutting an anchor, intentional grounding, entering a port of refuge, extinguishing a fire, transporting by a substitute vessel, salvage, etc.

479. With respect to the (iii) above, legislative principles are divided as to the extent to which damage and costs should be considered as General Average. The common safety theory recognizes that only sacrificial damages or expenses paid to ensure the safety of the voyage property may be shared in General Average. The common benefit theory recognizes the sharing of damages or expenses necessary for the safe completion of a joint voyage. The sacrifice theory of the opfersystem recognizes a share in General Average if the damage or expense has a reasonable causal connection with the disposition, even if it does not promote either the common safety or the common benefit. According to scholars, the Japanese Com. Code adopts the common safety principle or the opfersystem.

480. With respect to the (iv) above, if either the vessel or the cargo, etc. is preserved, General Average is established. The Com. Code prior to the amendment in 2018 required that there be a causal connection between the Common Risk Avoidance Disposition and the result of preservation of the vessel or cargo (Article 789 of the Com. Code prior to the amendment). However, the amended Code stipulates that a causal connection is not required between the Common Risk Avoidance Disposition and the result of preservation (Article 810 paragraph 1 of the Com. Code). The reasons for this are that the York Antwerp Rules do not require a causal connection, and that it would be inequitable if the cargo owner who suffered damage due to the jettison does not have the right to claim for a share of the General Average when the grounded vessel jettisoned the cargo but did not float and then refloated by a tug.

III. Effects

481. Once the requirements for the establishment of General Average have been met, the damages and costs belonging to General Average constitute a receiving fund (*see* §3 below), and the property sharing the General Average constitutes a contributing fund (*see* §4 below). Establishing the scope and amount of respective funds and determining the proportion and amount to be shared is referred to as the settlement of the General Average.

482. An interested party of a receiving fund acquires a right to claim for contribution of the General Average against an interested party of the contributing funds. With respect to the claim for contribution of the General Average, the vessel owner may not limit its liability under the Limit. Act (Article 4 item 1 of the Limit. Act).

483. The claim for the General Average contribution shall be extinguished by limitation in one year from the time of completion of the calculation (Article 812 of the Com. Code).

484. The claim for contribution of General Average belonging to the burden of the vessel is secured by a maritime lien under Japanese law (Article 842 item 2 of the Com. Code, although there is a dispute as to the governing law of a vessel's lien, it is secured when Japanese law is applied).

§3. The Receiving Fund

485. Damages constituting a receiving fund are provided for in Article 809 of the Com. Code, and costs are provided for in Article 808 of the Com. Code.

486. The amount of damage to a *vessel* that constitutes General Average shall be calculated based on the price of the vessel at the time and place of arrival (Article 809 paragraph 1 item 1 of the Com. Code). This is the same purpose as the York Antwerp Rules.

487. The amount of damage to the *cargo* that constitutes General Average loss shall be calculated based on the price of the cargo at the time and place of discharge (Article 809 paragraph 1 item 2 of the Com. Code). This is also the same purpose as the York Antwerp Rules. However, the amount of all expenses that are no longer required to be paid due to loss or damage of the cargo shall be deducted (Article 809 paragraph 1 of the Com. Code). If a value lower than the actual value of the cargo is stated in a B/L or any other document sufficient to assess the value of the cargo, the amount of damage caused to the cargo shall be determined by the value stated in such a document. The same shall apply to the case where a false statement is made in the same document with respect to any matter affecting the value of the cargo, which statement would result in a lower value than the actual value of the cargo being assessed (Article 809 paragraph 2 of the Com. Code).

488. The amount of damage to *property in a vessel other than cargo* that constitutes General Average shall be calculated based on the price of the property at the time and place of arrival (Article 809 paragraph 1 item 3 of the Com. Code). Since the Com. Code was amended in 2018 to allow for the establishment of General Average for property onboard a vessel other than cargo, a new provision has been added.

489. The amount of damage to the *freight* constitutes General Average shall be calculated based on the amount of freight which may be claimed at the time and place of discharge (Article 809 paragraph 1 item 4 of the Com. Code). However, the amount of all expenses that are no longer required to be paid due to the loss of or damage to the cargo shall be deducted (Article 809 paragraph 1 of the Com. Code).

490. The amount of costs that constitute General Average is the amount of costs incurred by the Common Risk Avoidance Disposition (Article 808 paragraph 1 of the Com. Code).

491. However, the following damage or costs are not required to be shared by the interested parties: (1) damage to cargo loaded without the vessel owner's consent; (2) damage to cargo intentionally misrepresented at the time of loading; (3) damage to cargo which is valuable goods and of which the shipper or charterer has not notified its type and value at the time of consignment of carriage (except where the carrier knew at the time of conclusion of the contract of carriage of goods that the goods to be carried were valuable goods); (4) damage to cargo on deck (except where there is a commercial practice of loading on deck); (5) damage to equipment not listed in the list of equipment; and (6) special compensation (Article 808 paragraph 3 of the Com. Code). The provisions were improved in the Com. Code Amendment of 2018, and (1), (2), (4) and (6) were made based on the York Antwerp Rules.

492. Court precedents and prevailing academic view is that statutory interest should be paid on the amount of General Average damage or the General Average contribution claim.

§4. The Contributing Fund

493. Article 810 of the Com. Code provides for a contributing fund. Of these, Article 810 paragraph 1 of the Com. Code establishes the basic contribution ratio.

494. First, the parties interested in the *vessel* shall share the General Average in proportion to the price of the vessel at the time and place of arrival (Article 810 paragraph 1 item 1 of the Com. Code).

495. Second, the parties interested in the *cargo* shall share the General Average in proportion to the following prices:

Price = (the price of the said cargo at the time and place of discharge) minus (the amount of freight and other expenses that would not be required to be paid by the interested parties of the said cargo if all of the said cargo had been lost at the time of the Common Risk Avoidance Disposition) (Article 810 paragraph 1 item 2 of the Com. Code).

496. However, if a value exceeding the actual value of the cargo is stated in the B/L or any other document sufficient for assessing the price of the cargo, the parties interested in the cargo shall share the General Average in proportion to such value.

The same shall apply to the case where a false statement is made in the same document with respect to a matter affecting the price of the cargo, which statement would result in a price exceeding the actual value of the cargo being assessed (Article 810 paragraph 4 of the Com. Code).

497. Third, the parties interested in *property onboard a vessel other than cargo* (except weapons provided onboard a vessel) shall share the General Average in proportion to the price of such properties at the time and place of arrival (Article 810 paragraph 1 item 3 of the Com. Code).

498. Fourth, the *carrier* shall share the General Average in proportion to the following prices:

Price = (the amount of the claim existing at the time and place of discharge, out of the freight that would not be required to be paid by the interested party of the aforementioned cargo if all of the aforementioned cargo had been lost at the time of the Common Risk Avoidance Disposition) minus (the amount that the carrier would not be required to pay if the vessel and all of the aforementioned cargo had been lost at the time and place of the Common Risk Avoidance Disposition, out of the crew's wages and other expenses necessary for the voyage (excluding expenses that would be General Average)) (Article 810 paragraph 1 item 4 of the Com. Code).

499. The Com. Code prior to the amendment in 2018 provided that the carrier shall share the General Average in the proportion of half of the freight claim (Article 789 of the Com. Code prior to the amendment). The amount was set at half in order to avoid complications in calculation. However, since the York Antwerp Rules stipulate that the share of General Average shall be determined on the basis of net freight, the same rule was revised.

500. Fifth, *Seafarers* and *passengers* shall not share the General Average (Article 810 paragraph 1 of the Com. Code). Prior to the amendment of the Com. Code in 2018, it was stipulated that the wages of seafarers and the food and clothing of seafarers and passengers shall not share in the General Average (the main text of Article 792 of the Com. Code prior to the amendment). However, this was changed by the amendment.

501. If, after the Common Risk Avoidance Disposition, necessary or beneficial expenses are expended with respect to the vessel or the cargo, etc. before arrival or discharge, the parties shall share the General Average in proportion to the amount obtained by deducting the amount of such expenses (excluding the expenses that constitute General Average) from the price set forth in Article 810 paragraph 1 of the Com. Code (Article 810 paragraph 2 of the Com. Code). For example, if necessary or beneficial expenses are expended by repairing the vessel after the Common Risk Avoidance Disposition but before the arrival, the parties interested in the vessel shall share the General Average on the basis of the amount remaining after deducting the amount of necessary or beneficial expenses (excluding the expenses that constitute General Average) from the price of the vessel at the time and place of arrival. The rule is similar to the York Antwerp Rules.

502. If a party interested in a vessel, a party interested in a cargo, a party interested in property onboard a vessel other than cargo or a carrier suffers damage to its property as a result of a Common Risk Avoidance Disposition, the General Average shall be shared in proportion to the amount of the damage added together (Article 810 paragraph 3 of the Com. Code). This provision has been newly established in the Com. Code Amendment of 2018. A provision has been established that is in line with the practical method of calculation (the calculation method of calculating the proportion of sharing by adding the amount of damage of the interested party to the value of the property at the end of the adventure).

503. There is an upper limit to the liability of those who should share the General Average (Article 811 of the Com. Code). In other words:

(1) A party interested in a vessel shall be liable only to the extent of the value existing at the time of the arrival of the vessel.
(2) A party interested in a cargo shall be liable only to the extent of the value existing at the time the discharge of the cargo.
(3) A party interested in a property onboard the vessel other than the cargo shall be liable only to the extent of the value existing at the time of arrival of the vessel.
(4) The carrier shall be liable only to the extent of the value existing at the time of discharge of the cargo.

§5. Settlement

504. In the event of an accident giving rise to General Average and the vessel owner settle damage and expenses as General Average, the vessel owner shall send General Average declaration letter to the interested parties and appoint General Average adjuster. The vessel owner then requires the interested parties to submit an Average Bond and the insurer to submit an Average Guarantee. If these documents are not submitted, the cargo will not be delivered to the interested parties of the cargo. After these documents are obtained and the cargo is delivered, the General Average adjuster prepares a General Average statement based on various documents. Based on the entries in the statement, the General Average contribution are collected and paid.

505. Who is obliged to settle the General Average? The majority of the academic theories hold that it is the Master of the vessel, while the influential theory holds that it is the vessel owner. However, as stated above paragraph 504, in practice, a specialist of General Average adjuster is appointed as an assistant, and neither the vessel owner nor the Master settles himself.

506. If there is a special agreement, the place of settlement shall be the agreed place of settlement. If there is no special agreement, the place of settlement is the place where the voyage ends, that is, the port of discharge of the last cargo. However, if the voyage is interrupted, the place of settlement is considered to be the place where the voyage ends by the interruption.

507. There is no provision in the Com. Code for cases where there are plural General Average during the same voyage. Academic view is that respective General Average is separate and the order of settlement is as follows: first, the later General Average are settled and the amount of sharing needs to be established, the amount is deducted from the value of each property and then, pursuant to the amount after the deduction, the earlier General Average are settled and the amount of sharing is determined.

§6. Quasi General Average

508. Article 799 of the Com. Code prior to the amendment in 2018 provided that the provisions of General Average shall apply *mutatis mutandis* to the expenses necessary for a vessel to anchor at a port of departure or on a voyage due to force majeure. For example, when a vessel was forced to anchor due to a blockade or quarantine, it was considered unreasonable to make only one vessel owner bear the cost, and the provision of General Average was applied *mutatis mutandis*.

509. However, the amended Code has deleted this provision. The reason for this is that, in principle, the expenses incurred due to force majeure are to be borne by the party which expended the expenses. Further, in practice, it is sufficient for the vessel owner to set the amount of freight in anticipation of the occurrence of force majeure and take out insurance.

§7. Particular Average

510. The Com. Code does not provide a definition of Particular Average. However, academically, it is explained that (i) damage and costs arising from an emergency cause are called ‘Average’ (Average in a narrow sense), (ii) there are two types of Average: General Average and Particular Average, and (iii) Particular Average is what does not fall under the category of General Average.

511. The Com. Code contains provisions of vessel collision, which are the provisions relating to Particular Average. There are no provisions for other types of Particular Average.

Chapter 12. Collisions

§1. DEFINITIONS

I. 1910 Collision Convention

512. Japan has ratified the 1910 Convention for the Unification of Certain Rules of Law with Respect to Collisions between Vessels (Brussels, 23 September 1910).

513. The Convention does not specify the definition of 'collision'. Japanese academic theories interpret the term 'collision' in the Convention as 'a case where damage is caused by contact between vessels'.

514. Article 1 of the Convention stipulates that the Convention applies to collisions between a sea-going vessel and a sea-going vessel, or between a sea-going vessel and a vessel of inland navigation. The definition of a vessel of inland navigation is not specified, but Japanese academic view constructs that an oar-oared vessel is included in a vessel of inland navigation. Article 11 of the Convention also stipulates that it does not apply to ships of war and government vessels appropriated exclusively to a public service. Japanese academic theories construct that the Convention does not apply to collisions between a vessel of inland navigation and a vessel of inland navigation. It is also constructed that the Convention does not apply to collisions between Japanese flag vessel and Japanese flag vessel.

515. In addition, Article 13 of the Convention provides that the Convention may apply even if there is no 'collision'.

II. Commercial Code

516. The Com. Code contains provisions relating to collision of vessels (Articles 788–791 of the Com. Code). However, Article 788 of the Com. Code only defines 'collision of vessels' as 'a collision between a vessel and another vessel' and does not provide any more detailed definition than that. Scholarly theories interpret 'collision' as 'two or more vessels coming into contact with each other on the water surface and causing damage.

517. With respect to the 'two or more vessels' requirement, the provisions on collision of vessels in the Com. Code shall apply to collision between a sea-going vessel (a vessel used for navigation at sea, excluding oar-oared vessels, Article 684 of the Com. Code and Article 35 paragraph 1 of the Vessel Act) and a sea-going vessel, and collision between a sea-going vessel and a non-sea-going vessel (a vessel used for navigation solely at river, port and any other water area other than sea, excluding oar-oared vessel, Article 747 of the Com. Code and Article 35 paragraph 2 of the Vessel Act) (Article 791 of the Com. Code).

518. On the other hand, the provisions of the Com. Code do not apply to collision between a sea-going vessel and a public vessel (a vessel used for public purposes) (Article 35 paragraph 1 proviso of the Vessel Act), collision between a non-sea-going vessel and an oar-oared vessel, collision between a non-sea-going vessel and a public vessel (Article 35 paragraph 1 proviso of the Vessel Act), collision between an oar-oared vessel and an oar-oared vessel, collision between an oar-oared vessel and a public vessel (Article 35 paragraph 1 proviso of the Vessel Act), and collision between a public vessel and a public vessel (Article 35 paragraph 1 of the Vessel Act).

519. Regarding the collision between a sea-going vessel and an oar-oared vessel, the prevailing theory denies the application of the Com. Code, but the influential theory affirms the application of analogy. As for the collision between a non-sea-going vessel and a non-sea-going vessel, the academic theories are divided into the negative theory and the affirmative theory of analogical application. As for the collision between a non-sea-going vessel and an oar-oared vessel, the academic theories are divided into the negative theory and the affirmative theory of analogical application.

520. Contact between a vessel and anything other than a vessel shall not constitute a collision of vessels. If a vessel collides with a port facility, floating dock, platform, hotel on the water or vessel under construction, the provisions of the Com. Code relating to collision of vessels do not apply.

521. As for the 'water surface' requirement, it is sufficient that it is the surface of the water, regardless of the type of water body where the collision occurred.

522. As for the 'damage' requirement, damage is not limited to damage to the hull of the vessel, but includes damage to crew, passengers, cargo, or any other person or property onboard the vessel.

523. In addition, Article 790 of the Com. Code recognizes the case where the provisions of the Com. Code are applied even when there is no 'collision of vessels'. In other words, Articles 788 and 789 of the Com. Code shall apply *mutatis mutandis* to an accident in which a vessel, by its act in connection with its navigation or handling, or by its act in violation of laws and regulations relating to vessels, significantly approaches another vessel and causes damage to such other vessel or to persons or property in such other vessel.

§2. Statutory Provisions

I. Application of Conventions and National Laws

524. As noted above paragraph 512, Japan has ratified the 1910 Collision Convention.

525. However, Japan has not ratified the Convention Internationale pour l'unification de certaines regles concernant les Immunites des navires d' Etad and the International convention for the unification of certain rules relating to Civil Jurisdiction in matters of collision.

526. In the event of a court case in Japan, first, the Convention is directly applicable to collisions between vessels of parties to the 1910 Collision Convention (excluding collisions between Japanese flag vessels). Even in cases where the Convention is applicable, the Convention does not have provisions covering all matters relating to vessel collisions. Japanese law shall apply to any matter not covered by the Convention.

527. Second, in the case of a vessel collision to which the 1910 Collision Convention does not apply, the law applicable to the concerned parties' claims for compensation for damages is determined based upon the Act on General Rules for Application of Laws. As a general rule, the law of the place where the result of tortious act occurred is applied (main clause of Article 17 of the Act), and if it is a foreign law, Japanese law is superimposed (Article 22 of the Act). The governing law for claims for compensation for damages in collisions on the high seas is not clear. For details, please refer to the literature on conflict of law rules of Japan.

528. Third, if the governing law is Japanese law, the Com. Code is applicable if the said 'collision of vessels' exists (*see* paragraph 516 above). If neither the 1910 Collision Convention nor the Com. Code applies to a vessel collision case, the case will be dealt with according to the Civ. Code or the State Redress Act.

II. Damages and Procedure

A. Basic Rules on Liability, Japanese Law: Negligence

529. In terms of lectures, there are four types of collisions: (1) collisions caused by incident, (2) collisions with unknown causes, (3) collisions caused by negligence of one party, and (4) collisions caused by negligence of both parties.

530. An 'incident' is an accident by chance, which can be classified into two types: a collision caused by force majeure (a collision that occurs outside the business, the occurrence of which cannot normally be foreseen, and which cannot be prevented even by taking preventive measures that are socially accepted as appropriate), and a collision caused by accidental incidents arising from within the business. As an example of the latter, the case of a collision caused by a sudden change of course due to a sudden heart attack of the helmsman, where the helmsman's accident was unforeseeable, is given.

531. In the case of (1) and (2), the victim cannot claim for compensation for damages (however, in the case of (2), there is room for the victim of the cargo to claim for compensation for damages against the carrier based on the contract of carriage. *See* §2, II, D below).

532. In the case of (3), the victim can claim for compensation for damages against the negligent seaman (Article 709 of the Civ. Code), against the Master (Article 713 of the Com. Code), and against the vessel owner (Article 690 of the Com. Code).

533. In the case of (4), the court shall determine the liability for compensation for damages and the amount thereof of each vessel owner by taking into consideration of degree of negligence of the vessel owner and the seamen. If it is not possible to determine the degree of the negligence, the liability for compensation for damages and the amount thereof shall be borne by each vessel owner in equal proportions (Article 788 of the Com. Code). This provision shall apply to the case where the owner of a vessel claims compensation for damages against the owner of the other vessel in collision, and to the case where each owner of a vessel in collision owes an inauthentic joint and several obligations to a third party and each owner shall determine the portion of the obligation to be borne by each of them.

534. With regard to (4) above, there is a dispute as to whether two liabilities for compensation for damages exist between the owners of the colliding vessels (cross-liability theory) or only one liability for compensation for damages exists between the owners of the vessels (single liability theory). In the past, the court ruled that only one liability for damages existed (Nagasaki C.A. Judgment dated 30 September 1919; Asahikawa D.C. Judgment dated 6 April 1956). However, the current majority theory and recent judicial precedents (Tokyo D.C. Judgment dated 20 July 1965) hold that two obligations for compensation for damages exist.

B. Basic Rules on Liability, Japanese Law: Creditors

535. Potential creditors in vessel collision cases include vessel owners, vessel co-owners, vessel lessees, time charterers, cargo owners, families of the deceased, and injured parties.

536. With respect to vessel co-ownership, under Japanese law, a vessel manager must be appointed (Article 697 paragraph 1 of the Com. Code) and the claim for compensation for damages is exercised by the vessel manager (Article 698 paragraph 1 of the Com. Code).

537. When a vessel is under bareboat charter, the vessel lessee has the same rights and obligations to the third party as the vessel owner (Article 703 paragraph 1 of the Com. Code), so the vessel lessee can exercise the claim for compensation for damages. However, since the vessel lessee only has the right of possession of the vessel, there is a theory that the vessel lessee can only claim compensation for the damage caused by being prevented from using the vessel, and cannot claim compensation for the damage caused to the vessel's hull by the collision.

538. A time charterer can claim for compensation for damage due to non-operation and loss of profits due to a vessel collision, but only for the period until a replacement vessel can be reasonably deployed (Tokyo C.A. judgment dated 14 April 2016).

539. As to whether the cargo owner, the family of the deceased, the injured party, etc., can claim all damages from the vessel owner, *see below* sections I and K.

C. Basic Rules on Liability, Japanese Law: Debtors

540. The parties who can be the debtor in a vessel collision case are the vessel owner, the vessel manager, the vessel co-owner, the vessel lessee, the time charterer, the Master and the pilot. Since Japan does not have a system of action in rem, a vessel itself cannot be a debtor.

541. The vessel owner is liable to compensate for damages caused to another person by the intentional or negligent act of the Master or other seamen in the performance of their duties (Article 690 of the Com. Code). The vessel owner is not exempted from liability even if it has exercised due diligence in appointing and supervising the Master and/or other seamen.

542. If a vessel owner has concluded a vessel management contract with a vessel manager, and the vessel manager neglects to perform maintenance, repair or other work on the vessel, and this causes a vessel collision, the vessel manager is liable to compensate for damages to the victim (Article 709 of the Civ. Code).

543. A vessel co-owner is liable for damages to third parties in proportion to the value of its interest (Article 695 of the Com. Code).

544. If a vessel is bareboat chartered to a lessee and a collision occurs due to the intentional or negligent act of a seaman appointed by the vessel lessee, the vessel lessee is liable to compensate for damages (Articles 690 and 703 paragraph 1 of the Com. Code).

545. There is a dispute as to whether a time charterer can be found liable for collision. Looking at the published court decisions, there are three affirmative decisions but no negative decision.

546. In the Tokyo D.C. Judgment of 17 June 1974 (*The Full Moon* case), a cargo vessel collided with a fishing boat, resulting in the death of the fishing boat's crew, and the fishing boat's owner and the deceased's family claimed damages against the cargo vessel's time charterer. The cargo vessel owner was not a defendant. The court held that the time charterer of the cargo vessel was liable for damages to the fishing vessel owner and the deceased's family by analogy application of Article 704 paragraph 1 of the Com. Code (equivalent to Article 703 paragraph 1 of the current Com. Code). In this case, the Baltime form was used for the time charter of the cargo vessel.

547. In the Osaka D.C. Judgment of 12 August 1983 (*The Shinko Maru* case), a cargo vessel collided with a fishing boat and crew of the fishing boat passed away. The owner of the fishing boat and the bereaved family of the deceased claimed compensation for damages against the owner, time charterer and the Master of the cargo vessel. The court ruled that the owner of the cargo vessel was not liable for damages, the time charterer was liable for damages under Article 704 paragraph 1 of the Com. Code (equivalent to Article 703 paragraph 1 of the current Com. Code), and the Master was liable for damages under Article 709 of the Civ. Code. The cargo vessel was a domestic cargo vessel, and the contents of the time charter were unknown.

548. In the Supreme Court Judgment on 28 April 1992, vessel A (Kamiyama Maru No. 5) connected vessel B (Izumi Maru No. 3) with a rope, and vessel B was towing a barge, and the barge collided with a minesweeper, and the State, the owner of the minesweeper, claimed compensation for damages against (i) the Master of the vessel A, (ii) the Master of the vessel B which was also the owner of the vessel B and (iii) the time charterer of vessel A which was also the time charterer of vessel B. The Supreme Court affirmed the judgment of the C.A. court that the time charterer was liable for the same damages as the vessel owner under Article 690 of the Com. Code by analogy application of Article 704 paragraph 1 of the Com. Code (equivalent to Article 703 paragraph 1 of the present Com. Code). In this case, respective time charter was one page contract written in Japanese, and not a typical contract form such as New York Produce Exchange Time Charter (NYPE) or Baltime.

549. There is a case in which a vessel collided with a breakwater when evacuating from a port to the outside of the port, and it was disputed whether the time charterer had the authority and responsibility to decide whether or not to evacuate the vessel from the port. In this case, the time charter was in the form of NYPE. The court ruled that the time charterer had neither the authority nor the responsibility to do so (Tokyo D.C. Judgment of 20 June 2013). It will be interesting to see how this will affect future vessel collision cases.

550. Looking at the scholarly theories, the majority theory affirms time charterer's liability, but the influential theory denies.

551. The Master of a vessel shall be liable to compensate for damage caused to another person by a seaman's intentional or negligent act in performing his duties. However, if the Master proves that he was not negligent in the supervision of the seamen, he shall not be liable (Article 713 of the Com. Code).

552. It is understood that a pilot is merely an advisor to the Master of the vessel. If a vessel collision occurs as a result of the pilot's erroneous advice, it is theoretically possible for the creditor to claim compensation for damages against the pilot (Article 709 of the Civ. Code). In practice, however, it is more likely to pursue the liability of the vessel owner. Sometimes, the owner of a vessel who has compensated the victim for damages may claim recourse against the pilot, but this is not easy because the Japanese standard pilotage agreement contains a provision exempting the pilot from negligence. A case in which the liability of the pilot was denied is the judgment of the Osaka C.A. dated 14 October 2018.

D. Basic Rules on Liability, Japanese Law: Extinctive Prescription of Claims

553. Claims for compensation for damages for a tort caused by a collision of a vessel are subject to the extinctive prescription of two years from the time of the tort (the date of the collision) for those relating to the infringement of property rights (Article 789 of the Com. Code). On the other hand, claims for compensation for damages for bodily injury are subject to the extinctive prescription of five years from the time when the victim became aware of the damage and the wrongdoer, or to the extinctive prescription of twenty years from the time of the tort (the date of the collision) (Article 724-2 of the Civ. Code).

E. Basic Rules on Liability, 1910 Collision Convention

554. It stipulates similar contents to the Com. Code. In case of (1) collisions caused by incident or (2) collisions with unknown causes, claim for compensation for damage is not possible (Article 2 paragraph 1 of the 1910 Collision Convention). In case of (3) collisions caused by negligence of one party, the victim may claim damages against the owner of the negligent vessel (Article 3 of the Convention). In case of (4) collisions caused by negligence of both parties, the liability of each vessel is in proportion to the degree of the faults respectively committed and if it is not possible to establish the degree, the responsibility shall be equal (Article 4 paragraph 1 of the Convention).

555. The claim for compensation for damages is subject to an extinctive prescription of two years from the date of the accident (Article 7 paragraph 1 of the Convention).

F. Evaluation of Fault

556. In determining the negligence of the vessel owner and the vessel's crew, the Japanese courts have focused on whether the vessel violated the navigational rules prescribed by law. This has been adopted both where the 1910 Collision Convention applies and where the Com. Code or other Japanese law applies.

557. The general rule of navigation is the Prevention of Collisions at Sea Act. This is in accordance with the provisions of the International Regulations for Preventing Collisions at Sea, 1972, attached to the Convention on the International Regulations for Preventing Collisions at Sea, 1972.

558. Special rules of navigation are provided in the Maritime Traffic Safety Act and the APR. The Maritime Traffic Safety Act provides special rules for areas where there is particularly heavy vessel traffic, such as Tokyo Bay, Ise Bay, and the Seto Inland Sea. The APR sets forth special rules in ports.

G. Liability for Damage to Other Vessels Where the Japanese Law Applies

559. In the event of a collision caused by the negligence of one of the vessels, the owner of the non-faulting vessel may claim damages against the owner of the negligent vessel (Article 690 of the Com. Code). In the case of a collision caused by the negligence of both vessels, the owner of one vessel may claim damages against the owner of the other vessel in proportion to the negligence of the other vessel (Article 788 of the Com. Code).

560. The damages that can be claimed are the damages that have a reasonable causal connection with the negligence.

561. If a vessel is damaged, it is possible to claim compensation for repair costs, inspection costs, towing costs, salvage costs, general average contribution, loss of earnings, etc.

562. If a vessel becomes total loss, it is possible to claim compensation for value of the lost vessel, wreck removal costs, and the vessel owner's property onboard the vessel. As for loss of earnings, it is possible to claim compensation for the amount of unreceived freight for the voyage on which the collision occurred. As for the loss of earnings for a reasonable period of time until a replacement vessel is acquired, the Supreme Court Judgment of 22 May 1926 denied the claim for a cargo vessel case and the Miyazaki D.C. Judgment of 12 March 2010 affirmed for a fishing vessel case.

H. Liability for Damage to Other Vessels Where 1910 Collision Convention Applies

563. In the event of a collision caused by the negligence of one vessel, the victim may claim damages against the owner of the negligent vessel (Article 3 of the Convention). In the event of a collision caused by the negligence of both vessels, the owner of one vessel may claim damages against the owner of the other vessel in proportion to the negligence of the other vessel (Article 4 paragraph 1 of the Convention).

564. There is no provision in the Convention as to the damages that may be claimed. The Japanese courts will apply the laws of Japan in making their decisions.

I. Liability for Cargo Claims Where Japanese Law Applies

565. Suppose that a cargo vessel A carrying cargo collides with another vessel B. The cargo owner's claim against the owner of vessel A and the claim against the owner of vessel B must be considered separately.

1. Claims Against the Owner of Vessel A

566. Where the port of loading and the port of discharge are outside Japan, where the port of loading is outside Japan or where the port of discharge is outside Japan, the Carriage of Goods by Sea Act (COGSA) shall apply.

567. If the owner of vessel A is the carrier under the contract of carriage, it is likely that the cargo owner cannot claim damages against the owner of vessel A due to the application of the exemption of error in navigation (Article 3 paragraph 2 of the COGSA).

568. If the owner of vessel A is not the carrier under the contract of carriage, the owner of the vessel A vessel may be able to avail itself of the carrier's exemption of error in navigation by virtue of the Himalaya clause contained in the contract of carriage and, again, it is likely that the cargo owner will not be able to claim damages against the owner of the vessel A.

569. If both the port of loading and the port of discharge are in Japan, the Com. Code shall apply. The Com. Code does not provide for exemption of error in navigation.

570. If the owner of vessel A is the carrier under the contract of carriage, the owner of the cargo may claim damages against the owner of vessel A. However, the cargo owner may not do so if the owner of vessel A proves that it was not negligent in the receipt, carriage, storage and delivery of the goods carried (Article 575 of the Com. Code). In addition, the Standard Terms and Conditions of Carriage for Domestic Navigation have a clause that allows the carrier to be exempted from liability for damage arising from navigation after departure, if it is proved that the seaman was not malicious or grossly negligent (Article 18 paragraph 5). Therefore, if this clause exists in the contract of carriage in question, the cargo owner may be able to claim damages against the owner of vessel A, but if the owner of vessel A proves the reason for the exemption under the contract of carriage, the cargo owner cannot be compensated for the damages.

571. The amount for which compensation may be claimed is basically limited. Namely, the amount shall be determined by the market price of the cargo at the place and time when delivery is to be made, or, if there is no market price, by the normal price of the goods of the same kind and quality at the place and time (Article 576 paragraph 1 of the Com. Code). Lost resale profits are outside the scope of compensation. However, this does not apply where the cargo is lost or damaged due to intentional or gross negligent act of the owner of Vessel A, the carrier (Article 576 paragraph 3 of the Com. Code).

572. If the owner of vessel A is not the carrier under the contract of carriage, the owner of the cargo may claim damages against the owner of vessel A if the crew of vessel A is intentional or negligent (Article 690 of the Com. Code). However, if the contract of carriage contains the Himalaya clause and the carrier's exemption clause, the owner of Vessel A may rely on them. The owner of the cargo can claim damages against the owner of vessel A only to the same extent as against the carrier.

2. Claims Against the Owner of Vessel B

573. The owner of the cargo can claim compensation for damages against the owner of vessel B (Article 690 of the Com. Code). The damage that can be claimed is the full amount. However, if the contract of carriage concluded by the cargo owner contains an exemption clause, or if the law applicable to the contract of carriage contains a statutory exemption provision, there is a dispute as to whether the owner of Vessel B can claim that the amount of its compensation is only the percentage of the fault of Vessel B by taking advantage of this clause or provision. The Tokyo D.C. Judgment of 25 April 1930 affirms this. Old theories deny the application, but recent majority theories affirm the application. In practice, it is often the case that only the percentage of negligence of vessel B is claimed.

J. Liability for Cargo Claims Where the 1910 Collision Convention Applies

574. Suppose that a cargo vessel A carrying cargo collides with another vessel B. The cargo owner's claim against the owner of vessel A and the claim against the owner of vessel B must be considered separately.

1. Claims Against the Owner of Vessel A

575. Under the Convention, the cargo owner can claim damages from the owner of vessel A according to the percentage of negligence of vessel A (Article 4 paragraph 2 of the Convention). However, for the following reasons, it is likely to be difficult to claim in practice.

576. If the owner of vessel A is the carrier under the contract of carriage, it is likely that the cargo owner will not be able to claim damages against the owner of vessel A due to the error in navigation defence (Article 4 Rule 2a of H.V.R.).

577. If the owner of vessel A is not the carrier under the contract of carriage, it is likely that the owner of vessel A can use the carrier's exemption of error in navigation by the Himalaya clause contained in the contract of carriage, and again, it is likely that the cargo owner cannot claim damages against the owner of vessel A.

2. Claims Against the Owner of Vessel B

578. The cargo owner may claim damages against the owner of vessel B according to the percentage of negligence of vessel B (Article 4 paragraph 2 of the Convention).

579. As for the amount of damages, there is no provision in the Convention, and the Japanese court will judge it in accordance with Japanese law.

K. Liability for Personal Injury (Crew) Where Japanese Law Applies

580. Suppose that vessel A, with a crew onboard, collides with another vessel B. The basis of the crew's claim against the owner of vessel A and the basis of the claim against the owner of vessel B are both in tort.

581. If there is an employment contract between the crew and the owner of vessel A, breach of contract is also a basis for a claim. The content of the employment contract may affect the crew's tort claim against the owner of vessel A. However, on ocean-going vessels, a crew usually enters into an employment contract with a manning company and not with the owner of the A vessel. In addition, on domestic vessels, the employment contract often does not contain any special provisions regarding compensation for damages. Therefore, tort claims will be focused on herein below.

582. The crew may claim compensation for damages from the owner of Vessel A and the owner of Vessel B (Article 690 of the Com. Code). Both vessel owners are joint tortfeasors and are jointly and severally liable to compensate the crew for all damages (Article 719 of the Civ. Code).

583. With regard to the internal claim for indemnification between joint tortfeasors, it was conventionally held that one tortfeasor who paid the victim in excess of his own burden could claim indemnification from the other tortfeasor (Supreme Court Judgment of 1 July 1988). However, it is not clear, after 1 April 2020, when the amended Civ. Code entered into force, whether payment in excess of one's own burden is required, and it is necessary to wait for the accumulation of court cases.

584. The damages that can be claimed by a crew member are damages which have reasonable causal connection. In the case of an injury, the crew member can claim for medical expenses, medicine expenses, attendant care expenses, hospitalization expenses, transport expenses to and from the hospital, damage by absence from work, loss of earnings due to the aftereffects, consolation money for injuries, and consolation money for aftereffects. In the case of death, funeral expenses, dead body storage and transportation expenses, travel expenses for the bereaved family, loss of earnings due to death, and consolation money for death may be claimed.

585. If the victim, the crew member, is at fault, the amount of damages will be reduced (Article 722 paragraph 2 of the Civ. Code). In addition, if workers' compensation insurance money, survivor's pension, or non-life insurance money is paid, the amount of such money will be reduced from the amount of compensation for damages.

L. Liability for Personal Injury (Crew) Where the 1910 Collision Convention Applies

586. The crew may claim from the owner of each vessel compensation for the entire damage, irrespective of the percentage of fault of each vessel (Article 4 paragraph 3 of the Convention). The owner of one vessel may claim indemnity from the owner of the other vessel if he pays more than its burden of the damage (Article 4 paragraph 3 of the Convention).

587. As for the amount of damages, there is no provision in the convention, and the Japanese court will judge in accordance with Japanese law.

M. Procedure, Especially the Determination of Damages

588. In order for a Japanese court to hear a collision case, it must have international jurisdiction. Japan has not ratified the International Convention for the Unification of Certain Rules Relating to Civil Jurisdiction in Matters of Collision, 1952. Whether or not the Japanese courts have international jurisdiction is determined in accordance with the provisions of the CCP of Japan. If the point of collision is within Japan's territorial waters, the international jurisdiction of Japanese courts is affirmed (Article 3-3 item 8 of the CCP). Even if the point of collision is on the high seas, the international jurisdiction of the Japanese courts is affirmed if the place where the damaged vessel first arrived is in Japan (Article 3-3 item 9 of the CCP). Even if the point of collision is on the high seas or in the territorial waters of a foreign state, if the principal office of the defendant is located in Japan, the international jurisdiction of the Japanese courts is affirmed (Article 3-2 paragraph 3 of the CCP). However, it is denied if there are special circumstances (Article 3-9 of the CCP). There is a court case that denied the international jurisdiction of the Japanese court over a case where a vessel collision occurred at high seas and the damaged vessel firstly arrived at Japan (Sendai C.A. Judgment of 22 September 2011).

589. In Japan, vessel collision cases are tried in ordinary civil litigation, and there is no special litigation system such as admiralty litigation.

590. The normal flow of a civil litigation is as follows. The plaintiff files a complaint, the defendant files an answer, and the first date is held. Thereafter, both parties submit their arguments and evidence regarding liability and quantum. If the issues are clarified and it is judged that it is necessary to examine witnesses, the examination of witnesses is conducted. Thereafter, the parties submit their final briefs, the oral argument is concluded, and the court renders its judgment. Depending on the case, the court may precede the trial on liability issue and start the trial on quantum issue after issuing a judgment on the apportionment of liability (Tokyo D.C. Interim Judgment on 30 September 2011).

591. Damages are often established by documentary evidence. If there is a dispute, witnesses such as experts and victims may be examined.

III. Limitation of Liability

592. The Limit. Act defines a vessel used for navigation, other than a boat driven by oars or mainly by oars and a vessel used for public purposes, as a 'vessel' (Article 2 paragraph 1 item 1 of the Limit. Act). Judicial decisions are divided as to whether or not a vessel navigating only in a smooth water area constitutes a 'vessel'. The Tokyo C.A. decision on 10 December 1992 and the Tokyo C.A. decision on 17 October 1995 held t that such a vessel does not fall under a 'vessel'. The Fukuoka C.A. Decision on 4 February 2021 held that it is a 'vessel'.

593. Vessel owners, etc. or their employees, etc. may limit their liability for a claim subject to limitation pursuant to the provisions of the Limit. Act (Article 3 paragraph 1 item 1 of the said Act). A 'claim subject to limitation' includes a claim based on the damage caused by the harm to the life or body of a person or damage caused by loss of or damage to property other than the vessel which has arisen onboard or has arisen directly related to the operation of the vessel (Article 3 paragraph 1 item 1 of the said Act). Therefore, it is likely that claims arising from vessel collision fall under the category of claims subject to limitation. *See* Chapter 5 for details.

IV. Tugs and Collisions

594. For more information on tugs in general, *see* Chapter 9. Tugs and collisions are discussed in the following sections.

595. Where a tug and a towed vessel collide, this is dealt with as a matter of default under the tug contract. It also gives rise to liability in tort, so there is scope for the provisions on vessel collision to apply.

596. There is a debate about the case of collision between a towing line and a third vessel. There is an idea that a tug is an employee of a towed vessel and the owner of the towed vessel is responsible for the act of the tug, which was called the principle of unity of towing line. The Supreme Court Judgment of 10 September 1938 held in a collision case that a barge, which is a towed vessel, is not an independent vessel but consists of one unit with a tug. However, the current majority academic view holds that the subject of liability to third parties differs depending on whether a tug or a towed vessel has the command of a towing line.

Chapter 13. Marine Pollution

§1. Introduction

597. With the rapid industrialization of Japan after the World War II, various kinds of pollution occurred, and laws for environmental conservation were prepared to cope with them. Since the 1970s, international conventions for marine environmental protection have been concluded, and Japan has ratified these conventions and revised its domestic laws to conform to their content. With regard to civil liability, laws have been developed to reflect the CLC Convention, the FC Convention, the Bunker Convention, and the Nairobi Convention.

§2. Statutory Provisions

598. Japan has ratified the following various international conventions on the prevention of marine pollution:

(1) Protocol of 1978 to the International Convention for the Prevention of Pollution from Vessels, 1973;
(2) Protocol of 1997 to amend the International Convention for the Prevention of Pollution from Ships, 1973, as modified by the Protocol of 1978 relating thereto;
(3) Convention on the Prevention of Marine Pollution by Dumping of Wastes and Other Matter 1972;
(4) 1996 Protocol to the Convention on the Prevention of Marine Pollution by Dumping of Wastes and Other Matter, 1972;
(5) International Convention on Oil Pollution Preparedness, Response and Cooperation, 1990;
(6) Protocol on Preparedness, Response and Co-operation to Pollution Incidents by Hazardous and Noxious Substances, 2000;
(7) International Convention for the Control and Management of Ship's Ballast Water and Sediments, 2004;
(8) International Convention on the Control of Harmful Anti-fouling Systems on Vessels, 2001;
(9) Protocol to the International Convention on Civil Liability for Oil Pollution Damage, 1976 (Protocol to the International Convention on Civil Liability for Oil Pollution Damage of 29 November 1969;
(10) International Maritime Organization Protocol of 1992 to amend the International Convention on Civil Liability for Oil Pollution Damage of 29 November 1969;
(11) Protocol to the International Convention on the Establishment of an International Fund for Compensation for Oil Pollution Damage;
(12) The International Convention on the Establishment of an International Fund for Compensation for Oil Pollution Damage of 1992;
(13) Protocol of 2003 to the International Convention on the Establishment of an International Fund for Compensation for Oil Pollution Damage, 1992;

(14) International Convention on Civil Liability for Bunker Oil Pollution Damage, 2001;
(15) Nairobi International Convention on the Removal of Wrecks, 2007; and
(16) although not yet in force, Japan has also deposited a letter of accession to (16) Hong Kong International Convention for the Safe and Environmentally Sound Recycling of Ships, 2009.

599. In order to realize (1)–(7) listed above, in Japan, APMPMD (Act No. 136 of 1970) has been enacted and revised. The (3) and (4) above are also related to the Waste Management and Public Cleaning Act (Act No. 137 of 1970). In order to realize (8) in Japan, the Vessel Safety Act, the Enforcement Regulations of the Vessel Safety Act, and the Vessel Structure Regulations have been amended. In order to realize (9)–(15) in Japan, the OPDA (Act No. 95 of 1975) has been enacted and revised, and in order to realize (16), the Act on Proper Performance of Recycling and Dismantling of Vessel (Act No. 61 of 2018) has been enacted.

600. In addition, the Water Pollution Prevention Act (WPA, Act No. 138 of 1970) has been enacted to prevent pollution of public waters (including ports and coastal waters). For specific lakes and marshes, the Act on Special Measures concerning Conservation of Lake Water Quality (Act No. 61 of 1984) has been enacted.

§3. Sources of Pollution

I. Pollution from Vessels

601. The APMPMD establishes various regulations. The main regulations are as follows.

A. Regulations on Discharge of Oil from Vessels

602. Article 4 paragraph 1 of the APMPMD establishes the principle that no person shall discharge oil from a vessel in the sea area. Vessel owners are obliged, in principle, to instal equipment to prevent the discharge of bilge from their vessels (Article 5, paragraph 1 of the APMPMD. The exception is vessels that do not produce bilge, etc.). In addition, tankers are required to instal equipment to prevent the discharge of water ballast, etc. (Article 5 paragraph 2 of the APMPMD). Furthermore, crude oil tankers with a deadweight of 20,000 tons or more must be equipped with separate ballast tanks or a cargo hold crude oil cleaning system (Article 5 paragraph 3 of the APMPMD, Article 14 of the Ministerial Ordinance on Technical Standards). The owner of a tanker with a gross tonnage of 200 tons or more shall be obliged to appoint an Oil Pollution Prevention Manager from the vessel's personnel onboard (Article 6 of the APMPMD, Article 9 of the Enforcement Regulation of the APMPMD). The Owner of a tanker of 150 gross tons or more or a vessel of 400 gross tons or more other than a tanker (excluding a laid-up vessel) shall be obliged to establish the Oil Pollution Prevention Rules (Article 7 paragraph 1 of

APMPMD, Article 11 of the Enforcement Regulation of the APMPMD), and shall be obliged to prepare the Emergency Guide for Oil Pollution Prevention and keep it in the vessel (Article 7-2 of the APMPMD, Article 34 of the Ministerial Ordinance on Technical Standards). In addition, the Master shall keep the Oil Record Book in the vessel and make an entry in the Oil Record Book when the vessel discharges oil (Article 8 of the APMPMD). The owner of a tanker whose gross tonnage is 150 tons or more and which transships cargo oil in bulk with other tankers shall be obliged to prepare and keep onboard a manual for transshipment of cargo oil between vessels (Article 8-2 paragraph 1 of the APMPMD). The Master of a tanker of 150 gross tons or more that transships cargo oil between vessels in the inland waters, territorial waters or exclusive economic zones of Japan shall notify the Japan Coast Guard in advance of the time and area of transshipment (Article 8-3 paragraph 1 of the APMPMD and Article 11-4 of the Enforcement Regulation of the APMPMD). The regulations in Article 6 and Article 7 do not apply to foreign-flag vessels (Article 9 paragraph 3 of the APMPMD).

B. Regulations on Discharge of Hazardous Liquid Substances from Vessels

603. Article 9-2 paragraph 1 of the APMPMD establishes the principle that no person shall discharge hazardous liquid substances from vessels in the sea area. Owners of bulk carriers of hazardous liquid substances are obliged to instal equipment to prevent the discharge of hazardous liquid substances (Article 9-3 of the APMPMD and Article 21 paragraph 1 of the Ministerial Ordinance on Technical Standards, etc.). The owner of a vessel of 200 tons or more in gross tonnage transporting hazardous liquid substances shall be obliged to appoint an Hazardous Liquid Pollution Prevention Manager from the vessel's personnel onboard the vessel (Article 9-4 paragraph 1 of the APMPMD and Article 12-2-5 of the Enforcement Regulation of the APMPMD), and the owner of a vessel of 150 tons or more in gross tonnage transporting hazardous liquid substances shall be obliged to establish the Hazardous Liquid Pollution Prevention Rules and prepare an Emergency Guide for Hazardous Liquid Pollution Prevention and keep it onboard the vessel (Article 9-4 paragraphs 2 and 6 of the APMPMD and Article 12-2-27 of the Enforcement Regulations of the APMPMD). In addition, the Master of a vessel transporting hazardous liquid substances shall keep a hazardous liquid substances record book onboard, and shall make an entry in the record book when a hazardous liquid substance is discharged (Article 9-5 of the APMPMD).

C. Regulations on Discharge of Wastes from Vessels

604. Article 10 paragraph 1 of APMPMD establishes the principle that no person shall discharge waste materials from vessels in the sea area. Owners of vessels engaged in international voyages with a gross tonnage of 400 tons or more or with a maximum capacity of 16 people or more are obliged to instal equipment to prevent the discharge of faeces and urine into their vessels (Article 10-2 paragraph 1 of the APMPMD, Article 2 item 1 of the Enforcement Order of the APMPMD). In the case of a vessel in the Antarctic Ocean, the regulation is applied to a vessel with a gross tonnage of 400 tons or more or the maximum capacity of eleven people or more. Owners of vessels with a gross tonnage of 100 tons or more or a maximum capacity of fifteen people or more are obliged to establish Wastes Pollution Prevention Rules and keep them onboard (Article 10-3 paragraph 1 of the APMPMD, and Article 12-3-3 of the Enforcement Regulation of the APMPMD). The Master of a vessel with gross tonnage of 400 tons or more or with a maximum capacity of fifteen people or more onboard (except those engaged in mining of mineral resources on the seabed or under the seabed) shall keep onboard a Vessel Generated Wastes Record Book and shall make entries in the record book when certain operations related to the handling of vessel generated wastes are carried out (Article 10-4 paragraph 1 of the APMPMD and Article 12-3-5 of the Enforcement Regulation of the APMPMD). Any person who intends to dispose of certain wastes from vessels in the sea shall obtain permission from the Minister of the Environment (Article 10-6 paragraph 1 of the APMPMD). In addition, a person who intends to discharge certain wastes from a vessel shall obtain confirmation of the discharge plan from the Director-General of the Japan Coast Guard before loading the wastes into the vessel (Article 10-12 paragraph 1 of the APMPMD).

605. For the disposal of oil, hazardous liquid substances or wastes under the seabed, *see* section III below.

D. Regulations on Discharge of Harmful Water Ballast from Vessels

606. Article 17 paragraph 1 of the APMPMD establishes the principle that no person shall discharge harmful water ballast from vessels in the sea area. In addition, in principle, the owner of every vessel shall be obliged to instal a harmful water ballast treatment equipment onboard the vessel (Article 17-2 paragraph 1 of the APMPMD, with five exceptions listed in Article 12-14-12 of the Enforcement Regulation of the APMPMD), and shall be obliged to appoint a Harmful Water Ballast Pollution Prevention Manager from the vessel's personnel onboard the vessel (Article 17-3 paragraph 1 of the APMPMD, with three exceptions listed in Article 12-14-13 of the Enforcement Regulation of the APMPMD), and to prepare and keep in the vessel a Guide for Prevention of Pollution of Harmful Water Ballast (Article 17-3 paragraph 2 of the APMPMD). As a general rule, the Master of every vessel shall keep a Water Ballast Record Book onboard and make an entry in the record book when discharging harmful water ballast (Article 17-4 paragraphs 1 and 2 of the APMPMD; three exceptions are listed in Article 12-14-15 and 12-14-13 of the Enforcement Regulation of the APMPMD).

E. Regulations on the Emission of Exhaust Gas from Vessels

607. Article 19-21 paragraph 1 of the APMPMD establishes the principle that when any person uses fuel oil for vessels in the sea area, it must use fuel oil whose sulphur content and other qualities conform to the standards specified by the Cabinet Order for each sea area. However, this principle does not apply when sulphur oxide emission reduction equipment is installed and used in accordance with the provisions of the Ministerial Ordinance (Article 19-21 paragraph 2 of the APMPMD). The owner of a vessel who intends to change the fuel to be used while the vessel is in navigation shall be obliged to prepare and keep in the vessel a Guide for Operation to Change Fuel Oil (Article 19-21-2 of the APMPMD). The Master of a vessel of 400 gross tons or more engaged in international voyage shall keep a fuel oil supply certificate and a sample onboard for a certain period of time when the vessel is loaded with fuel oil (Article 19-22 of the APMPMD, Article 12-17-7 to Article 12-17-10 of the Enforcement Regulation of the APMPMD).

608. The Minister of Land, Infrastructure, Transport and Tourism may designate a port as a port regulated for the release of volatile substances (Article 19-13 paragraph 1 of the APMPMD). The owner of a vessel which loads cargoes which emit volatile organic compounds at the port is obliged to instal equipment to prevent the emission of volatile substances on the vessel (Article 19-24 paragraph 1 of the APMPMD). The owner of a crude oil tanker shall be obliged to prepare a Guide for Prevention of Volatile Substance Release and keep it in the tanker (Article 19-24-2 of the APMPMD).

609. The owner of an ocean-going vessel of Japanese registry with a gross tonnage of 400 tons or more shall prepare a Carbon Dioxide Emission Control Guide and obtain the approval of the Minister of Land, Infrastructure, Transport and Tourism (Article 19-25 paragraph 1 and Article 19-32 paragraph 1 of the APMPMD and Article 1-20 of the Regulations Concerning the Inspection etc. of Equipment, etc. of Vessels under the Provisions of the APMPMD). When the Minister of Land, Infrastructure, Transport and Tourism approves it, the Minister shall be obliged to issue a Certificate for International CO_2 Emission Reduction Vessel (Article 19-27 paragraph 1 of the APMPMD) and the owner of the vessel who has received the said Certificate shall be obliged to keep the said Certificate and the Guide onboard (Article 19-29 paragraph 1 of the APMPMD).

610. When owners of vessels instal engines on their vessels, they shall, as a general rule, instal engines for which they have obtained an International Air Pollution Prevention Engine Certificate (Article 19-7 paragraph 1 of the APMPMD). In addition, engines to be installed on vessels shall be installed in accordance with a Guide for Handling Engines approved by the Minister of Land, Infrastructure, Transport and Tourism so that they conform to certain technical standards (Article 19-7 paragraph 4 of the APMPMD). When a vessel owner has installed engines on a vessel, the vessel owner shall keep onboard the vessel a Certificate for Engines for Prevention of International Air Pollution and an approved Guide for Handling Engines (Article 19-8 of the APMPMD). This regulation does not apply to engines installed on foreign-flagged vessels (Article 19-16 paragraph 1 of the APMPMD).

F. Prohibition of Disposal of Vessels

611. No person shall abandon a vessel in the sea. However, this shall not apply in the case of abandoning a vessel in distress which is difficult to remove (Article 43 paragraph 1 of the APMPMD).

G. Penalties

612. Violations of the various regulations are subject to criminal penalties. For example, a person who intentionally discharges oil in violation of Article 4 paragraph 1 of the APMPMD is subject to a fine of up to JPY 10 million, and a person who negligently discharges oil is subject to a fine of up to JPY 5 million (Article 55 paragraph 1 item 1 and Article 55 paragraph 2 of the APMPMD). When a representative or an employee of a juridical person commits any of these violations with respect to the business of the juridical person, the same fine is imposed on the juridical person (Article 59 of the APMPMD).

H. Ordinance for Enforcement of the Vessel Safety Act

613. In response to the AFL Convention, Article 64 of the Vessel Structure Regulations stipulates that antifouling methods must not use organotin compounds that exceed the tin content rate specified in the Notification. Notification No. 1035 of the MLIT stipulates that the content rate shall be 0.25% by mass when the paint is sufficiently dry. The definition of antifouling method is given in Article 19 paragraph 3 item 3, sub-item 2 of the Enforcement Regulations of the Vessel Safety Act.

II. Pollution from Land-Based Sources

614. The WPA aims to prevent water pollution in public waters and groundwater. Public waters include rivers, ports, and coastal waters (Article 2 paragraph 1 of the WPA).

A. Regulations on Discharged Water

615. A person who discharges water from a specified workplace to a public water shall not discharge water that does not conform to the effluent standards at the drainage outlet of the specified workplace (Article 12 paragraph 1 of the WPA). A specified workplace is a factory or a workplace where specified facilities are installed (Article 2 paragraph 6 of the WPA), and a specified facility is a facility that (i)(a) discharges sewage or wastewater that contains harmful substances or (i)(b) discharges sewage or wastewater that contains items which are likely to cause damage to the life environment with respect to the items specified by a Cabinet Order such as ‘hydrogen ion concentration’ and (ii) facilities specified by a Cabinet Order such as coal selection facilities used for mining (Article 2 paragraph 2 of the WPA, Article 1, Article 3 and Appended Table 1 of the Enforcement Order of the WPA). Harmful substances mean substances specified by Cabinet Order such as cadmium, cadmium compounds and cyanide compounds (Article 2 paragraph 2 item 1 of the WPA and Article 2 of the Enforcement Order of the WPA). Effluent standards are set by the Ministerial Ordinance of the Ministry of the Environment (Article 3 paragraph 1 of the WPA), but prefectures may set more stringent permissible limits (Article 3 paragraph 3 of the WPA).

616. In order to ensure compliance with the regulation, there are systems such as: (a) obligation of notification by business operator when setting up the specified facility (Article 5 paragraph 1 of the WPA) and plan change order by prefectural governor (Article 8 paragraph 1 of the WPA); (b) improvement measure order by prefectural governor when a discharged water which does not comply with effluent standards is likely to be discharged (Article 13 paragraph 1 of the WPA); (c) obligation to measure, record and preserve records of the state of pollution of the discharged water of the person who discharges the discharged water (Article 14 paragraph 1 of the WPA); (d) obligation to report and take emergency measures by the business operator when it discharged the discharged water which does not conform to the effluent standards due to an accident (Article 14-2 paragraph 1 of the WPA) and emergency measures order by the prefectural governor (Article 14-2 paragraph 4 of the WPA); (e) constant monitoring by prefectural governors (Article 15 of the WPA) and (f) emergency measures orders by prefectural governors in the event of significant water pollution due to abnormal droughts, etc. (Article 18 of the WPA).

B. Total Volume Control in Designated Areas

617. The establisher of a workplace in a designated area shall comply with the total volume control standards pertaining to said workplace (Article 12-2 of the WPA). A workplace in a designated area means a specified workplace in an area designated by the Minister of the Environment with an average daily effluent volume of 50 m^3 or more (Article 4-5 paragraph 1 of the WPA, Article 1-4 of the Enforcement Regulations of the WPA). The total volume control standard is a standard for the amount of pollutant load of discharged water established by the prefectural governor based on the total volume reduction basic policy set by the Minister of the Environment and the total volume reduction plan set by the prefectural governor (Article 4-2 paragraph 1, Article 4-3 paragraph 1 and Article 4-5 paragraph 1 of the WPA).

618. In order to ensure compliance with the total volume control standards, there are the following systems: (a) obligation of notification by business operators when setting up specified facilities (Article 5 paragraph 1 of the WPA) and prior action orders by prefectural governors (Article 8-2 of the WPA); (b) improvement measure orders by prefectural governors when there is a risk of discharging effluent that does not comply with the total volume control standards (Article 13 paragraph 3 of the WPA); (c) obligation to measure, record and preserve records of the pollution load of discharged water by those who discharge discharged water from a workplace in a designated areas (Article 14 paragraph 2 of the WPA); (d) constant monitoring by prefectural governors (Article 15 of the WPA); and (e) emergency measures orders by prefectural governors in the event of significant water pollution due to abnormal droughts, etc. (Article 18 of the WPA).

C. Regulations on Underground Seepage Water

619. A person who discharges water from a specified workplace where hazardous substances are used shall not allow specified underground seepage water that satisfies certain requirements to seep in (Article 12-3 of the WPA). Specified underground seepage water means water that seeps underground from a factory or workplace where a specified facility using a hazardous substance is installed (a Specified Workplace Using a Hazardous Substance) and that is sewage or waste water pertaining to the Specified Facility Using a Hazardous Substance (Article 2 paragraphs 7 and 8 of the WPA). A Specified Facility Using a Hazardous Substances means a specific facility that manufactures, uses or treats hazardous substances, but excludes a Designated Regional Specified Facility (Article 2 paragraph 8 of the WPA).

620. In order to ensure compliance with the above regulations, there are the following systems: (a) obligation of notification by the business operator when setting up the specified facility (Article 5 paragraph 1 of the WPA) and plan change order by prefectural governor (Article 8 paragraph 1 of the WPA); (b) improvement measure order by the prefectural governor when there is a risk of infiltrating the specified underground seepage water (Article 13-2 paragraph 1 of the WPA); (c) obligation of the person who percolates the specified underground seepage water to measure, record, and preserve records of the state of contamination of the specified underground water (Article 14 paragraph 1 of the WPA); (d) obligation of the business operator to notify and take emergency measures when water containing hazardous substances percolates underground due to an accident (Article 14-2 paragraph 1 of the WPA) and emergency measure orders by prefectural governor (Article 14-2 paragraph 4 of the WPA); (e) constant monitoring by prefectural governor (Article 15 of the WPA); and (f) emergency measure orders by prefectural governor in the event of significant water pollution due to an abnormal drought, etc. (Article 18 of the WPA).

D. Designated Facilities and Measures to Be Taken in the Event of an Accident

621. In the event that water containing a hazardous substance is discharged into a public water or infiltrates underground due to an accident, the person who set up a factory or workplace (designated workplace) that instals a designated facility shall immediately notify the prefectural governor of the circumstances of the accident and take emergency measures to prevent the discharge or infiltration (Article 14-2 paragraph 2 of the WPA). Designated facilities are facilities that store or use hazardous substances, or that manufacture, store, use or treat substances specified by a Cabinet Order, such as formaldehyde (Article 2 paragraph 4 of the WPA, Article 3-3 of the Enforcement Regulation of the WPA).

E. Oil Storage Facilities and Measures to Be Taken in the Event of an Accident

622. In the event that water containing oil is discharged into the public water or infiltrates underground due to an accident, the person who set up a factory or workplace (oil storage workplace) that instals oil storage facilities, etc. shall immediately notify the prefectural governor of the circumstances of the accident and take emergency measures to prevent the discharge or infiltration (Article 14-2 paragraph 3 of the WPA). Oil storage facilities, etc. means oil storage facilities that store oil specified by a Cabinet Order such as crude oil and heavy oil, or oil-water separation facilities that treat water containing the same oil (Article 2 paragraph 5 of the WPA, Article 3-4 and 3-5 of the Enforcement Order of the WPA).

F. Compensation for Damages

623. In the event that the life or body of a person is injured due to the discharge or infiltration into the ground of a hazardous substance contained in sewage or waste water resulting from business activities at a factory or workplace, the business operator involved in such discharge or infiltration into the ground shall be liable to compensate for the damage resulting therefrom (Article 19 paragraph 1 of the WPA). In the event of a natural disaster or other force majeure that competes with the occurrence of such damage, the court may take this into consideration when determining the responsibility for damages and the amount of damages (Article 20-2 of the WPA). The right to claim compensation for damages shall be extinguished by the statute of limitations in five years from the time when the victim or his/her/its legal representative becomes aware of the damage and the person who is liable for compensation. In addition, it is extinguished by the statute of limitations in twenty years from the time of occurrence of damage (Article 20-3 of the WPA). However, when the Mining Act and the Act on Washing Coal Industry are applied, it shall be as prescribed in those Acts (Article 20-4 of the WPA). In addition, this law does not apply to the work-related injury, illness or death of a person engaged in the business conducted by the business operator (Article 20-5 of the WPA).

G. Criminal Penalties

624. Criminal penalties have been established for violations of each regulation. For example, a person who intentionally violates Article 12 paragraph 1 of the WPA shall be punished by imprisonment for not more than six months or a fine of not more than JPY 500,000. A person who negligently violates Article 12 paragraph 1 of the WPA shall be punished by imprisonment for not more than three months or a fine of not more than JPY 300,000 (Article 31 paragraph 1 item 1 and Article 31 paragraph 2 of the WPA). If a representative, employee or other worker of a juridical person commits an act in violation of Article 31 of the WPA in connection with the business of the juridical person, the juridical person shall also be punished by a fine under Article 31 (Article 34 of the WPA).

H. Regulations of the Waste Management and Public Cleaning Act

625. General wastes shall not be disposed of in the ocean (Article 6-2 paragraph 2 of the said Act, Article 3 item 4 of the Enforcement Order of the Act). General wastes mean wastes other than industrial wastes (Article 2 paragraph 2 of the Act).s

626. With regard to industrial wastes, only industrial wastes specified by a Cabinet Order, such as sludge generated from construction work, may be disposed of in the sea from a vessel, provided that the method specified by the Cabinet Order is followed for collection and transportation (Article 12 paragraph 1 of the Act, Article 6 paragraph 1 item 4 of the Enforcement Order of the Act).

III. Pollution from Seabed Activities

A. Outline

627. Many of the seabed activities are likely to be conducted through offshore facilities. Under the APMPMD, 'offshore facilities' means, in outline, structures established in the sea area that have a structure capable of accommodating people and structures established in the sea area that are used for the processing, transportation or storage of materials (Article 3 item 10 of the APMPMD and Article 1-7 paragraph 1 of the Enforcement Order of the APMPMD). A person who intends to instal offshore facilities shall notify the Director-General of the Japan Coast Guard of the name and address of the installer and the location and outline of the offshore facilities (Article 18-3 paragraph 1 of the APMPMD).

B. Regulation of the Discharge of Oil, Hazardous Liquid Substances and Wastes from Offshore Facilities

628. Article 18 paragraph 1 of the APMPMD establishes the principle that no person shall discharge oil, hazardous liquid substances or wastes from offshore facilities in the sea area. The manager of offshore facilities which can accommodate 15 people or more shall establish guide for waste pollution prevention generated in the offshore facilities and keep it on the offshore facilities (Article 18-5 paragraph 1 of the APMPMD, Article 12-17-3 of the Enforcement Regulation of the APMPMD). A manager of lay-up facilities that is used for transportation of oil or hazardous liquid substance shall keep an oil record book or a hazardous liquid substance record book in the facility, and shall make an entry in the oil record book or the hazardous liquid substance record book when certain work related to the handling of oil or hazardous liquid substances is performed (Article 18-4 paragraphs 1 and 2 of the APMPMD, Article 12-17-3 paragraph 1 of the Enforcement Regulation of the APMPMD). Any person who intends to dispose of certain wastes in the sea from offshore facilities shall obtain a permit from the Minister of the Environment (Article 18-2 paragraph 1 of the APMPMD). In addition, a person who intends to discharge certain wastes from offshore facilities shall obtain confirmation of the discharge plan from the Director-General of the Japan Coast Guard prior to loading the wastes into the offshore facility (Article 18-2 paragraph 2 of the APMPMD).

C. *Regulations on the Disposal of Oil, Hazardous Liquid Substances and Wastes under the Seabed*

629. Article 18-7 of the APMPMD establishes the principle that no person shall dispose of oil, hazardous liquid substances or waste materials under the seabed. The disposal of certain carbon dioxide gases below the seabed is possible with the permission of the Minister of the Environment (Article 18-8 paragraph 1 of the APMPMD). The Minister of the Environment shall not grant permission unless all the requirements specified in the law are met (Article 18-9 of the APMPMD). In addition, even after issuing a permit, the Minister may issue a business improvement order to the licensee in accordance with the law (Article 18-10 paragraph 1 of the APMPMD) or revoke the permit (Article 18-11 of the APMPMD).

D. *Regulation of Disposal of Offshore Facilities*

630. No person shall dump any offshore facilities into the sea. However, this shall not apply to the case of dumping with the permission of the Minister of the Environment, or to the case of leaving offshore facilities in distress that are difficult to remove (Article 43 paragraph 1 of the APMPMD).

E. *Penalties*

631. Violations of the various regulations are subject to criminal penalties. For example, a person who intentionally discharges oil in violation of Article 18 paragraph 1 of the APMPMD is subject to a fine of up to JPY 10 million, while a person who discharges oil through negligence is subject to a fine of up to JPY 5 million (Article 55 paragraph 1 item 7 and paragraph 2 of the APMPMD). When a representative or an employee of a juridical person commits any of these violations with respect to the business of the juridical person, the same fine is imposed on the juridical person (Article 59 of the APMPMD).

IV. Prevention of Marine Pollution and Marine Disaster

A. Duty to Report

632. In the event of discharge of oil, etc. from a vessel, the Master of such vessel shall, in principle, report the date, time, place, etc. of discharge to the nearest office of the Japan Coast Guard (Article 38 paragraph 1 of the APMPMD). In the event of a marine accident such as a collision of vessels and there is a risk of discharge of oil, etc. from a vessel, the Master of the said vessel shall, in principle, immediately notify the nearest office of Japan Coast Guard of the date, time, place, etc. of the said marine accident (Article 38 paragraph 2 of the APMPMD).

633. In the event of discharge of oil, etc. from an offshore facility, etc., the manager of the relevant offshore facility shall, in principle, report the date, time, place etc. of discharge to the nearest office of the Japan Coast Guard (Article 38 paragraph 3 of the APMPMD). In the event of an abnormal phenomenon such as damage to offshore facilities, etc., and there is a risk of discharge of a large quantity of oil, etc., the manager of the relevant offshore facility shall, in principle, immediately report the date, time, place etc. of the abnormal phenomenon to the nearest office of the Japan Coast Guard (Article 38 paragraph 4 of the APMPMD).

634. In the event of a discharge of dangerous goods, if there is a risk of a fire at sea due to the discharged dangerous goods, the Master of the vessel on which the discharged dangerous goods were loaded, the manager of the facility where the discharged dangerous goods were managed, and the person who committed the act causing the discharge of the dangerous goods shall immediately notify the nearest office of the Japan Coast Guard of the date, time, place etc. of the discharge of the dangerous goods (Article 42-2 paragraph 1 of the APMPMD).

635. In the event of a fire at sea onboard a vessel carrying dangerous goods in bulk as cargo, a fire at sea at an offshore facility managing dangerous goods, or a fire at sea involving dangerous goods, the Master of the vessel, the manager of the offshore facility or the Master of the vessel on which the dangerous goods were loaded, the manager of the offshore facility at which the dangerous goods were loaded, and the person who committed the act that caused the fire at sea shall immediately notify the nearest office of the Japan Coast Guard of the date, time, place etc. of the occurrence of the fire at sea (Article 42-3 paragraph 1 of the APMPMD).

636. In the event of collision, grounding, engine failure or other marine casualty of a vessel, or in the event of damage to an offshore facility managing dangerous goods or other abnormal phenomena pertaining to the said facility, if there is a risk of discharge of dangerous goods from the said vessel or facility, the Master of said vessel or the manager of said offshore facility shall immediately notify the nearest office of the Japan Coast Guard of the date, time, place etc. of the occurrence of the marine casualty or the abnormal phenomena (Article 42-4-2 paragraph 1 of the APMPMD).

B. Measures to Be Taken in the Event of Discharge, Etc.

637. In the event of a discharge of a large quantity of oil or hazardous liquid substances, (i) the Master of the vessel in which the oil or hazardous liquid substances were loaded, the manager of the facility in which the oil or hazardous liquid substances were managed, or the person who committed the act causing the discharge shall immediately take emergency measures that are necessary for prevention and removal thereof (Article 39 paragraph 1 of the APMPMD) and (ii) the owner of the vessel in which the oil or hazardous liquid substances were loaded, the installer of the facility in which the oil or hazardous liquid substances were managed, or the employer of the person who committed the act causing the discharge in connection with the business shall immediately take measures that are necessary for prevention and removal thereof (Article 39 paragraph 2 of the APMPMD).

638. In the event of a discharge of dangerous goods, the Master of the vessel on which the discharged dangerous goods were loaded, the manager of the facility where the discharged dangerous goods were managed, and the person who committed the act causing the discharge of the dangerous goods (the person prescribed in Article 42-2 paragraph 1, *see* section IV, A above) shall take emergency measures to prevent further discharge of dangerous goods and to prevent the occurrence of a fire and shall take measures to alert persons or vessels in the vicinity of the scene of the discharge (Article 42-2 paragraph 3 of the APMPMD).

639. In the event of a fire at sea onboard a vessel carrying dangerous goods in bulk as cargo, a fire at an offshore facility managing dangerous goods, or a fire at sea involving dangerous goods, the Master of the vessel, the manager of the offshore facility, the Master of the vessel on which the dangerous goods were loaded, the manager of the offshore facility at which the dangerous goods were loaded or the person who committed the act causing the fire at sea shall take emergency measures to extinguish the fire, prevent the spread of the fire, and save lives, and shall also take measures to alert persons or vessels in the vicinity of the scene of the fire at sea (Article 42-3 paragraph 2 of the APMPMD).

C. Authority of the Director-General of the Japan Coast Guard

640. As discussed below, the Director-General of the Japan Coast Guard is granted a variety of powers.

641. The Director-General of the Japan Coast Guard may order the Master of the vessel in which the discharged oil or hazardous liquid substances were loaded, the manager of the offshore facility in which they were managed, or the employer of the person who committed the act causing the discharge in connection with the business (the person referred to in Article 39 paragraph 2 of the APMPMD, *see* section IV, B above) to take the necessary measures for the prevention and removal of the discharged oil or hazardous liquid substances, if the Director-General finds that these persons have not taken the measures (Article 39 paragraph 3 of the APMPMD).

642. In the event of a marine disaster, such as a collision of vessels, or in the event of an abnormal phenomenon pertaining to offshore facilities, when the Director-General finds that there is a risk of discharge of a large quantity of oil or hazardous liquid substances from them and that it is urgently necessary to prevent such discharge, the Director-General of the Japan Coast Guard may order the Master or the owner of the vessel or the manager or the installer of the offshore facilities to take necessary measures to prevent the discharge (Article 39 paragraph 5 of the APMPMD).

643. In the event of a discharge of a large quantity of oil or hazardous liquid substances, when the Director-General finds it necessary to take urgent measures for prevention or removal, the Director-General may order the Master of a vessel in the sea area where the measures are taken to remove the vessel from the sea area, order the Master of a vessel entering the sea area to refrain from entering the sea area and may restrict the navigation of vessels navigating in the said sea area (Article 39-2 of the APMPMD).

644. The Director-General of the Japan Coast Guard may order the person who discharged the wastes or other materials (excluding oil and hazardous liquid substances) or the owner of the vessel to take necessary measures to prevent pollution, if the marine environment is polluted or is likely to be polluted due to the discharge of wastes or other materials (excluding oil and hazardous liquid substances) or due to the sinking or grounding of the vessel, and if such pollution causes or is likely to cause significant damage to the preservation of the marine environment (Article 40 of the APMPMD).

645. In the event that the Director-General of the Japan Coast Guard finds that the persons who should have taken the above-mentioned measures (persons referred to in Article 39 paragraph 1–3, 5 and Article40, *see above*) do not take the measures, or that it is difficult to prevent marine pollution only by the measures taken by such persons, and that the Director-General has taken the measures necessary for the prevention of marine pollution, the Director-General may, in principle, have the owner of the vessel on which the oil or hazardous liquid substance were loaded, the installer of the offshore facilities etc. in which the oil or hazardous liquid substance were managed, or the owner of the sunken vessel or the grounded vessel bear a certain amount of the cost of the measures (Article 41 paragraph 1 of the APMPMD). With regard to the amount borne pursuant to the provision, the owner of the vessel or the installer of the offshore facilities, etc. shall have the right of recourse against the person who is responsible for the discharge, threat of discharge, sinking or grounding of vessel (Article 41 paragraph 4 of the APMPMD).

646. In the event that the Director-General of the Japan Coast Guard finds that the persons who should have taken the above-mentioned measures (persons referred to in Article 39 paragraph 1–3, 5 and Article 40, *see above*) do not take the measures, or in the event of discharge of large quantity of oil or hazardous liquid substance from the specified foreign vessel in the sea out of the territorial waters of Japan (foreign vessel engaging in exploration or development of natural resources in the continental shelf of Japan, foreign vessel engaging in drilling the continental shelf of Japan or foreign vessel that navigates between Japanese ports only), the Director-General may request the head of relevant administrative organ, etc. to take necessary measure to prevent marine pollution (Article 41-2 of the APMPMD). When the head of the relevant administrative organ, etc. has taken the measures requested by the Director-General, the head of the relevant administrative organ, etc. may, in principle, have the owner of the vessel in which the discharged materials were loaded, the installer of the offshore facilities, etc. in which the discharged materials were managed, or the owner of the sunken vessel or grounded vessel bear a certain range of the costs of the measures (Article 41-3 paragraph 1 of the APMPMD). With regard to the amount borne pursuant to the provision, the owner of the vessel or the installer of the offshore facilities, etc. has the right of recourse against the person who is responsible for the discharge, threat of discharge, sinking or grounding (Article 41-3 paragraph 8 and Article 41 paragraph 4 of the APMPMD).

647. The Director-General of the Japan Coast Guard may, when the sea is significantly polluted by an extremely large quantity of oil or hazardous liquid substances discharged in the coastal waters of Japan, and the pollution causes significant disturbance to the preservation of the marine environment in a wide area of coastal waters, and when it is necessary to take urgent measures of prevention or removal of the discharged oil etc. to prevent such disturbance, the Director-General may destroy the vessel on which the discharged oil or hazardous liquid substance were loaded or dispose property in the sea area in vicinity of the scene, to the extent that it is unavoidable for the purpose (Article 42 of the APMPMD).

648. The Director-General of the Japan Coast Guard may, when there has been a discharge of dangerous goods and it is necessary to prevent the occurrence of a fire at sea, order the Master of the vessel on which the discharged dangerous goods were loaded, the manager of the offshore facility where the discharged dangerous goods were managed, and the employer of the person who committed the act that caused the discharge of the dangerous goods in connection with the business, to take necessary measures to prevent further discharge of the dangerous goods, to prevent the occurrence of fire caused by the discharged dangerous goods, and to prevent other maritime disasters (Article 42-2 paragraph 4 of the APMPMD).

649. In the event of a fire at sea onboard a vessel carrying dangerous goods in bulk as cargo, a fire at sea at an offshore facility managing dangerous goods, or a fire at sea involving dangerous goods, when it is necessary to prevent the spread of a maritime disaster, the Director-General may order the Master of the vessel, the manager of the offshore facility, the Master of the vessel on which the dangerous goods were loaded, the manager of the offshore facility at which the dangerous goods were loaded, and the employer of the person who committed act causing the fire in connection with his/her duties, to extinguish the fire, prevent the spread of the fire, or otherwise prevent the spread of maritime disaster (Article 42-3 paragraph 3 of the APMPMD).

650. In the event of a collision, grounding, engine failure or other marine disaster of a vessel, or in the event of damage to an offshore facility managing dangerous goods or other abnormal phenomena pertaining to the said facility, when the Director-General finds it necessary to prevent discharge of the dangerous goods urgently for prevention of the occurrence of a marine disaster, the Director-General may order the Master of the vessel, the owner of the vessel, the manager of the offshore facility or the installer of the offshore facility to remove the dangerous goods or to take any other measure to prevent the discharge (Article 42-4-2 paragraph 2 of the APMPMD).

651. In the event of discharge of dangerous goods and the possibility of a fire at sea caused by the discharged dangerous goods is significantly high and a fire at sea would cause a significant maritime disaster, the Director-General may restrict or prohibit the use of fire by persons in the sea area where a fire at sea is likely to occur, order the Master of a vessel in the sea area to remove the vessel from the sea area, and order the Master of a vessel entering the sea area to stop entering the sea area (Article 42-5 paragraph 1 of the APMPMD).

652. In the event of a fire at sea, the Director-General of the Japan Coast Guard may order the Master of a vessel in the sea area where the fire occurred to remove the vessel from the sea area, and may order the Master of a vessel entering the sea area to stop entering the sea area (Article 42-5 paragraph 2 of the APMPMD).

653. The Director-General may use, move, dispose of, or restrict the use of a vessel, an offshore facility managing dangerous goods, or any other property in which a has occurred or is about to occur, if it is necessary for extinguishing the fire, preventing the spread of the fire, or saving human lives. In addition, when it is unavoidable in order to prevent the spread of fire, the Director-General may use, move, dispose of, or restrict the use of vessels, offshore facilities managing dangerous goods, and other property in the sea area (Article 42-6 of the APMPMD).

D. Penalties

654. Violations of the various regulations are subject to criminal penalties. For example, a person who fails to report a violation of Article 38 paragraph 1 of the APMPMD is subject to a fine of up to JPY 500,000 (Article 57 item 15 of the APMPMD). If a representative or employee of a judicial person commits any of these violations in connection with the judicial person's business, the judicial person is also subject to the same fine (Article 59 of the APMPMD).

V. Tanker Oil Pollution Damage

A. Tanker Owner's Liability for Damages

655. In the event of Tanker Oil Pollution Damage, the Tanker Owner of the Tanker in which the Crude Oil, etc. pertaining to the said Tanker Oil Pollution was loaded shall be liable to compensate for the damage (Article 3 paragraph 1 main clause of the OPDA, Liability for Vessel Oil Pollution Damage Act).

656. Tanker Oil Pollution Damage means the damage in the territory or exclusive economic zone of a contracting state of the International Convention on Civil Liability for Oil Pollution Damage 1992 (Liability Convention) caused by Tanker or the damage in the waters prescribed in Article 2 (a)(ii) of the Liability Convention of a foreign state which is a contracting state of the Liability Convention, the cost required for reasonable measures taken to prevent or mitigate the damage after the occurrence of the fact which causes the damage, and the damage caused by such measures (Article 2 item 14 of the OPDA). 'Crude Oil, etc.' means crude oil, heavy oil, lubricating oil or other oil that is difficult to evaporate and is specified by a Cabinet Order (Article 2 item 6 of the OPDA). 'Tanker' means a vessel for carriage by sea of the Crude Oil, etc. in bulk (Article 2 item 9 of the OPDA). 'Tanker Owner' means the owner of a Tanker (Article 2 item 11 of the OPDA).

657. However, if the Tanker Oil Pollution Damage is caused by (i) war, civil war or insurrection, (ii) abnormal natural disaster, (iii) solely malicious act of a person other than the Tanker Owner or the person who is used by the Tanker Owner, or (iv) solely defective management of navigation signs or signal facilities for traffic control by the nation or a public entity (Article 3 paragraph 1 proviso of the OPDA).

658. In the case of Tanker Oil Pollution Damage caused by the Crude Oil, etc. loaded on two or more Tankers, if it is impossible to distinguish which Tanker's Crude Oil etc. caused the Tanker Oil Pollution Damage, each Tanker Owner shall be jointly and severally liable for damages (Article 3 paragraph 2 main clause of the OPDA).

659. In the event of occurrence of Tanker Oil Pollution Damage or occurrence of Tanker Oil Pollution Damage by the Crude Oil, etc. loaded on two or more Tankers, the following parties shall not be liable for damages in principle: (i) the person who is used by the Tanker Owner; (ii) the lessee of the Tanker and the person who is used by the lessee; (iii) the charterer, manager or operator of the Tanker which is provided in Article 3 paragraph 4(c) of the Liability Convention and the person who is used by them; (iv) the person who undertakes to repair the Tanker or to provide other services pertaining to the Tanker and the person who is used by the said person; (v) the person who, with the consent of the Tanker Owner or in accordance with the instructions of the administrative agency, provides services directly related to the salvage of human lives, cargo or the Tanker and the person who is used by the said person; (vi) the person who takes reasonable measures to prevent or mitigate the damage after the occurrence of the fact which causes the damage, and the person who is used by the said person. However, this shall not apply when the Tanker Oil Pollution Damage is caused by their intentional act or their reckless act with knowledge that the damage would probably result (Article 3 paragraph 4 of the OPDA). In this way, Japanese law also concentrates the responsibility on the owner, but this does not prevent the Tanker Owner which has compensated for the damage from exercising the right of recourse to a third party (Article 3 paragraph 5 of the OPDA).

660. When the Tanker Oil Pollution Damage is caused by the intentional act or negligence of the victim, the court may take it into consideration in determining the responsibility and amount of damages (Article 4 of the OPDA).

661. The right to claim for compensation for damages against the Tanker Owner shall be extinguished if no judicial claim is made within three years from the date when the Tanker Oil Pollution Damage occurred. The right to claim for damages against the Tanker Owner shall also be extinguished if no judicial claim is made within six years from the date when the first fact causing the Tanker Oil Pollution Damage occurred (Article 10 of the OPDA).

662. It is understood that the international jurisdiction of the Japanese courts over an action against the Tanker Owner is determined in accordance with the provision of Article 9 of the Liability Convention, not with domestic law. Namely, if an accident has caused pollution damage in the territory or exclusive economic zone of Japan, or if preventive measures have been taken to prevent or minimize the pollution damage in the territory or exclusive economic zone of Japan, the jurisdiction is affirmed (Article 9 paragraph 1 of the Liability Convention). The domestic jurisdiction of the Japanese court is in accordance with the provisions of the CCP of Japan and if the court which has jurisdiction is not specified in the Code, the Tokyo District Court or the Tokyo Summary Court has the jurisdiction (Article 11 of the OPDA, Article 1 of the Rules of Procedure for Limitation of Liability for Vessel Oil Pollution Damage, etc.).

663. A final and binding judgment rendered by a foreign court having jurisdiction pursuant to Article 9 paragraph 1 of the Limitation Convention shall be effective unless (i) the said judgment was obtained by fraud, (ii) the defendant was not served with a summons or order necessary for commencement of the action and was not given a fair opportunity to state its claim (Article 12 paragraph 1 of the OPDA).

B. Compulsory Conclusion of Security Contract and Insurer's Responsibility

664. No tanker having Japanese nationality shall be used for transportation of Crude Oil, etc. in bulk exceeding 2,000 tons unless a security contract for compensation for Tanker Oil Pollution Damage is concluded (Article 13 paragraph 1 of the

OPDA). A Tanker shall not be used for transportation of Crude Oil, etc. in bulk exceeding 2,000 tons unless a certificate of the security contract is kept onboard (Article 20 paragraph 1 of the OPDA).

665. With respect to other Tankers, unless the security contract for compensation for Tanker Oil Pollution Damage is concluded, she shall not enter or leave any port in Japan or use any mooring facility in Japan loaded with Crude Oil, etc. in bulk exceeding 2,000 tons (Article 13 paragraph 2 of the OPDA). In addition, she shall not enter a port in Japan, depart from a port in Japan or use mooring facilities in Japan unless (i) a certificate of the security contract, (ii) a document in the form of an annex to the Liability Convention issued by a foreign state which is a Contracting Party to the Liability Convention certifying that a security contract is concluded for her, or (iii) a document stating the matters described in the certificate prescribed in Article 7 paragraph 12 of the Liability Convention issued by a foreign state, is kept onboard (Article 20 paragraph 2 of the OPDA).

666. The security contract is an insurance contract to cover the damage caused to the Tanker Owner by the performance of the obligation of compensation or a contract to secure the performance of the obligation of compensation in the case the Tanker Owner is liable to compensate for the Tanker Oil Pollution Damage caused by the Crude Oil, etc. loaded on the Tanker (Article 14 paragraph 1 of the OPDA). In the security contract, the party who covers the damage of the Tanker Owner or secures the performance of the obligation of compensation (Insurer, etc.) must be the Japan Ship Owners' Mutual Protection & Indemnity Association, the Japan Fishing Vessel Insurance Association, the non-life insurance company under the Insurance Business Act of Japan or the foreign non-life insurance company under the Insurance Business Act of Japan (Article 14 paragraph 2 of the OPDA and Article 3 paragraph 1 of the Enforcement Order of the OPDA). The amount of insurance to cover the damage of the Tanker Owner or the amount of the Tanker Oil Pollution Damage for which the performance of the obligation of compensation is secured in the security contract shall not be less than the limit of liability of the Tanker Owner (Article 14 paragraph 3 of the OPDA).

667. The Minister of Land, Infrastructure, Transport and Tourism shall, when there is an application from the person who has a security contract with Insurer, etc. with regard to Tanker (except for Tanker whose nationality is that of a foreign state which is a Contracting Party to the Liability Convention), issue a document certifying that the security contract is concluded for the Tanker (Article 17 paragraph 1 of the OPDA).

668. When the Tanker Owner's liability to compensate for damages pursuant to the provision of Article 3 paragraph 1 or paragraph 2 of the OPDA has occurred, the victim may claim the payment of the amount of damages to the Insurer, etc. However, this shall not apply when the damage was caused by the bad faith of the Tanker Owner (Article 15 paragraph 1 of the OPDA). The Insurer, etc. may oppose the victim only with the defence that the Tanker Owner can assert against the victim (Article 15 paragraph 2 of the OPDA). For example, the Insurer, etc. cannot claim that the Tanker Owner did not pay the insurance premiums and therefore the Insurer, etc. is not responsible for the payment to the victim by cancelling the insurance contract. The provisions concerning the right of recourse against a third party and extinguishment of the right shall apply *mutatis mutandis* to the Insurer, etc. (Article 15 paragraph 3 of the OPDA).

C. Limitation of Liability of Tanker Owners and Insurers, Etc.

669. The Tanker Owner who is liable to compensate for the Tanker Oil Pollution Damage may limit the liability for the claim based on the Tanker Oil Pollution Damage pursuant to the provision of the OPDA. However, this shall not apply if the Tanker Oil Pollution Damage was caused by the Tanker Owner's intentional act or by the Tanker Owner's reckless act with the knowledge that such damage would probably result (Article 5 of the OPDA).

670. The limit of liability is 4,510,000 SDR for Tanker with a gross tonnage of 5,000 tons or less, and for Tanker with a gross tonnage exceeding 5,000 tons, an amount equal to 631 SDR per ton in excess of 5,000 tons (the upper limit is 89,770,000 SDR) (Article 6 of the OPDA).

671. The limitation of liability extends to all claims subject to limitation against the Tanker Owner and the Insurer, etc. regarding each Tanker arising out of the same accident (Article 8 of the OPDA).

672. With regard to the limitation of liability cases, it is understood that the international jurisdiction of the Japanese courts is determined in accordance with the provisions of the Liability Convention, not with domestic law. Namely, if an accident has caused pollution damage in the territory or exclusive economic zone of Japan, or if preventive measures have been taken to prevent or minimize the pollution damage in the territory or exclusive economic zone of Japan, the jurisdiction is affirmed (Article 5 paragraph 3 and Article 9 paragraph 1 of the Liability Convention). The domestic jurisdiction shall be as follows: (i) if the Tanker Oil Pollution Damage occurred in Japan, the district court which has jurisdiction over the place where the Tanker Oil Pollution Damage occurred; (ii) if the Tanker Oil Pollution Damage occurred in the Exclusive Economic Zone, the district court which has jurisdiction over the location of the general venue of the known claimant of the claim subject to limitation (if there is no such court, the Tokyo District Court); or (iii) if measures to prevent damage in Japan or in the Exclusive Economic Zone of Japan are taken outside of Japan or the Exclusive Economic Zone of Japan and no damage occurs in Japan or the Exclusive Economic Zone in Japan, the district court with jurisdiction over the location of the general venue of the person who took the measures (or the Tokyo District Court if this court is not available) (Article 31 of the OPDA, Article 3 of Rules of Procedure for Limitation of Liability for Vessel Oil Pollution Damage, etc.). The International Fund may participate in the procedure for limitation of liability (Article 33 of the OPDA). Basically, the provisions of Chapter III of the Limit. Act are applied *mutatis mutandis* to the procedure for the limitation of liability (Article 38 of the OPDA).

673. This provision on limitation of liability is also applied *mutatis mutandis* to Insurers, etc. (Article 15 paragraph 3 of the OPDA).

674. The claim for which the Tanker Owner or the Insurer, etc. may limit its liability under the OPDA is considered to be a Claim Subject to Limitation (Article 2 item 22 of the OPDA). The Claimant of the Claim Subject to Limitation pertaining to the Tanker Oil Pollution Damage has a statutory lien on the vessel and its equipment pertaining to the accident with respect to the Claim Subject to Limitation (Article 55 paragraph 1 of the OPDA). This statutory lien is considered to be second to the statutory lien of Article 842 item 5 of the Com. Code, has priority over the vessel mortgage, and will be extinguished after one year from the occurrence (Article 55 paragraphs 2 and 3 of the OPDA and Articles 846 and 848 paragraph 1 of the Com. Code).

675. In the case a fund is formed pursuant to the provision of Article 5 of the Liability Convention in a foreign country which is a Contracting State of the Liability Convention, with respect to the Claim Subject to Limitation that can receive payment from the said fund, the claimant of the Claim Subject to Limitation with respect to Tanker Oil Pollution Damage may not exercise their rights against the property of the Tanker Owner or the Insurer, etc. other than the said fund (Article 56 paragraph 1 of the OPDA).

D. Claims Against the International Fund

676. The victim may request the International Fund to indemnify the amount of the Tanker Oil Pollution Damage that could not be compensated, as prescribed in Article 4 paragraph 1 of the International Fund Convention (Article 22 of the OPDA). The International Fund Convention means the International Convention on the Establishment of an International Fund for Compensation of Oil Pollution Damage, 1992 (Article 2 item 2 of the OPDA). International Fund means the International Fund for Compensation of Oil Pollution Damage of 1992 provided in Article 2 paragraph 1 of the International Fund Convention (Article 2 item 20 of the OPDA).

677. With regard to claims against the International Fund, it is understood that the international jurisdiction of the Japanese courts is determined in accordance with the provisions of Article 7, paragraphs 1 and 3 of the International Fund Convention, not domestic law. Namely, if an accident has caused pollution damage in the territory or exclusive economic zone of Japan, if preventive measures have been taken to prevent or minimize the pollution damage in the territory or exclusive economic zone of Japan, or if a lawsuit against the Tanker Owner or Insurer etc. on these grounds is pending in the Japanese courts, the jurisdiction is affirmed. The domestic jurisdiction is, in principle, vested in the court having jurisdiction over the action against the Tanker Owner (Article 26 paragraph 1 of the OPDA).

678. A final and binding judgment rendered by a foreign court having jurisdiction pursuant to Article 7 paragraph 1 or Article 7 paragraph 3 of the International Fund Convention shall be effective unless (i) such judgment was obtained by fraud, or (ii) the defendant was not served with a summons or order necessary for the commencement of the action and was not given a fair opportunity to state its case (Article 27 and Article 12 paragraph 1 of the OPDA).

679. The International Fund may participate in a lawsuit against a Tanker Owner or an Insurer, etc. as a party (Article 24 paragraph 1 of the OPDA). It may also participate in the procedure for limitation of liability (Article 33 of the OPDA).

E. Claims Against the Additional Fund

680. The victim may request the Supplementary Fund to indemnify the amount of Tanker Oil Pollution Damage for which the compensation and the indemnification from the International Fund could not be received, as prescribed in Article 4 paragraph 1 of the Supplementary Fund Protocol (Article 30-2 of the OPDA). Supplementary Fund Protocol means the Protocol of 2003 to the International Convention on the Establishment of an International Fund for Compensation of Oil Pollution Damage, 1992 (Article 2 item 3 of the OPDA). Supplementary Fund means the Supplemental International Fund for Compensation for Pollution Damage Caused by Oil of 2003, as provided for in Article 2 paragraph 1 of the Supplementary Fund Protocol (Article 2 item 21 of the OPDA).

681. With regard to claims against the Supplementary Fund, it is understood that the international jurisdiction of the Japanese courts is determined in accordance with the provision of Article 7 of the Supplementary Fund Protocol, not with domestic law. Namely, if an accident has caused pollution damage in the territory or exclusive economic zone of Japan, if preventive measures have been taken to prevent or minimize the pollution damage in the territory or exclusive economic zone of Japan, or if a lawsuit against the Tanker Owner or Insurer, etc. on these grounds is pending in the Japanese courts, the jurisdiction is affirmed. Domestic jurisdiction is, in principle, vested in the court having jurisdiction over the action against the Tanker Owner (Article 30-3 and Article 26 paragraph 1 of the OPDA).

682. A final and binding judgment rendered by a foreign court having jurisdiction pursuant to Article 7 of the Supplementary Fund Protocol shall be effective unless (i) such judgment was obtained by fraud, or (ii) the defendant was not served with a summons or order necessary for the commencement of the action and was not given a fair opportunity to state its case (Articles 30-3, 27, and 12 paragraph 1 of the OPDA).

683. The Supplementary Fund may participate in the lawsuit against the Tanker Owner or the Insurer, etc. as a party to the lawsuit (Articles 30-3 and 24 paragraph 1 of the OPDA). It may also participate in the procedure for limitation of liability (Articles 37-2 and 33 of the OPDA).

VI. Oil Pollution Damage of General Vessel, Etc.

A. Liability for Compensation for Damages of the Owner of Tanker or General Vessel

684. When Oil Pollution Damage of General Vessel, etc. has occurred, the owners, etc. of the tanker or general vessel in which the Bunker Oil, etc. pertaining to the Oil Pollution Damage of General Vessel etc. was loaded (including the manager and operator of the vessel prescribed in Article 1 paragraph 3 of the Bunker Oil Convention) shall be jointly and severally liable to compensate for the damage (Article 39 paragraph 1 of the OPDA).

685. Oil Pollution Damage of General Vessel, etc. means (i) damage in the territory of Japan or in the Exclusive Economic Zone of Japan caused by pollution by Bunker Oil, etc. spilled or discharged from a tanker or general vessel, (ii) damage in the territory or in the water area prescribed in Article 2(a)(ii) of the Bunker Oil Convention of a foreign state which is a Contracting Party to the Bunker Oil Convention caused by pollution by Bunker Oil, etc. spilled or discharged from a tanker or general vessel, or (iii) cost of reasonable measures taken to prevent or mitigate the damage after the occurrence of the fact that causes the damage listed in the (i) or (ii) above, or damage caused by such measures (Article 2 item 16 of the OPDA). Bunker Oil, etc. means bunker oil, lubricating oil and other oil used for navigation of a vessel and specified by Cabinet Order (Article 2 item 7 of the OPDA). Bunker Oil Convention means the International Convention on Civil Liability for Bunker Oil Pollution Damage 2001 (Article 2 item 4 of the OPDA).

686. However, if the Oil Pollution Damage of General Vessel, etc. is caused by (1) war, civil war or riot, (2) abnormal natural disaster, (3) solely malicious intent of a person other than the owner of the vessel or the person who is used by the owner, or (4) defective management of a navigation sign or a signal facility for traffic control by the state or a public entity (Article 39 paragraph 1 proviso of the OPDA).

687. In the case Oil Pollution Damage of General Vessel, etc. occurred by Bunker Oil, etc. loaded on two or more tankers or general vessels, if it is impossible to distinguish which of the Bunker Oil, etc. loaded on the tanker or general vessel caused the Oil Pollution Damage of General Vessel etc., the owner, etc. of each tanker or general vessel shall be jointly and severally liable for damages (Article 39 paragraph 2 and Article 3 paragraph 2 main clause of the OPDA).

688. When the Oil Pollution Damage of General Vessel, etc. is caused by the intentional act or negligence of the victim, the court may take it into consideration in determining the responsibility for compensation for damages and the amount of damages (Article 39 paragraph 2 and Article 4 of the OPDA).

689. The claim for compensation for damages against the owners of the vessel etc. shall be extinguished when no judicial claim is made within three years from the day when the Oil Pollution Damage of General Vessel etc. is occurred. The claim shall also be extinguished if no judicial claim is made within six years from the day when the first fact causing the Oil Pollution Damage of General Vessel etc. is occurred (Article 39 paragraph 2 and Article 10 of the OPDA).

690. It is understood that the international jurisdiction of the Japanese courts over actions against the owners of the vessel etc. is determined in accordance with the provisions of Article 9 of the Bunker Oil Convention, not with domestic law. Namely, it is affirmed when the accident causes pollution damage in the territory or exclusive economic zone of Japan, or when preventive measures are taken to prevent or minimize pollution damage in the said territory or exclusive economic zone (Article 9 paragraph 1 of the Bunker Oil Convention). The domestic jurisdiction of the Japanese court is in accordance with the provisions of the CCP and if no court of jurisdiction is specified in the Code, the Tokyo District Court or the Tokyo Summary Court (Article 39 paragraph 2 and Article 11 of the OPDA and Article 1 of the Rules of Procedure for Limitation of Liability for Vessel Oil Pollution Damage, etc.).

691. A final and binding judgment rendered by a foreign court having jurisdiction pursuant to Article 9 paragraph 1 of the Bunker Oil Convention on an action for compensation for damages for Oil Pollution Damage of General Vessel, etc. shall be effective unless (i) the said judgment was obtained by fraud, (ii) the defendant was not served with a summons or order necessary for commencement of the action and was not given a fair opportunity to state his/her claim except in cases where the defendant was not given a fair opportunity to state his or her case (Article 39 paragraph 2 and Article 12 paragraph 1 of the OPDA).

B. Compulsory Conclusion of Security Contract and Insurer's Responsibility

692. A tanker or a general vessel having Japanese nationality and of exceeding 1,000 gross tons (except those which are not required to use Bunker Oil etc. for navigation; hereinafter 'Type I Specified Vessel') shall not be engaged in all voyages unless a security contract for compensation for oil pollution damage of general vessel, etc. (Security Contract) is concluded (Article 41 paragraph 1 item 1 of the IPDA). They shall not engage in any voyage unless they have a certificate of the Security Contract onboard (Article 45 paragraph 1 item 1 of the OPDA).

693. A general vessel having Japanese nationality and of 100 gross tons or more but less than 1,000 gross tons (excluding those that are not required to use Bunker

Oil etc. for navigation; hereinafter 'Type II Specified Vessel') shall not engage in international voyages unless a Security Contract is concluded (Article 41 paragraph 1 item 2 of the OPDA). They shall not engage in international voyages unless they have a certificate of the Security Contract onboard (Article 45 paragraph 1 item 2 of the OPDA).

694. A Type I Specified Vessel with foreign nationality and a Type II Specified Vessel with foreign nationality shall not enter a port in Japan, leave a port in Japan, or use a mooring facility in Japan unless the Security Contract is concluded (Article 41 paragraph 2 of the OPDA). A Type I Specified Vessel with foreign nationality shall not enter a port in Japan, leave a port in Japan, or use a mooring facility in Japan without (1) a certificate of Security Contract, (2) a document in the form of an annex to the Bunker Oil Convention issued by a foreign state which is a Contracting Party to the Bunker Oil Convention certifying that a security contract on has been concluded for the said vessel, or (3) a document stating the matters described in the certificate prescribed in Article 7 paragraph 14 of the Bunker Oil Convention issued by a foreign state (Article 45 paragraph 2 item 1 of the OPDA). Type II Specified Vessels with foreign nationality shall not enter a port in Japan, leave a port in Japan or use a mooring facility in Japan unless a certificate of Security Contract is kept onboard (Article 45 paragraph 2 item 2 of the OPDA).

695. In case of Type I Specified Vessel, the Security Contract is a contract of insurance or a contract to secure the performance of the obligation of compensation to cover the damage caused to the owner of the vessel by the performance of the obligation in the case that the owner of the vessel is liable to compensate for the Oil Pollution Damage of General Vessel etc. caused by the Bunker Oil, etc. loaded on the vessel (Article 42 paragraph 1 item 1 of the OPDA). In the case of the Type II Specified Vessel, the Security Contract is the contract of insurance or the contract to secure the performance of the obligation of compensation to cover the damage caused to the owner of the vessel by the performance of the obligation in the case that the owner, etc. of the vessel is liable to compensate for the Oil Pollution Damage of General Vessel, etc. caused by the Bunker Oil, etc. loaded on the vessel (Article 42 paragraph 1 item 2 of the OPDA). In the security contract, the party who covers the damage of the owners, etc. of the vessel or secures the performance of the obligation of compensation of the owners etc. of the vessel (Insurer, etc.) must be the Japan Ship Owners' Mutual Protection and Indemnity Association, the Japan Fishing Vessel Insurance Association, the non-life insurance company under the Insurance Business Act of Japan or the foreign non-life insurance company under the Insurance Business Act of Japan (Article 42 paragraph 2 of the OPDA and Article 3 paragraph 2 of the Enforcement Order of the OPDA). The amount of insurance to cover the damage of the owners etc. of the vessel or the amount of the Oil Pollution Damage of General Vessel etc. for which the performance of the obligation of compensation is secured in the security contract shall not be less than the limit of liability of the owners etc. of the vessel (Article 42 paragraph 3 of the OPDA). The limit of liability is the vessel owner's limit of liability including damage to person and damage to property, which is 4,530,000 SDR for a vessel of 2,000 tons or less, and for a vessel of exceeding 2,000 tons, 4,530,000 SDR and 1,812

SDR per ton for the part of the vessel exceeding 2,000 tons up to 30,000 tons, 1,359 SDR per ton for the part of the vessel exceeding 30,000 tons up to 70,000 tons and 906 SDR per ton for the portion exceeding 70,000 tons.

696. The Minister of Land, Infrastructure, Transport and Tourism will, when there is an application from a person who has concluded a Security Contract with Insurer, etc. for a Type I Specified Vessel (excluding those who have the nationality of a foreign state that is a Contracting Party to the Bunker Oil Convention) or a Type II Specified Vessel, issue a document certifying that the Security Contract is concluded for the vessel (Articles 44 and 17 paragraph 1 of the OPDA).

697. When the liability generates to compensate for damages of the owner of the vessel of a Type I Specified Vessel pursuant to the provision of Article 39 paragraph 1 of the OPDA or Article 3 paragraph 2 as applied *mutatis mutandis* pursuant to the provision of Article 39 paragraph 2 of the OPDA, the victim may demand the payment of the amount of damages to the Insurer, etc. However, this shall not apply when the damage was caused by the bad faith of the owner of the vessel (Article 43 paragraph 1 of the OPDA). When the liability generates to compensate for damages of the owner etc. of the Type II Specified Vessel, there is no provision that allows the victim to claim directly to the Insurer, etc. The Insurer etc. may oppose to the victim only with the defence that the owner of the vessel of the Type I Specified Vessel may assert against the victim (Article 43 paragraph 2 of OPDA). For example, the Insurer, etc. cannot claim that the owner of the vessel did not pay the insurance premiums, and therefore, the Insurer, etc. cancels the insurance contract and is not responsible for payment to the victim. The provisions concerning extinguishment of rights are also applied *mutatis mutandis* to the insurer (Article 43 paragraph 4 and Article 10 of the OPDA).

C. Limitation of Liability of Owners, Etc.of the Vessel and Insurers, Etc.

698. Limitation of Liability of Owners etc. of Vessel: The owners, etc. of a tanker or general vessel which is liable to compensate for Oil Pollution Damage of General Vessel, etc. may limit the liability for the claim based on the Oil Pollution Damage of General Vessel, etc. pursuant to the provisions of the Limit. Act (Article 40 of the OPDA). Amount of limit of liability, case where it is not possible to limit liability, scope of limitation of liability, international jurisdiction of the Japanese courts, the domestic jurisdiction etc. shall be subject to the provisions and construction of the Limit. Act.

699. Limitation of Liability of Insurer, etc.: An insurer, etc. that pays the amount of compensation for damages based on a claim from a victim may limit its liability for claims related to payment to the maximum amount of liability as provided for in the OPDA (Article 43 paragraph 3 of the OPDA). The details of the amount of limit of liability are as described above. The scope of the limitation of liability extends to all the claims subject to limitation against the owner of the vessel and the Insurer etc. pertaining to the Type I Specified Vessel arising from the same accident for each

Type I Specified Vessel (Article 43 paragraph 4 and Article 8 of the OPDA). As for the case of limitation of liability, it is constructed that the international jurisdiction of the Japanese court is affirmed (i) when the Oil Pollution Damage of General Vessel, etc. has occurred in Japan, (ii) when the Oil Pollution Damage of General Vessel, etc. has occurred in the Exclusive Economic Zone, (3) when the reasonable measures to prevent or mitigate the damage in Japan or in the exclusive economic zone are taken outside of Japan and no damage are occurred in Japan or in the exclusive economic zone (Article 43 paragraph 5 and Article 31 of the OPDA). As for the procedure for limitation of liability, the provisions of Chapter III of the Limit. Act apply *mutatis mutandis* (Article 43 paragraph 6 of the OPDA).

VII. Wreckage Removal Damage

A. Liability for Compensation for Damages of Owner of Tanker or General Vessel

700. When the Wreckage Removal Damage occurs, the owner of the tanker or the general vessel pertaining to the Wreckage Removal Damage shall be liable to compensate for the damage (Article 47 paragraph 1 of the OPDA). 'Wreck Removal Damage' means the damage caused by the cost of the following measures in the territory of Japan or in the exclusive economic zone of Japan, or in the territory of a foreign state which is a Contracting Party to the Wreck Removal Convention and has given notice pursuant to the provision of Article 3 paragraph 2 of the Wreck Removal Convention, or in the waters prescribed in Article 1 paragraph 1 of the Wreck Removal Convention of a foreign state which is a Contracting Party to the Wreck Removal Convention (excluding Tanker Oil Pollution Damage and Oil Pollution Damage of General Vessel, etc.). This includes: (i) identification of the location of the wreck, (ii) marking of the wreck in the event that removal of the wreck or other measures become necessary pursuant to the provisions of the PHA (Port and Harbour Act) or other laws and regulations or the decision made pursuant to the provisions of Article 6 of the Wreck Removal Convention, (iii) removal of the wreck or other measures in the case of the (ii) above (Article 2 item 17 of the OPDA). Wreck is (i) a sunken or grounded vessel or part thereof, (ii) objects lost from a vessel at sea that have sunk, grounded or been drifting, and (iii) a vessel that is likely to sink or be grounded (limited to those for which the necessary salvage has not been carried out), caused by a marine disaster (Article 2 item 8 of the OPDA). Wreck Removal Convention refers the Nairobi International Convention on the Removal of Wrecks, 2007 (Article 2 item 5 of the OPDA).

701. However, if the Wreck Removal Damage is caused by (i) war, civil disturbance or riot, (ii) abnormal natural disaster, (iii) solely malicious intent of a person other than the owner of the vessel or the person used by the owner, or (iv) defective management of navigation signs or signal facilities for traffic control by the State or a public entity (Article 47 paragraph 1 proviso of the OPDA).

702. If Wreck Removal Damage is caused by the intentional or negligent act of the victim, the court may take this into consideration when determining the responsibility and amount of damages (Article 47 paragraph 2 and Article 4 of the OPDA).

703. The right to claim for compensation for damages against the owner of the vessel shall be extinguished if no judicial claim is made within three years from the date of occurrence of the Wreck Removal Damage. The right to claim for compensation for damages against the owner of the vessel shall also be extinguished if no judicial claim is made within six years from the date on which the first fact causing the Wreck Removal Damage (Article 47 paragraph 2 and Article 10 of the OPDA).

704. With respect to the action against the owner of the vessel, the international jurisdiction of the Japanese court is affirmed when the wreck has generated in the territory or exclusive economic zone of Japan (Article 48 paragraph 1 of the OPDA). The domestic jurisdiction of the Japanese court shall be in accordance with provisions of the CCP and if the court of jurisdiction is not specified in the Code, the Tokyo District Court or the Tokyo Summary Court has jurisdiction (Article 48 paragraph 2 and Article 11 of the OPDA, Article 1 of the Rules of Procedure for Cases of Limitation of Liability for Vessel Oil Pollution Damage, etc.).

B. Compulsory Conclusion of Security Contract and Insurer's Responsibility

705. A tanker or general vessel of 300 gross tons or more having Japanese nationality (hereinafter 'Class I Specified Vessels') shall not be engaged in all voyages unless they have a security contract for compensation for Wreck Removal Damage (Security Contract) (Article 49 paragraph 1 item 1 of the OPDA). Further, the vessel shall not be engaged in all voyages unless a certificate of the Security Contract is kept onboard (Article 53 paragraph 1 item 1 of the OPDA).

706. A general vessel of 100 gross tons or more but less than 300 gross tons having Japanese nationality (hereinafter 'Class II Specified Vessels') shall not be engaged in international voyages unless they have a Security Contract (Article 49 paragraph 1 item 2 of the OPDA). Further, the vessel shall not engage in an international voyage unless a certificate of the Security Contract is kept onboard (Article 53 paragraph 1 item 2 of the OPDA).

707. A Class I Specified Vessel with foreign nationality and a Class II Specified Vessel with foreign nationality shall not enter a port in Japan, depart from a port in Japan, or use a mooring facility in Japan unless the Security Contract has been concluded (Article 49 paragraph 2 of the OPDA). In addition, a Class I Specified Vessel with foreign nationality shall not enter a port in Japan, leave a port in Japan, or use a mooring facility in Japan without (1) a certificate of Security Contract, (2) a document in the form of an annex to the Wreck Removal Convention issued by a foreign state that is a Contracting Party to the Wreck Removal Convention, which certifies that a Security Contract has been concluded, or (3) a document stating the matters in the certificate prescribed in Article 12 paragraph 14 of the Wreck

Removal Convention issued by a foreign state, is kept onboard (Article 53 paragraph 2 item 1 of the OPDA). Class II Specified Vessels with foreign nationality shall not enter a port in Japan, leave a port in Japan or use a mooring facility in Japan unless a certificate of Security Contract is kept onboard (Article 53 paragraph 2 item 2 of the OPDA).

708. In the case of a Class I Specified Vessel, the Security Contract is an insurance contract or a contract to secure the performance of the obligation of compensation to cover the damage caused to the owner of the vessel by the performance of the obligation of compensation when the owner is liable to compensate for the Wreck Removal Damage by the vessel (Article 50 paragraph 1 item 1 of the OPDA). In case of a Class II Specified Vessel, the Security Contract is an insurance contract or a contract to secure the performance of the obligation of compensation to cover damage caused to the owner, etc. of the vessel by the performance of the obligation of compensation when the owner, etc. is liable to compensate for the Wreck Removal Damage by the vessel (limited to the damage caused by the identification of the location of the wreck in the territory of Japan, the marking of the wreck when the removal of the wreck and other measures are necessary in the territory of Japan, and the cost required for the removal of the wreck and other measures in the territory of Japan) (Article 50 paragraph 1 item ii of the OPDA). In the Security Contract, the party who covers the damage of the owners etc. of the vessel or secures the performance of the obligation of compensation of the owners etc. of the vessel (Insurer, etc.) must be the Japan Ship Owners' Mutual Protection & Indemnity Association, the Japan Fishing Vessel Insurance Association, the non-life insurance company under the Insurance Business Act of Japan or the foreign non-life insurance company under the Insurance Business Act of Japan (Article 50 paragraph 2 of the OPDA, Article 3 paragraph 2 of the Enforcement Order of the OPDA). The amount of insurance to cover the damage of the owners, etc. of the vessel or the amount of the Wreck Removal Damage for which the performance of the obligation of compensation is secured in the security contract shall not be less than the limit of liability of the owners etc. of the vessel (Article 50 paragraph 3 of the OPDA). The limit of liability is the vessel owner's limit of liability for property damage, which is 1,510,000 SDR for a vessel of 2,000 tons or less, and for a vessel of exceeding 2,000 tons, 1,510,000 SDR and 604 SDR per ton for the part of the vessel exceeding 2,000 tons up to 30,000 tons, 453 SDR per ton for the part of the vessel exceeding 30,000 tons up to 70,000 tons and 302 SDR per ton for the portion exceeding 70,000 tons.

709. The Minister of Land, Infrastructure, Transport and Tourism will, when there is an application from a person who has concluded a Security Contract with Insurer, etc. for a Class I Specified Vessel (excluding those having the nationality of a foreign state which is a Contracting Party to the Wreck Removal Convention) or a Class II Specified Vessel, issue a document certifying that the Security Contract is concluded for the vessel (Articles 52 and 17 paragraph 1 of the OPDA).

710. When the liability generates to compensate for damages of the owner of a Class I Specified Vessel pursuant to the provision of Article 47 paragraph 1 of the

OPDA, the victim may demand the payment of the amount of compensation of damages to the Insurer, etc. However, this shall not apply when the damage was caused by the bad faith of the owner of the vessel (Article 51 paragraph 1 of the OPDA). The Insurer, etc. may oppose the victim only with the defences that the owner of the vessel can assert against the victim (Article 51 paragraph 2 of the OPDA). The provisions concerning extinguishment of rights shall apply *mutatis mutandis* to the Insurer, etc. (Article 51 paragraph 4 and Article 10 of the OPDA). With respect to liability to compensate for damage of the owner etc. of a Class II Specified Vessel, there is no provision that allows the victim to make a direct claim to the Insurer etc.

C. Limitation of Liability of Insurer, Etc.

711. Limitation of Liability of Insurer, etc.: With respect to the liability to compensate for damages of the owner of Class I Specified Vessel, the Insurer, etc. who have received the claim directly from the victim may limit its liability for the same claim up to the amount of the limit of liability pursuant to the provisions of the OPDA (Article 51 paragraph 3 of the OPDA). The specific details of the limit of liability are as above.

712. The limitation of liability extends to all claims subject to limitation against the owner and the Insurer etc. pertaining to the Class I Specified Vessel arising from the same accident for each of the Class I Specified Vessels (Article 51 paragraph 4 and Article 8 of the OPDA).

713. With respect to the limitation of liability cases, the international jurisdiction of the Japanese courts is considered to be affirmed when (i) the Wreck Removal Damage occurs in Japan, or (ii) the Wreck Removal Damage occurs in the exclusive economic zone of Japan (Article 51 paragraph 5 and Article 31 of the OPDA). As for the procedures for limitation of liability, the provisions of Chapter III of the Limit. Act apply *mutatis mutandis* (Article 51 paragraph 6 of the OPDA).

714. Limitation of Liability of Owners, etc. of Vessel: In accession of the Convention on Limitation of Liability for Maritime Claims, 1976, Japan has exercised the right of reservation granted by the Convention, which excludes the application of the claim for wreck removal costs (Article 2 paragraph 1 item (d) and (e) of the 1976 Convention). Accordingly, no provision has been made to allow the owner etc. of the vessel to limit their liability for claims for compensation for Wreck Removal Damage.

Chapter 14. The Arrest of Vessels

§1. Sources of Law

715. There are two sources of law to arrest a vessel in Japan: (1) CEA (auction procedure) and (2) Civil Provisional Remedy Act (PRA) (provisional seizure of vessel). Of these, (1) can be used when there is (a) statutory lien, (b) a mortgage or (c) a final and binding judgment. In practice, the most common type of arrests for ocean-going vessels is (1)(a) vessel auction based on a statutory lien.

716. Japan has not ratified the International Convention for the Unification of Certain Rules Relating to the Arrest of Sea-going Ships, Brussels, 1952, nor the International Convention on Arrests of Ships, 1999.

717. In the following, explanation is in the following order: a vessel auction based on a statutory lien, a vessel auction based on a mortgage, a vessel auction based on a final judgment, and a provisional seizure of a vessel.

§2. Vessel Auction Based on a Statutory Lien

I. Requirement for an Arrest of Vessels

718. The CEA establishes a system to precede only vessel detention without security in order to cope with the situation where it is not possible to arrest a vessel by filing an auction petition after her entrance to the port due to the speeding up of port operations and shortening of berthing time.

719. This system is available by petitioning a Japanese court when there is a risk that execution against a vessel may become extremely difficult if the vessel nationality certificate etc. is not taken up before the petition for execution against a vessel is filed (Article 189 and Article 115 paragraph 1 of the CEA).

720. The subject vessel is a vessel with a gross tonnage of 20 tons or more, but even if the gross tonnage is 20 tons or more, vessels operated with oars or mainly with oars are excluded (Articles 189 and Article 112 of the CEA). The nationality of the vessel and whether or not it is registered are irrelevant.

II. Judicial Procedure

721. A creditor shall file a petition with the district court that has jurisdiction over the location of the vessel's registry in the case of a Japanese-flagged vessel, or with twelve district courts, including the Tokyo District Court, in the case of a foreign-flagged vessel. If there are urgent circumstances, a petition may also be filed with the court that has jurisdiction over the location of the vessel (Articles 189 and 115 paragraph 1 of the CEA and Article 77 of the Civil Execution Rules (CER)).

722. At the time of filing, the creditor must submit a final and binding judgment proving the existence of the statutory lien, a certified copy of a notarial deed prepared by a notary public proving the existence of the statutory lien, or a document proving the existence of the statutory lien (Article 189, Article 115 paragraph 3 and Article 181 paragraph 1 of the CEA). The degree of proof must be such that the court is convinced of the existence of the statutory lien (Sendai C.A. Judgment of 11 November 2005, regarding statutory lien). In addition, it should be prima facie established that execution against the vessel may become extremely difficult if the vessel nationality certificate etc. is not taken up prior to the filing of the petition for execution against the vessel (Article 189 and Article 115 paragraph 3 of the CEA).

723. The creditor is required to concretely specify the secured claim, security rights and vessel at the time of filing the petition. Of these, with respect to security rights, there are some debates as to under which governing law a statutory lien needs to be affirmed, and court decisions are divided. Please refer to the literature on conflict of law rules for this point. If Japanese law is the governing law, a person who has the following claims would have a lien on the vessel and her equipment (maritime lien): (i) a claim for compensation for damage caused by an infringement of a person's life or body directly related to the operation of the vessel (Article 842 item 1 of the Com. Code), (ii) a claim for a salvage remuneration or a claim for General Average contribution to be borne by the vessel (Article 842 item 2 of the Com. Code), (iii) a claim that may be collected in accordance with the National Tax Collection Act or the examples of national tax collection, and which arise in connection with the entry of a vessel into a port, use of a port or other navigation of a vessel, or a claim pertaining to pilotage fees or tug fees (Article 842 item 3 of the Com. Code), (iv) a claim pertaining to expenses necessary to continue a voyage (Article 842 item 4 of the Com. Code), (v) a claim of the Master and other seamen arising from contracts of employment (Article 842 item 5 of the Com. Code), (vi) a claim subject to limitation which a limited creditor has under the Limit. Act (limited to claims relating to damage to property) (Article 95 paragraph 1 of the Limit. Act), (vii) a claim subject to limitation which a limited creditors relating to Tanker Oil Pollution Damage has under the OPDA has (Article 55 paragraph 1 of the OPDA).

724. As a practical matter, the court will interview the creditor and then determine whether required items are established and proved.

725. If the court determines that there is proof, it will issue an order for delivery of vessel nationality certificate, etc. (Article 189 and Article 115 paragraph 1 of the CEA). The said order is enforceable even before it is served upon the other party, but it is not enforceable if two weeks have passed since it was notified to the petitioner (Article 189, Article 115 paragraph 7, Article 55 paragraph 8 and Article 55 paragraph 9 of the CEA).

726. On the other hand, if the court determines that there is no proof, it will request the creditor to submit additional evidence, to identify the claim, or partially withdraw the claim, and if the claim is still not corrected, it will issue an order of dismissal. The creditor may file an appeal against the order of dismissal by filing an ordinary appeal (Article 189 and 20 of the CEA and Article 328 paragraph 1 of the CCP).

III. Security and Counter Security

727. A creditor is not required to deposit a security to the court in order to obtain an order for delivery of vessel nationality certificate, etc.

IV. Enforcement of the Arrest Order

728. After the vessel that is the subject of the order for delivery of vessel nationality certificate, etc. has arrived at a port, the creditor shall file a petition for execution of the order for delivery of vessel nationality certificate, etc. with court execution officer of the court that has jurisdiction over the port where the vessel is actually located. It is not possible to file a petition for execution prior to the vessel's arrival at port. The court execution officer shall visit the vessel and take away the vessel nationality certificate, etc. and keep it. As a result, the vessel shall not sail from the port.

729. However, the creditor shall submit to a court execution officer a document proving that the creditor has filed a petition for execution against a vessel (auction) within five days from the day on which the court execution officer took delivery of the vessel nationality certificate, etc. If the creditor fails to do so, the court execution officer shall return the vessel nationality certificate, etc. to the debtor (Articles 189 and 115 paragraph 4 of the CEA). This petition for execution against a vessel shall be filed with the district court having jurisdiction over the location of the vessel (Articles 189 and 113 of the CEA). At the time of filing a petition for execution against a vessel, the creditor shall submit a final and binding judgment proving the existence of the statutory lien, a certified copy of a notarial deed prepared by a notary public proving the existence of the statutory lien, or a document proving the existence of the statutory lien (Articles 189 and 181 paragraph 1 of the CEA).

V. Appeal by Debtor

A. Outline

730. When the court execution officer takes up the vessel nationality certificate etc., the order for delivery of vessel nationality certificate etc. will be served upon the debtor. Thereafter, the creditor files a petition for execution against a vessel and pay a prepayment to the court (Article 14 paragraph 1 of the CEA). Then, the court issues a decision of commencement of the auction as execution of security rights, declares seizure of the vessel and prohibits the debtor from sailing the vessel (Articles 189 and 114 paragraphs 1 and 2 of the CEA). Then, the procedure of the vessel auction proceeds further.

731. In the above process, the debtor may file (1) an immediate appeal against the order for the delivery (Articles 189 and 115 paragraph 5 of the CEA) and (2) an objection to execution against the decision of the commencement (Articles 189 and 182 of the CEA). Of these, the (1) above must be filed within a period of one week from the day on which the order is notified (Article 332 of the CCP). For the (2) above, there is no time limit. However, neither (1) nor (2) has the effect of releasing the vessel from detention by itself.

732. The methods of releasing the vessel from detention include (a) court's rescission of the auction procedure by providing security (Articles 189 and 117 paragraph 1 of the CEA, (b) court's permission for navigation (Articles 189 and 118 of the CEA), and (c) creditor's withdrawal of the petition for auction by making a settlement.

B. Rescission of Auction Procedure by Provision of Security

733. The (a) above requires that the debtor (i) submit to the court an authenticated copy of the judicial decision ordering a temporary stay of the procedure, and (ii) provide security equivalent to the total amount of claims and execution costs of the creditor effecting a seizure and the creditor who has demanded distribution by the time of provision of security, prior to the filing of the purchase offer (Articles 189 and 117 paragraph 1 of the CEA). With regard to the (i) above, the debtor does not have the right to file a petition for said judicial decision, and the court shall do so ex officio based on its discretion. However, the debtor may request the court to exercise its authority in the objection to the execution set forth in the (2) above. The court shall make a judgment based on its reasonable discretion, taking into consideration the type and degree of damage suffered by the debtor as a result of the execution and the type and degree of disadvantage suffered by the creditor as a result of the stay of execution. If the court considers it appropriate to issue the order, it shall order the debtor to provide security and stay execution (Article 11 paragraph 2, Article 10 paragraph 6, Article 39 paragraph 1 item 7 of the CEA). The amount of security required by the court is determined on a case-by-case basis. Security can be provided in the form of a cash deposit, a deposit of securities etc., or, with the permission of the court, a payment guarantee consignment agreement with a bank or insurance company, etc. licensed in Japan (Article 15 paragraph 1 of the CEA and Article 10 of the CER). With regard to the (ii) above, the following methods of providing the security are possible; a cash deposit, a deposit of securities etc., or, with the permission of the court, a payment guarantee consignment contract with a bank or insurance company etc. licensed in Japan (Article 117 paragraph 5 and Article 15 of the CEA and Article 78 paragraph 1 of the CER). If (i) and (ii) are satisfied, the court will cancel the auction procedure except for the procedures for distribution, etc. (Articles 189 and 117 paragraph 1 of the CEA).

734. The court will then decide on the objection to execution. If the court accepts the objection, the execution against the vessel procedure shall be terminated and the security shall be returned to the debtor. On the other hand, if the court does not accept the objection and the judicial decision ordering the temporary stay of the procedure becomes ineffective, the court shall implement the distribution of the secured amount. If the court does not accept the objection, the debtor may further file a security with the court and obtain a provisional disposition order (provisional disposition order to temporary stay the procedure for exercise of security rights) to stop the implementation of the distribution (Articles 189 and 183 paragraph 1 item 7 of the CEA), and file a lawsuit for declaration of non-existence of security rights (Mito D.C. Judgment of 20 March 2014).

C. Court's Permission for Navigation

735. The (b) above shall be permitted by the court upon petition by the debtor if there is a business necessity or other reasonable grounds and the consent of each creditor and the highest purchase offeror or purchaser and the next-highest purchase offeror is obtained (Articles 189 and 118 paragraph 1 of the CEA). The court should limit the purpose, scope and duration of the navigation as much as possible. Once the order of permission becomes final and binding, the vessel nationality certificate, etc. is returned to the Master by the court, and the execution against the vessel (auction procedure) effectively ceases. Any loss of or damage to the vessel during the course of navigation will be to the detriment of the creditors etc. who agreed to the navigation. If the vessel returns to the port and the vessel nationality certificate etc. is resubmitted, the execution procedure will be continued. If it is not resubmitted, the court shall issue an order for resubmission upon the petition of an interested party (Article 81 of the CER). If the vessel does not return to the port and is not expected to do so, the court cancels the procedure (Articles 189, 121 and 53 of the CEA).

D. Settlement with Creditor

736. If a settlement is reached with the creditor and the creditor withdraws the petition for auction, the vessel is released from detention. A settlement may be reached by providing a letter of guarantee to the creditor.

VI. Remedies for Wrongful Arrest

737. When a vessel is illegally detained, there is room for the debtor to claim compensation for damages against the creditor. If the requirements of Japanese tort (intentional or negligent act, infringement of rights or illegality, damage, and reasonable causation) are satisfied, it is highly likely that the amount of damage with reasonable causation can be claimed. However, there is possibility that the amount is reduced by fault in common.

VII. Costs

738. The creditor is required to pay a petition fee for an order for delivery of vessel nationality certificate, etc. prior to the filing of a petition for execution against a vessel (section II above), a prepayment for a court execution officer (section IV above), a petition fee for execution against a vessel (sections IV and V above), and a prepayment for execution against a vessel (section V above). The amount of the fee for filing a petition with the court is stipulated in the Act on the Costs of Civil Proceedings, while the prepayment for a court execution officer and prepayment for execution against a vessel are determined on a case-by-case basis. In many cases, travel expenses are also incurred. At the very least, a petition for execution of the order for delivery of vessel nationality certificate etc. must be filed with the court execution officer of the district court that has jurisdiction over the location of the vessel. There are 50 district courts in Japan, and it is necessary to travel to the court where the vessel is located to file the petition. If a lawyer is appointed, lawyer's fee will be incurred. These costs are usually borne by the creditor.

739. If the debtor or the owner of the vessel disputes the case, a fee for filing an immediate appeal (section V above) and a fee for filing an objection to execution (section V above) will be charged. These amounts are provided for in the Act on the Costs of Civil Proceedings. In addition, if the method of cash deposit is used for security necessary to obtain a judicial decision ordering a temporary stay of proceedings or for a security equivalent to the total amount of claims and execution costs (section V above), such cash is also required. These amounts are determined on a case-by-case basis. If a lawyer is appointed, lawyer's fee will also be incurred.

§3. Vessel Auction Based on Vessel Mortgages

I. Requirement for an Arrest of Vessels

740. Same as the arrest based on a statutory lien, the system of an order of delivery of vessel nationality certificate, etc. prior to the filing of a petition for execution against a vessel is to be used. This system is available by petitioning a Japanese court when there is a risk that execution against a vessel may become extremely difficult if the vessel nationality certificate, etc. is not taken up before the petition for execution against a vessel is filed (Articles 189 and 115 paragraph 1 of the CEA).

741. The subject vessel is a vessel with a gross tonnage of 20 tons or more, but even if the gross tonnage is 20 tons or more, vessels operated with oars or mainly with oars are excluded (Articles 189 and 112 of the CEA). The nationality of the vessel and whether or not it is registered are irrelevant.

II. Judicial Procedure

742. A creditor shall file a petition with the district court that has jurisdiction over the location of the vessel's registry in the case of a Japanese-flagged vessel, or with twelve district courts, including the Tokyo District Court, in the case of a foreign-flagged vessel. If there are urgent circumstances, a petition may also be filed with the court that has jurisdiction over the location of the vessel (Articles 189 and 115 paragraph 1 of the CEA and Article 77 of the CER).

743. At the time of filing, the creditor must submit a final and binding judgment proving the existence of the mortgage, a certified copy of a notarial deed prepared by a notary public proving the existence of the mortgage, or a certificate of registered matters concerning the registration of the mortgage (Article 189, Article 115 paragraph 3 and Article 181 paragraph 1 item 1-3 of the CEA).

744. In addition, it should be prima facie established that execution against the vessel may become extremely difficult if the vessel nationality certificate, etc. is not taken up prior to the filing of the petition for execution against the vessel (Articles 189 and 115 paragraph 3 of the CEA).

745. The creditor is required to concretely specify the secured claim, security rights and vessel at the time of filing the petition. With respect to security rights, there are no disputes that the applicable law to establishment of mortgage is the law of the flag state of the vessel. As for the effect of the mortgage, the dominant academic view is that it is governed by the law of the flag state.

746. As a practical matter, the court will interview the creditor and then determine whether required items are established and proved.

747. If the court determines that there is proof, it will issue an order for delivery of vessel nationality certificate, etc. (Articles 189 and 115 paragraph 1 of the CEA). The said order is enforceable even before it is served upon the other party, but it is not enforceable if two weeks have passed since it was notified to the petitioner (Article 189, Article 115 paragraph 7, Article 55 paragraph 8 and Article 55 paragraph 9 of the CEA).

748. On the other hand, if the court determines that there is no proof, it will request the creditor to submit additional evidence, to identify the claim, or partially withdraw the claim, and if the claim is still not corrected, it will issue an order of dismissal. The creditor may file an appeal against the order of dismissal by filing an ordinary appeal (Articles 189 and 20 of the CEA and 328 paragraph 1 of the CCP).

III. Security and Counter Security

749. A creditor is not required to deposit a security to the court in order to obtain an order for delivery of vessel nationality certificate, etc.

IV. Enforcement of the Arrest Order

750. After the vessel that is the subject of the order for delivery of vessel nationality certificate etc. has arrived at a port, the creditor shall file a petition for execution of the order for delivery of vessel nationality certificate, etc. with court execution officer of the court that has jurisdiction over the port where the vessel is actually located. It is not possible to file a petition for execution prior to the vessel's arrival at port. The court execution officer shall visit the vessel and take away the vessel nationality certificate, etc. and keep it. As a result, the vessel shall not sail from the port.

751. However, the creditor shall submit to a court execution officer a document proving that the creditor has filed a petition for execution against a vessel (auction) within five days from the day on which the court execution officer took delivery of the vessel nationality certificate etc. If the creditor fails to do so, the court execution officer shall return the vessel nationality certificate etc. to the debtor (Articles 189 and 115 paragraph 4 of the CEA). This petition for execution against a vessel shall be filed with the district court having jurisdiction over the location of the vessel (Articles 189 and 113 of the CEA). At the time of filing a petition for execution against a vessel, the creditor shall submit a final and binding judgment proving the existence of the mortgage, a certified copy of a notarial deed prepared by a notary public proving the existence of the mortgage, or a certificate of registered matters concerning the registration of the mortgage (Articles 189 and 181 paragraph 1 item 1-3 of the CEA).

V. Appeal by Debtor

A. *Outline*

752. When the court execution officer takes up the vessel nationality certificate, etc., the order for delivery of vessel nationality certificate, etc. will be served upon the debtor. Thereafter, the creditor files a petition for execution against a vessel and pays a prepayment to the court (Article 14 paragraph 1 of the CEA). Then, the court issues a decision of commencement of the auction as execution of security rights, declares seizure of the vessel and prohibits the debtor from sailing the vessel (Article 189 and 114 paragraphs 1 and 2 of the CEA). Then, the procedure of the vessel auction proceeds further.

753. In the above process, the debtor may file (1) an immediate appeal against the order for the delivery (Articles 189 and 115 paragraph 5 of the CEA) and (2) an objection to execution against the decision of the commencement (Articles 189 and 182 of the CEA). Of these, the (1) above must be filed within a period of one week from the day on which the order is notified (Article 332 of the CCP). For the (2) above, there is no time limit. However, neither (1) nor (2) has the effect of releasing the vessel from detention by itself.

754. The methods of releasing the vessel from detention include (a) court's rescission of the auction procedure by providing security (Articles 189 and 117 paragraph 1 of the CEA), (b) court's permission for navigation (Articles 189 and 118 of the CEA), and (c) creditor's withdrawal of the petition for auction by making a settlement.

B. Rescission of Auction Procedure by Provision of Security

755. The (a) above requires that the debtor (i) submit to the court an authenticated copy of the judicial decision ordering a temporary stay of the procedure, and (ii) provide security equivalent to the total amount of claims and execution costs of the creditor effecting a seizure and the creditor who has demanded distribution by the time of provision of security, prior to the filing of the purchase offer (Articles 189 and 117 paragraph 1 of the CEA). With regard to the (i) above, the debtor does not have the right to file a petition for said judicial decision, and the court shall do so ex officio based on its discretion. However, the debtor may request the court to exercise its authority in the objection to the execution set forth in the (2) above. The court shall make a judgment based on its reasonable discretion, taking into consideration the type and degree of damage suffered by the debtor as a result of the execution and the type and degree of disadvantage suffered by the creditor as a result of the stay of execution. If the court considers it appropriate to issue the order, it shall order the debtor to provide security and stay execution (Article 11 paragraph 2, Article 10 paragraph 6, Article 39 paragraph 1 item 7 of the CEA). The amount of security required by the court is determined on a case-by-case basis. Security can be provided in the form of a cash deposit, a deposit of securities etc., or, with the permission of the court, a payment guarantee consignment agreement with a bank or insurance company etc. licensed in Japan (Article 15 paragraph 1 of the CEA and Article 10 of the CER). With regard to the (ii) above, the following methods of providing the security are possible; a cash deposit, a deposit of securities, etc., or, with the permission of the court, a payment guarantee consignment contract with a bank or insurance company etc. licensed in Japan (Article 117 paragraph 5 and Article 15 of the CEA and Article 78 paragraph 1 of the CER). If (i) and (ii) are satisfied, the court will cancel the auction procedure except for the procedures for distribution, etc. (Articles 189 and 117 paragraph 1 of the CEA).

756. The court will then decide on the objection to execution. If the court accepts the objection, the execution against the vessel procedure shall be terminated and the security shall be returned to the debtor. On the other hand, if the court does not accept the objection and the judicial decision ordering the temporary stay of the procedure becomes ineffective, the court shall implement the distribution of the secured amount. If the court does not accept the objection, the debtor may further file a security with the court and obtain a provisional disposition order (provisional disposition order to temporary stay the procedure for exercise of security rights) to stop the implementation of the distribution (Articles 189 and 183 paragraph 1 item 7 of the CEA), and file a lawsuit for declaration of non-existence of security rights (Mito D.C. Judgment of 20 March 2014).

C. Court's Permission for Navigation

757. The (b) above shall be permitted by the court upon petition by the debtor if there is a business necessity or other reasonable grounds and the consent of each creditor and the highest purchase offeror or purchaser and the next-highest purchase offeror is obtained (Articles 189 and 118 paragraph 1 of the CEA). The court should limit the purpose, scope and duration of the navigation as much as possible. Once the order of permission becomes final and binding, the vessel nationality certificate etc. is returned to the Master by the court, and the execution against the vessel (auction procedure) effectively ceases. Any loss of or damage to the vessel during the course of navigation will be to the detriment of the creditors etc. who agreed to the navigation. If the vessel returns to the port and the vessel nationality certificate etc. is resubmitted, the execution procedure will be continued. If it is not resubmitted, the court shall issue an order for resubmission upon the petition of an interested party (Article 81 of the CER). If the vessel does not return to the port and is not expected to do so, the court cancels the procedure (Articles 189, 121 and 53 of the CEA).

D. Settlement with Creditor

758. If a settlement is reached with the creditor and the creditor withdraws the petition for auction, the vessel is released from detention. A settlement may be reached by providing a letter of guarantee to the creditor.

VI. Remedies for Wrongful Arrest

759. When a vessel is illegally detained, there is room for the debtor to claim compensation for damages against the creditor. If the requirements of Japanese tort (intentional or negligent act, infringement of rights or illegality, damage, and reasonable causation) are satisfied, it is highly likely that the amount of damage with reasonable causation can be claimed. However, there is possibility that the amount is reduced by fault in common.

VII. Costs

760. The creditor is required to pay a petition fee for an order for delivery of vessel nationality certificate etc. prior to the filing of a petition for execution against a vessel (section II above), a prepayment for a court execution officer (IV above), a petition fee for execution against a vessel (sections IV and V above), and a prepayment for execution against a vessel (section V above). The amount of the fee for filing a petition with the court is stipulated in the Act on the Costs of Civil Proceedings, while the prepayment for a court execution officer and prepayment for execution against a vessel are determined on a case-by-case basis. In many cases, travel expenses are also incurred. At the very least, a petition for execution of the order for delivery of vessel nationality certificate etc. must be filed with the court execution officer of the district court that has jurisdiction over the location of the vessel. There are fifty district courts in Japan, and it is necessary to travel to the court where the vessel is located to file the petition. If a lawyer is appointed, lawyer's fee will be incurred. These costs are usually borne by the creditor.

761. If the debtor or the owner of the vessel disputes the case, a fee for filing an immediate appeal (section V above) and a fee for filing an objection to execution (section V above) will be charged. These amounts are provided for in the Act on the Costs of Civil Proceedings. In addition, if the method of cash deposit is used for security necessary to obtain a judicial decision ordering a temporary stay of proceedings or for a security equivalent to the total amount of claims and execution costs (section V above), such cash is also required. These amounts are determined on a case-by-case basis. If a lawyer is appointed, lawyer's fee will also be incurred.

§4. Vessel Auction Based on a Final and Binding Judgment

I. Requirement for an Arrest of Vessels

762. Same as the arrest based on a statutory lien, the system of an order of delivery of vessel nationality certificate etc. prior to the filing of a petition for execution against a vessel is to be used. This system is available by petitioning a Japanese court when there is a risk that execution against a vessel may become extremely difficult if the vessel nationality certificate, etc. is not taken up before the petition for execution against a vessel is filed (Article 115 paragraph 1 of the CEA).

763. The subject vessel is a vessel with a gross tonnage of 20 tons or more, but even if the gross tonnage is 20 tons or more, vessels operated with oars or mainly with oars are excluded (Article 112 of the CEA). The nationality of the vessel and whether or not it is registered are irrelevant. The subject vessel must be owned by the debtor.

II. Judicial Procedure

764. A creditor shall file a petition with the district court that has jurisdiction over the location of the vessel's registry in the case of a Japanese-flagged vessel, or with twelve district courts, including the Tokyo District Court, in the case of a foreign-flagged vessel. If there are urgent circumstances, a petition may also be filed with the court that has jurisdiction over the location of the vessel (Article 115 paragraph 1 of the CEA and Article 77 of the CER).

765. The creditor is required to submit an enforceable authenticated copy of the title of obligation at the time of filing the petition (Article 115 paragraph 3 of the CEA). An example of an enforceable authenticated copy of a title of obligation is a final and binding judgment of a Japanese court to which a sentence of execution has been granted (Article 51 paragraph 1, Article 25 and Article 22 paragraph 1 of the CEA). A final and binding judgment of a foreign court shall become an enforceable authenticated copy of a title of obligation if the execution decision issued by a Japanese court with respect thereto becomes final and binding and a sentence of execution is granted (Article 22 item 6 of the CEA). An arbitral award (including foreign arbitral awards) will become an enforceable authenticated copy of a title of obligation if the execution decision rendered in relation to it by a Japanese court becomes final and binding and if a sentence of execution is granted (Article 22 item 6-2 of the CEA and Article 3 paragraph3 and Article 46 paragraph 1 of the Arbitration Act).

766. In addition, it should be prima facie established that execution against the vessel may become extremely difficult if the vessel nationality certificate etc. is not taken up prior to the filing of the petition for execution against the vessel (Article 115 paragraph 3 of the CEA).

767. The creditor is required to concretely specify the secured claim and vessel at the time of filing the petition.

768. As a practical matter, the court will interview the creditor and then determine whether required items are established and proved.

769. If the court determines that there is proof, it will issue an order for delivery of vessel nationality certificate, etc. (Article 115 paragraph 1 of the CEA). The said order is enforceable even before it is served upon the other party, but it is not enforceable if two weeks have passed since it was notified to the petitioner (Article 115 paragraph 7, Article 55 paragraph 8 and Article 55 paragraph 9 of the CEA).

770. On the other hand, if the court determines that there is no proof, it will request the creditor to submit additional evidence, to identify the claim, or partially withdraw the claim, and if the claim is still not corrected, it will issue an order of dismissal. The creditor may file an appeal against the order of dismissal by filing an ordinary appeal (Article 20 of the CEA and Article 328 paragraph 1 of the CCP).

III. Security and Counter Security

771. A creditor is not required to deposit a security to the court in order to obtain an order for delivery of vessel nationality certificate, etc.

IV. Enforcement of the Arrest Order

772. After the vessel that is the subject of the order for delivery of vessel nationality certificate, etc. has arrived at a port, the creditor shall file a petition for execution of the order for delivery of vessel nationality certificate etc. with court execution officer of the court that has jurisdiction over the port where the vessel is actually located. It is not possible to file a petition for execution prior to the vessel's arrival at port. The court execution officer shall visit the vessel and take away the vessel nationality certificate etc. and keep it. As a result, the vessel shall not sail from the port.

773. However, the creditor shall submit to a court execution officer a document proving that the creditor has filed a petition for execution against a vessel (auction) within five days from the day on which the court execution officer took delivery of the vessel nationality certificate, etc. If the creditor fails to do so, the court execution officer shall return the vessel nationality certificate etc. to the debtor (Article 115 paragraph 4 of the CEA). This petition for execution against a vessel shall be filed with the district court having jurisdiction over the location of the vessel (Article 113 of the CEA). At the time of filing a petition for execution against a vessel, the creditor shall submit an enforceable authenticated copy of the title of obligation at the time of filing the petition for execution against a vessel (Article 74 of the CER).

V. Appeal by Debtor

A. *Outline*

774. When the court execution officer takes up the vessel nationality certificate etc., the order for delivery of vessel nationality certificate etc. will be served upon the debtor. Thereafter, the creditor files a petition for execution against a vessel and pays a prepayment to the court (Article 14 paragraph 1 of the CEA). Then, the court issues a decision of commencement of the auction as execution of security rights, declares seizure of the vessel and prohibits the debtor from sailing the vessel (Article 114 paragraphs 1 and 2 of the CEA). Then, the procedure of the vessel auction proceeds further.

775. In the above process, the debtor may file (1) an immediate appeal against the order for the delivery (Article 115 paragraph 5 of the CEA) and (2) an action to oppose execution (Article 35 paragraph 1 of the CEA). Of these, the (1) above must be filed within a period of one week from the day on which the order is notified (Article 332 of the CCP). For the (2) above, there is no time limit. Further, if debtor is not the owner of the vessel, the owner may file (3) third-party action against execution (Article 38 paragraph 1 of the CEA). However, none of (1), (2) or (3) has the effect of releasing the vessel from detention by itself.

776. The methods of releasing the vessel from detention include (a) court's rescission of the auction procedure by providing security (Article 117 paragraph 1 of the CEA), (b) court's permission for navigation (Article 118 of the CEA), and (c) creditor's withdrawal of the petition for auction by making a settlement.

B. Rescission of Auction Procedure by Provision of Security

777. The (a) above requires that the debtor (i) submit to the court an authenticated copy of the judicial decision ordering a temporary stay of the procedure, and (ii) provide security equivalent to the total amount of claims and execution costs of the creditor effecting a seizure and the creditor who has demanded distribution by the time of provision of security, prior to the filing of the purchase offer (Article 117 paragraph 1 of the CEA). In the Article, the party who provide the authenticated copy of the judicial decision and the security is stipulated as 'the debtor', and it is not clear whether or not the owner of the vessel, who is not the debtor, can be the party. With regard to the (i) above, the judicial decision is issued by the court in its discretion when the circumstances alleged for objection appear to be legally justified and a prima facie case is made on the factual points. If the court considers the issuance to be reasonable, it shall order the debtor to provide security and stay execution (Article 36 paragraph 1 and Article 39 paragraph 1 item 7 of the CEA). The amount of security required by the court is determined on a case-by-case basis. Security can be provided in the form of a cash deposit, a deposit of securities, etc., or, with the permission of the court, a payment guarantee consignment agreement with a bank or insurance company etc. licensed in Japan (Article 15 paragraph 1 of the CEA, Article 10 of the CER). With regard to the (ii) above, the following methods of providing the security are possible; a cash deposit, a deposit of securities etc., or, with the permission of the court, a payment guarantee consignment contract with a bank or insurance company etc. licensed in Japan (Article 117 paragraph 5 and Article 15 of the CEA and Article 78 paragraph 1 of the CER). If (i) and (ii) are satisfied, the court will cancel the auction procedure except for the procedures for distribution, etc. (Article 117 paragraph 1 of the CEA).

778. The court will then decide on the action to oppose execution. If the court affirms the action, the execution against the vessel procedure shall be terminated and the security shall be returned to the debtor. On the other hand, if the court does not affirm the action and the judicial decision ordering the temporary stay of the procedure becomes ineffective, the court shall implement the distribution of the secured amount.

C. Court's Permission for Navigation

779. The (b) above shall be permitted by the court upon petition by the debtor if there is a business necessity or other reasonable grounds and the consent of each creditor and the highest purchase offeror or purchaser and the next-highest purchase offeror is obtained (Article 118 paragraph 1 of the CEA). The court should limit the purpose, scope and duration of the navigation as much as possible. Once the order of permission becomes final and binding, the vessel nationality certificate etc. is returned to the Master by the court, and the execution against the vessel (auction procedure) effectively ceases. Any loss of or damage to the vessel during the course of navigation will be to the detriment of the creditors, etc. who agreed to the navigation. If the vessel returns to the port and the vessel nationality certificate, etc. is resubmitted, the execution procedure will be continued. If it is not resubmitted, the court shall issue an order for resubmission upon the petition of an interested party (Article 81 of the CER). If the vessel does not return to the port and is not expected to do so, the court cancels the procedure (Articles 121 and 53 of the CEA).

D. Settlement with Creditor

780. If a settlement is reached with the creditor and the creditor withdraws the petition for auction, the vessel is released from detention.

VI. Remedies for Wrongful Arrest

781. When a vessel is illegally detained, there is room for the debtor to claim compensation for damages against the creditor. If the requirements of Japanese tort (intentional or negligent act, infringement of rights or illegality, damage, and reasonable causation) are satisfied, it is highly likely that the amount of damage with reasonable causation can be claimed. However, there is possibility that the amount is reduced by fault in common.

VII. Costs

782. The creditor is required to pay a petition fee for an order for delivery of vessel nationality certificate etc. prior to the filing of a petition for execution against a vessel (section II above), a prepayment for a court execution officer (section IV above), a petition fee for execution against a vessel (sections IV and V above), and a prepayment for execution against a vessel (section V above). The amount of the fee for filing a petition with the court is stipulated in the Act on the Costs of Civil Proceedings, while the prepayment for a court execution officer and prepayment for execution against a vessel are determined on a case-by-case basis. In many cases, travel expenses are also incurred. At the very least, a petition for execution of the order for delivery of vessel nationality certificate etc. must be filed with the court execution officer of the district court that has jurisdiction over the location of the vessel. There are fifty district courts in Japan, and it is necessary to travel to the court where the vessel is located to file the petition. If a lawyer is appointed, lawyer's fee will be incurred. These costs are usually borne by the creditor.

783. If the debtor or the owner of the vessel disputes the case, a fee for filing an immediate appeal (section V above) and a fee for filing an objection to execution (section V above) will be charged. These amounts are provided for in the Act on the Costs of Civil Proceedings. In addition, if the method of cash deposit is used for security necessary to obtain a judicial decision ordering a temporary stay of proceedings or for a security equivalent to the total amount of claims and execution costs (section V above), such cash is also required. These amounts are determined on a case-by-case basis. If a lawyer is appointed, lawyer's fee will also be incurred.

§5. Provisional Seizure of Vessels

I. Requirement for an Arrest of Vessels

784. The requirements for a provisional seizure of a vessel based on the PRA are (a) a claim for the payment of money (claim to be preserved), (b) risk of being unable to enforce compulsory execution or risk of causing significant difficulty in enforcing compulsory execution (necessity of preservation) (Article 20 paragraph 1 of the PRA). Further, (c) a debtor must be the owner of the vessel subject to the provisional seizure order (Article 20 paragraph 2 item ha of the Civil Provisional Remedy Rule (PRR)), and (d) a creditor must provide security (Article 14 paragraph 1 of the PRA).

II. Judicial Procedure

785. A provisional seizure of a vessel is possible only when an action on the main case can be filed with a Japanese court or when the vessel to be provisionally seized is located in Japan (Article 11 of the PRA). Even where there is an arbitration agreement between a creditor and a debtor that designates Japan or a foreign country as the place of arbitration, a provisional seizure of a vessel is possible if the vessel to be provisionally seized is located in Japan (Articles 3 and 15 of the Arbitration Act).

786. A creditor shall file a petition for an order of provisional seizure with the court having jurisdiction over the main case or the district court having jurisdiction over the location of the vessel to be provisionally seized (Article 12 paragraph 1 of the PRA).

787. A creditor shall file a petition by clarifying the purpose of the petition, the existence of the claim to be preserved and the necessity of preservation (Article 13 paragraph 1 of the PRA). The petition shall include a certificate of the registered matters of the vessel subject to the provisional seizure (in the case of a registered Japanese vessel), a document proving that the vessel subject to the provisional seizure is a vessel with a gross tonnage of 20 tons or more (excluding a paddle boat or any other boat operated by oars or mainly by oars) and a document proving that the vessel is owned by the debtor (in the case of a vessel other than a Japanese vessel) and the document proving the value of the vessel (Article 20 item 2 of the PRR). The creditor must prima facie establish the existence of the claim to be preserved and the necessity of preservation (Article 13 paragraph 2 of the PRA). In practice, in principle, a prima facie establishment should be made with the original evidence. If the governing law of the claim to be preserved is a foreign law, a prima facie establishment of the content of the foreign law may also be required.

788. The court will interview the creditor promptly after filing the petition. On the other hand, the court seldom interviews the debtor in a case involving an order for provisional seizure of a vessel.

789. If the court determines that there is no prima facie case, it shall issue an order of dismissal (Article 19 paragraph 1 of the PRA). In response to this, the creditor may file an immediate appeal within a period of two weeks from the date of receipt of the notice and contest it (Article 19 paragraph 1 of the PRA). The creditor may not further challenge the judicial decision to dismiss the immediate appeal (Article 19 paragraph 2 of the PRA).

790. If, on the other hand, the court determines that there is a prima facie case, it will require the creditor to post security within a certain period of time. *See* section III below for details of security. Where the creditor has put up security, the court will normally issue an order for provisional seizure of the vessel without hearing from the debtor.

III. Security and Counter Security

791. In the case of a provisional seizure of a vessel under the PRA, the court requires the creditor to post security within a certain period of time (Article 14 paragraph 1 of the PRA). The period for putting up security is often in practice three to five days. The amount of security is determined by considering the purpose of the preservation order, the type and value of the subject matter, etc., and then considering the nature of the claim to be secured, the occupation, property and creditworthiness of the debtor, as well as the extent of the damage that may occur and the degree of probability thereof, taking into consideration the degree of credibility of the prima facie evidence. The decision is made on a case-by-case basis. In principle, the method of providing security is (i) a cash deposit. A creditor is required to deposit cash with a depositary within the jurisdiction of the court that has ordered the provision of security. However, as exceptions, it is also possible to (ii) deposit securities that the court deems appropriate, or (iii) with the permission of the court, conclude a payment guarantee consignment agreement that satisfies the requirements set out in the PRR with a bank, insurance company or other entity licensed in Japan by the creditor (Article 4 paragraph 1 of the PRA and Article 2 of the PRR).

IV. Enforcement of the Arrest Order

792. There are two methods of execution of a provisional seizure of a vessel based on the PRA: (1) registration of provisional seizure and (2) ordering court execution officer to take up vessel nationality certificate and other documents necessary for the navigation of the vessel (vessel nationality certificate, etc.) and submit them to the court (Article 48 paragraph 1 of the PRA). The method of execution against a vessel of Japanese registry is (1), (2) or both. The method of execution against a vessel of foreign registry is (2) only.

793. In case of registration of provisional seizure, the court that has issued the order of provisional seizure has jurisdiction over the execution of the provisional seizure as the court for execution of preservation (Article 48 paragraph 2 of the

PRA). Specifically, the clerk of the said court shall commission the registration of the provisional seizure to the registry office that has jurisdiction over the registration of the relevant vessel, and the order of provisional seizure shall be entered in the registry (Article 48 paragraph 3, Article 47 paragraph 3 of the PRA and Article 48 of the CEA). The creditor is not required to file a petition.

794. In case of ordering court execution officer to take up seizure and retention of the certificate of the vessel nationality certificate, etc., the district court having jurisdiction over the location of the vessel shall have jurisdiction over the execution of the provisional seizure as the court for execution of preservation (Article 48 paragraph 2 of the PRA). The creditor is required to file a petition for an order of retention of the vessel nationality certificate, etc. with the said court (Articles 33 and 32 paragraph 2 of the PRR and Article 74 of the CER). The court shall issue an order to the court execution officer to take up and keep the vessel nationality certificate etc. The court execution officer shall go to the vessel, take the vessel nationality certificate etc. and submit it to the court. This execution may be carried out even before the order of provisional seizure of the vessel is served upon the debtor (Article 43 paragraph 3 of the PRA), but may not be carried out after two weeks have elapsed from the day on which the order is served upon the creditor (Article 43 paragraph 2 of the PRA). The execution of such provisional seizure may not be carried out against a vessel on voyage (excluding a vessel at anchor) (Article 689 of the Com. Code).

795. Upon the petition by a creditor, the court may, if it finds it necessary, appoint a custodian for the vessel for which an order of provisional seizure has been issued (Article 48 paragraph 3 of the PRA and Article 116 of the CEA).

796. Upon the petition by a debtor, the court may permit the navigation of a vessel if it finds that there is a business necessity or other reasonable grounds and if the creditor consents (Article 48 paragraph 3 of the PRA and Article 118 of the CEA).

V. Appeal by Debtor

A. *Outline*

797. A provisional seizure against a vessel takes the form of execution of the provisional seizure order issued by the court. A debtor may contest at two levels: appeal against the order of provisional seizure and revocation of the execution of the order.

B. *Appeal Against an Order of Provisional Seizure*

798. The debtor may file an appeal against an order of provisional seizure. The types of appeals are: (a) objection to a provisional seizure order (Article 26 of the RPA), (b) revocation of a provisional seizure order due to failure to file an action on the merits (Article 37 of the PRA), (c) revocation of a provisional seizure order due to a change in circumstances (Article 38 of the PRA), and (d) revocation of a provisional seizure order due to special circumstances (Article 39 of the PRA). The (a) above is to request re-examination of appropriateness of a provisional seizure order. The (b)–(d) above are to request examination of existence or non-existence of the cause of revocation which occurred after the issuance of the provisional seizure order. Among them, the (b) above is a procedure in which a debtor files a petition with a court, the court orders a creditor to file a suit and submit a document proving the filing of the suit within a period of two weeks or more, and if the creditor fails to submit the document within the said period, the court revokes the temporary restraining order based on the petition of the debtor (Article 37 paragraphs 1–3 of the PRA). The (c) above is a procedure in which a court revokes a provisional seizure order based on a petition by a debtor when there is extinguishment of the claim to be preserved or the necessity for preservation or any other change in circumstances (Article 38 paragraph 1 of the PRA). The (d) above is a procedure in which a court revokes a provisional seizure order based on a petition by a debtor and subject to the provision of security, when there is a risk of causing damage that cannot be compensated for by a provisional disposition or when there are other special circumstances (Article 39 paragraph 1 of the PRA).

799. In either of these procedures, the court shall render decision to uphold, modify or revoke the provisional seizure order after a hearing date on which both parties may be present (Article 27 paragraph 3, Article 29 and Article 40 paragraph 1 of the PRA). In the decision, the court may make it a condition for continuing the execution of the provisional seizure order that the creditor provides additional security for the increased amount within a certain period of time (Article 32 paragraph 2 of the PRA). This security may be provided by way of cash deposit, deposit of securities, or conclusion of a payment guarantee consignment contract with a bank or insurance company etc. licensed in Japan (Article 4 of the PRA and Article 2 of the PRR). The court may, in making a revocation decision, make it a condition that the debtor provides security (Article 32 paragraph 3 of the PRA).

800. If a debtor makes a prima facie showing of circumstances that are obvious as the cause of revocation of the provisional seizure order and that there is a risk of incurring damage that cannot be compensated for by execution of the provisional seizure order, the court may, upon petition by the debtor, order the debtor to provide security and stay the execution of the provisional seizure order or revoke the execution that has already been made until the decision to uphold, modify or revoke the provisional seizure order (Article 27 paragraph 1 and Article 40 paragraph 1 of the PRA). No appeal is allowed against such order (Article 27 paragraph 4 of the PRA).

801. A creditor and a debtor may file an appeal against court's decision to uphold, modify or revoke a provisional seizure order within two weeks from the date of service of the order (Article 41 paragraph 1 of the PRA). When the appeal is filed, the court of prior instance shall send the case to the appellate court (Article 41 paragraph 2 of the PRA). The provisions on objections to a provisional seizure order apply *mutatis mutandis* to the appeal procedure in terms of method of hearing and power of a court (Article 41 paragraph 4 of the PRA). A further appeal against a judicial decision on the appeal against the court's decision to uphold, modify or revoke a provisional seizure order may not be filed (Article 41 paragraph 3 of the PRA).

802. Where an appeal is filed against a decision to revoke a temporary seizure order, if a prima facie showing is made with regard to the circumstances that clearly constitute the cause of the revocation of the original decision and the possibility of causing damage that cannot be compensated for by the revocation, the appellate court may, until it renders a judicial decision, order a stay of the effect of the decision to revoke the provisional seizure order by providing security (Article 42 paragraph 1 of the PRA).

C. Revocation of the Execution of an Order of Provisional Seizure

803. The main cases in which the execution of an order of provisional seizure against a vessel may be rescinded are the following cases: (a) a creditor withdraws the petition for an order of provisional seizure (Article 18 of the PRA, in case of registration of a provisional seizure), (b) a creditor withdraws the petition for execution of an order of provisional seizure (in case of taking up vessel nationality certificate etc.), (c) a debtor makes a deposit of the provisional seizure release money (Article 51 paragraph 1 and Article 22 paragraph 1 of the PRA), (d) the court make a decision to revoke the order of provisional seizure, and the debtor submits an authenticated copy of the revocation decision to the execution court (Article 46 of the PRA and Article 40 paragraph 1 and Article 39 paragraph 1 item 1 of the CEA); (e) in objection to a provisional seizure, revocation of a provisional seizure due to a change in circumstances, or an order on appeal against a provisional seizure, the court orders a creditor to provide additional security within a certain period of time, but the creditor fails to submit to a provisional execution court a document showing that the creditor has provided security within one week from the last day of the period (Article 44 paragraphs 1 and 2 of the PRA; the debtor is required to submit an authenticated copy of the said decision to the provisional execution court); or (f) the debtor becomes bankrupt (Article 42 paragraph 2 of the Bankruptcy Act).

804. Of these, (a) and (b) are made when a settlement is reached between the creditor and the debtor. The amount of the release money from a provisional seizure set forth in (c) is stated in the order of provisional seizure and is usually the full amount of the claim. The provisional seizure release money must be deposited in cash at a depositary within the jurisdiction of the district court that has jurisdiction over the location of the court that has issued the provisional seizure order or the court for provisional execution (Article 22 paragraph 2 of the PRA). The method in which the debtor deposits securities or the method in which the debtor concludes a payment guarantee consignment contract with a bank or an insurance company licensed in Japan is not allowed. As to the details of the (d), please *see* section V. B (paragraphs 798–802) above.

VI. Remedies for Wrongful Arrest

805. The Supreme Court judgment of 24 December 1968 held that 'In general, when an order of provisional disposition is revoked in opposition or appeal proceedings, or when a judgment to defeat the plaintiff is rendered in the main suit and the judgment becomes final and binding, it is reasonable to assume that the applicant was negligent unless there are other special circumstances. However, if the applicant had reasonable grounds for act as such, the applicant cannot be said to have been negligent as a matter of course because of the revocation.' This holding is applicable not only to provisional dispositions but also to provisional seizures. Therefore, although it depends on the facts of each case, in cases where a provisional seizure order is revoked by an objection, the debtor may be able to claim compensation against the creditor for damages normally suffered due to the illegal seizure.

VII. Costs

806. In the case of a provisional seizure of a vessel, a creditor is required to pay a fee for petitioning the court for an order of provisional seizure of a vessel, a fee for petitioning the court for execution of an order of provisional seizure, and a prepayment to a court execution officer. The amount of the fee for petitioning the court is stipulated in the Act on the Costs of Civil Proceedings, while the prepayment for a court execution officer is determined on a case-by-case basis. If security is by way of cash deposit, the cash is necessary as well.

807. In many cases, travel expenses are also incurred. A petition for execution of an order of a provisional seizure of a vessel must be filed with the district court that has jurisdiction over the location of the vessel. There are fifty district courts in Japan, and it is necessary to travel to the court where the vessel is located to file the petition. If a custodian is appointed, the cost of the custodian will also be incurred. These costs are usually borne by the petitioner.

Chapter 15. Carriage of Passengers by Sea

§1. Introduction

808. Japan has not ratified either the Athens Convention relating to the Carriage of Passengers and their Luggage by Sea, 1974, or the Protocol of 2002 to the Athens Convention relating to the Carriage of Passengers and their Luggage by Sea, 1974.

809. Articles 589–594 of the Com. Code provide for the carriage of passengers. These provisions apply to land transportation, air transportation as well as sea transportation.

810. In addition, a general passenger liner service operator must establish conditions of carriage and obtain approval from the Minister of Land, Infrastructure, Transport and Tourism (Article 9 paragraph 1 of the Marine Transportation Act). If the operator sets the same conditions of carriage as the standard conditions of carriage set and published by the Minister of Land, Infrastructure, Transport and Tourism, the operator is deemed to have obtained an approval (Article 9 paragraph 3 of the Martine Transportation Act). The standard conditions of carriage established by the Minister of Land, Infrastructure, Transport and Tourism are revised in 2019.

811. Article 548-2 of the Civ. Code requires agreement or indication as a requirement for conditions to become the content of a contract. However, in the case of passenger transport transaction through a general passenger liner service business, a cargo liner service business carrying people and tramp service business carrying people, it is sufficient to announce in advance that conditions of carriage will be the content of the contract (Article 32-2 of the Marine Transportation Act).

812. It is likely that passenger vessels often fall under the category of 'vessels used for navigation for the purpose of conducting commercial activities' (Article 684 of the Com. Code). If they fall under this category, they are subject to the provisions of the Com. Code relating to vessel owning, vessel leasing, time charters, Master, vessel collisions, marine salvage, General Average, marine insurance, maritime liens and vessel mortgages.

813. For emigrant carriers, the Emigrant Protection Act provides special regulations.

§2. Statutory Provisions

I. Formation of Passenger Carriage Contract

814. A contract of carriage for a passenger shall become effective when the 'carrier' undertakes to carry the passenger and the 'other party' undertakes to pay the freight for the result (Article 589 of the Com. Code). The 'other party' may be other than the passenger.

815. In principle, a carrier has freedom to conclude a contract, but a general passenger liner service operator may not refuse to carry passengers, baggage and parcels on a designated section (Article 12 of the Maritime Transportation Law) (except when such carriage is contrary to the provisions of laws and ordinances or public order and morals, or when there are obstacles to carriage due to natural disasters or other unavoidable reasons, or when such carriage does not conform to the approved conditions of carriage).

II. Carrier's Obligations

816. There is no provision in the Com. Code that directly defines the carrier's obligations. In academic views, the following obligations are admitted: the obligation to provide a vessel, the obligation to determine the time of embarkation and to make the vessel ready for embarkation, the obligation to depart, the obligation to carry the passenger's body, the obligation to carry baggage, the obligation to sail directly, and the obligation to land the passenger at the place of embarkation.

817. Article 786 paragraph 1 and Article 738 of the Com. Code prior to the amendment in 2018 provided for the obligation to ensure that the vessel is capable of making a safe voyage as of the time of its departure. However, the said provisions were deleted by the amendment in 2018. Therefore, there is no provision that directly stipulates the carrier's obligation to ensure the vessel's capability. It is considered that the protection of passengers' life and body will be protected by Articles 590 and 591 of the Com. Code.

818. Article 779 of the Com. Code, which was in force prior to the amendment in 2018, provided for the obligation of free carriage of baggage. However, it has been deleted because, in practice, the conditions of carriage stipulate in detail whether the carriage is free of charge or not, and the amount of charge.

819. Article 778 of the Com. Code prior to the amendment in 2018 provided for the obligation to supply food; however, in practice, the cost of food is not included in freight and is separately paid for, so it has been deleted.

820. Before the amendment in 2018, Article 783 of the Com. Code provided for the obligation to provide housing and food during vessel repairs. However, it has been deleted because in practice, when a vessel is being repaired, either the carriage is suspended and the freight is not charged or the carriage is continued by another vessel.

821. Article 785 of the Com. Code, prior to its amendment in 2018, provided for the obligation of the Master to dispose of baggage in the event of the death of a passenger. However, it has been deleted because the procedures to be taken by the

Master are detailed in Article 16 of the Seamen's Act and Articles 6–8 of the Enforcement Rules of the Seamen's Act. Under the Act and the Rules, the Master of a vessel must examine the articles left behind in the presence of two relatives or other appropriate persons of the deceased person aboard the vessel and make a list of the articles left behind, take care of the articles left behind in a manner that is suitable for the interests of the heirs and other interested parties, and hand them over to the heirs and other right holders together with the list of articles left behind. In cases where the existence or whereabouts of the right holder is unknown, it shall be submitted to the nearest Regional Transport Bureau together with the list of articles left behind.

III. Carrier's Rights

822. A carrier shall have a right to claim freight against the other party (Article 589 of the Com. Code). It is also understood that the carrier may detain the baggage until it is reimbursed for the freight for the carriage of a passenger and a baggage (Article 295 of the Civ. Code). In addition, a transportation lien shall be recognized on the baggage in the possession of the carrier for the freight for the carriage of a passenger or a baggage and incidental expenses (Article 318 of the Civ. Code).

823. The period of extinctive prescription for the carrier's claim against the other party is one year from the time when the carrier can exercise the claim (Articles 594 and 586 of the Com. Code).

824. Article 780 of the Com. Code before the amendment in 2018 provided that if a passenger does not board the vessel by the time of embarkation, the Master may depart and the passenger shall be liable to pay the full freight. However, these have been deleted because they are as a matter of course.

825. Article 782 of the Com. Code prior to the amendment in 2018 provided, among other things, that if a passenger is unable to continue on a voyage due to force majeure such as death, the carrier may claim one-fourth of the freight. However, in practice, when a passenger is unable to board the vessel due to force majeure, the freight is not claimed, and when the passenger is unable to continue boarding the vessel after departure, the freight in proportion to the carriage is often claimed. For this reason, it has been deleted.

826. Article 786 paragraph 2 and Article 740 of the Com. Code prior to the amendment in 2018 provided that the Master of a vessel could land the baggage at any time if the baggage was loaded onboard in violation of law or not in accordance with the contract, and that if there was a risk of harm to the vessel or the cargo, the baggage could be abandoned. However, this provision has been deleted in view of the fact that the Master may abandon or take other measures if the passenger is in possession of dangerous goods, under Article 27 of the Seamen's Act.

827. Article 786 paragraph 2 and Article 764 of the Com. Code prior to the amendment in 2018 provided, among other things, that if the Master of a vessel uses a passenger's baggage for the purpose of navigation, the carrier may demand the full amount of the freight. However, in practice, it is difficult to assume that the Master of the vessel uses the passenger's baggage for the purpose of navigation, so these provisions have been deleted.

IV. Termination of Transportation Contract

828. No special cause of termination is provided for under the Com. Code. Therefore, the termination of a contract is subject to the general principles of the Civ. Code. For example, if all of the obligations under the contract of carriage are not possible to be fulfilled, one party may immediately terminate the contract (Article 542 paragraph 1 item 1 of the Civ. Code).

829. Article 781 paragraph 1 of the Com. Code prior to the amendment in 2018 provided that a passenger could cancel the contract by paying half of the freight before the departure. However, it has been deleted because in practice it is usual to accept almost full refund.

830. Article 781 paragraph 2 of the Com. Code prior to its amendment in 2018 provided that a passenger could cancel the contract by paying the full amount of the freight after the departure. However, this has been deleted because it is a matter of course.

831. Article 784 of the Com. Code prior to its amendment in 2018 provided that the contract of carriage would naturally terminate when the vessel became unable to be repaired. However, it has been deleted in consideration that it is not necessary to terminate the contract of carriage uniformly because it is easier to arrange a substitute vessel in modern times.

§3. Liability and Limitation of Liability

I. Carrier's Liability in General

832. A carrier shall be liable to compensate for damages sustained by a passenger due to carriage. However, the carrier shall not be liable if it is proved that the carrier is not negligent in his care with respect to the carriage (Article 590 of the Com. Code). The carrier bears the burden of proof of no fault.

833. Article 590 paragraph 2 of the Com. Code prior to the amendment in 2018 provided that the court shall take into consideration the situation of the victim and his/her family when determining the amount of compensation for damages to the passenger. However, it has been deleted because it was considered unreasonable to put this rule only for passenger transportation among various kinds of personal injury.

II. Liability for Injury of the Life or Body of a Passenger

834. A special provision exempting or reducing the carrier's liability to compensate for damages due to an injury to the life or body of a passenger (other than those primarily caused by delay in carriage) is invalid (Article 591 paragraph 1 of the Com. Code). However, this shall not apply (1) when carriage is performed in the event of a major fire, earthquake or other disaster, or in the event that such events are likely to occur, or (2) when carriage is performed for a person whose life or body is likely to be seriously endangered by vibrations or other circumstances normally caused by carriage (Article 591 paragraph 2 of the Com. Code).

835. Thus, by making the exemption clause invalid in principle, the Com. Code protects the lives and bodies of passengers. On the other hand, the rationale for holding the exemption clause valid in the case of delays is that delays often occur and it is not easy to determine whether or not the carrier is responsible for the delay, so that if the exemption clause is not admitted, a large number of disputes will arise each time a delay occurs and the rationality of the transportation business will be hindered. An example of the (1) above is a person who delivers relief goods to the disaster area, and that of the (2) above is a very sick person who needs hospital transfer. Their necessities of transportation are high, but if the exemption clause is not granted, the carrier may hesitate to accept the transportation, so it is provided as an exception.

836. This rule does not apply to the carrier's liability for damages due to infringement of the passenger's property rights.

III. Carrier's Liability in Respect of Delivered Baggage (Checked Baggage)

837. A carrier bears the same liability as a carrier under a contract of carriage of goods with respect to baggage delivered by a passenger, even when the carrier does not claim freight thereof (Article 592 paragraph 1 of the Com. Code). For this reason, the following provisions apply: the fixed amount of compensation (Article 576 of the Com. Code), special provisions for valuable goods (Article 577 of the Com. Code), extinction of liability upon receipt without objection (Article 584 paragraph 1 of the Com. Code), extinction of liability if no judicial claim is made within one year from the date of delivery (Article 585 paragraph 1 of the Com. Code), and reduction or exemption of the carrier's liability in tort (Article 587 of the Com. Code).

838. Even if the other party does not pursue the contractual liability against the carrier, but pursues the tort liability against the carrier's employee, it is subject to the same disciplines as the claim against the carrier, such as fixed amount of compensation, special provisions for valuable goods and extinguishment of rights etc. (Article 592 paragraph 2 and Article 588 paragraph 1 of the Com. Code). However, this is not the case if the carrier's employee is intentional or grossly negligent (Article 592 paragraph 2 and Article 588 paragraph 2 of the Com. Code).

839. If a passenger fails to claim delivery of baggage delivered to the carrier within one week from the date of arrival at the destination, the carrier may deposit the baggage or, after giving a reasonable period of notice, sell it at an auction (Article 592 paragraph 3 of the Com. Code). When a carrier has deposited or auctioned baggage, the carrier shall, without delay, notify the passenger of such deposit or auction (Article 592 paragraph 3 of the Com. Code). However, if the address or residence of the passenger is unknown, no notices shall be required (Article 592 paragraph 6 of the Com. Code). In addition, baggage that is likely to fall in value due to damage or other causes may be put up for auction without notice (Article 592 paragraph 4 of the Com. Code). In the event of an auction of baggage, the carrier shall make a deposit of the price, which may be applied to the freight (Article 592 paragraph 5 of the Com. Code).

IV. Carrier's Liability in Respect of Not-delivered Baggage (Unchecked Baggage)

840. A carrier shall not be liable for any loss of or damage to baggage (including personal effects) which was not delivered by a passenger, except where the carrier is intentional or negligent (Article 593 paragraph 1 of the Com. Code).

841. The carrier's liability for compensation for damages is subject to similar (though not identical) discipline to that of checked baggage. In other words, the fixed amount of compensation (Article 576 of the Com. Code), the extinction of liability upon receipt without objection (Article 584 paragraph 1 of the Com. Code), the extinction of liability if no judicial claim is made within one year from the date of termination of carriage (Article 585 paragraph 1 of the Com. Code), the reduction and exemption of the carrier's liability in tort (Article 587 of the Com. Code), and the reduction and exemption of the liability of the carrier's employee (Article 588 of the Com. Code) shall apply *mutatis mutandis*.

V. Limitation of Liability of Owners, etc.of Vessel

842. The Lim. Act provides that the owners etc. of vessel and their employees etc. may limit their liability with respect to the claim subject to limitation pursuant to the provisions of the said Act (Article 3 paragraph 1 of the Lim. Act). However, they may not limit their liability with respect to a claim relating to damage to a passenger (Article 3 paragraph 4 of the Lim. Act). A claim relating to damage of a passenger is defined as 'a claim against the owner etc. of a vessel or its employees etc.

based on damage to the life or body of a passenger carried by a vessel under a contract for carriage of passengers by sea or a person permitted to board a vessel together with a vehicle or a live animal carried by a vessel under a contract for carriage of goods by sea (Article 2 paragraph 1 item 6-2 of the Lim. Act).

Part III. Other Transport

Chapter 1. Transport by Road and Rail

§1. General

843. Under the Com. Code, transportation by road and rail are governed by the same regulations as land transport. Article 569(2) of the Com. Code defines land transport as the carriage of goods or passengers on land.

844. According to the Com. Code, a contract for the carriage of goods shall become effective when the carrier undertakes to receive certain goods from the consignor, to carry and to deliver them to the consignee, and the consignor undertakes to pay the freight for its result (Article 570 of the Com. Code). This means that (i) the contract of carriage of goods is a consensual contract, established by agreement between the consignor and the carrier and (ii) the contract of carriage of goods is a bilateral contract in which the carrier undertakes to receive goods from the consignor, to carry them and to deliver to the consignee and the consignor undertakes a promise to pay its freight. The consignee receives the goods at the destination, but the consignee is not a party to the contract. However, this does not mean that the consignee has no right regarding the contract of carriage. After goods arrived at the destination or were totally lost, the consignee acquires the rights of a consignor arising pursuant to a transportation contract (Article 581(1) of the Com. Code).

845. Article 569(1) of the Com. Code defines the 'carrier' as a person engaged in the business of undertaking land, marine, or air transport. Therefore, a freight forwarder who enters into a contract of carriage with the consignor but does not perform the actual carriage itself is the carrier under the Com. Code.

§2. Source of Law

I. The Commercial Code

846. The provisions of Book II, Chapter VIII 'Transportation Business' of the Com. Code apply to all contracts of carriage, irrespective of the type of transport (land, marine, or air). Therefore, the provisions of Book II, Chapter VIII ' Transportation Business' of the Com. Code apply to transport by road and rail. However, detailed regulations of transport by rail are set out in the Railway Operation Act

(Law No. 65 of 1900) (hereinafter the 'ROA') and the Regulations on Railway Transport (Order of Ministry of Railways No.3 of 1942) (hereinafter the 'RRT'). As these provisions shall apply first, there is little room to apply Com. Code in transport by rail. In the absence of provisions in the Com. Code or other special laws, the Civ. Code applies.

847. In principle, the provisions in the Com. Code regarding contracts of carriage are discretionary provisions (except for Articles 591 and 739). In other words, the parties can conclude a contract that does not correspond to the regulations of the Com. Code. Therefore, in land transport, the terms and conditions of contract play a major role in practice.

II. International Conventions

848. Japan has not ratified the convention applicable to land transport. There are two international conventions governing carriage on land: the 'Convention on the Contract for the International Carriage of Goods by Road' done at Geneva on 19 May 1956, and the 'Convention concerning International Carriage by Rail of 9 May 1980', both of which have a regional scope limited to European countries or their surroundings.

§3. Liability of the Carrier

I. Compensation for Damages

849. A carrier is liable to compensate for damage, loss, or delay of goods unless it proves that it has not neglected to exercise due care in the receipt, delivery, storage, or transportation of the goods (Article 575 of the Com. Code). In other words, the carrier is liable for loss or damage to the goods if (i) the arrival of the goods is delayed (i.e., the goods are not delivered by the time they should have been delivered), (ii) the goods are lost or damaged during carriage, or (iii) the cause of the loss or damage to the goods occurs during carriage. The consignor needs to prove one of those facts and the fact that the damage was caused by it. With regard to transport by rail, if the delivery is delayed for more than one month, compensation for a loss may be claimed (Article 13(1) of the ROA). Although this is not expressly stated in Article 575, the carrier is not released from liability even in the case where the person employed for transportation by the carrier is negligent. The loss in this context includes physical loss and the inability to deliver the goods.

850. Article 575 refers to loss, damage, or delay, but it is considered that liability to compensate for damages may also arise in other cases, for example, if the goods are mistakenly delivered to an unauthorized person.

851. The acts for which the carrier is held liable are those of the carrier and his assistants, agents, and servants. The carrier is also liable for the acts of persons used by the carrier for the carriage, even though they are not in the carrier's employment unless it is proved that they are not negligent.

852. In principle, the consignor has the right to claim compensation for damage. However, once the goods have arrived at their destination (or have been totally lost), the consignee has the same rights as the consignor (Article 581(1) of the Com. Code).

853. As Article 575 is a discretionary provision, it can be reduced or waived by agreement. In general, exemption clauses are often used to reduce the amount of compensation or release the carrier from liability.

II. Amount of Compensation for Damages

854. The amount of damages in the event of the total loss or damage to goods is determined based on the market price of the goods at the place and time at which the goods should have been delivered (or based on the commodity exchange price if such price is available). However, if such market price is not available, the amount of damages for the goods shall be determined by reference to the normal price of the goods of the same kind and quality at the place and time at which the goods should have been delivered (Article 576(1) of the Com. Code). The 'normal price' in this context is based on the price at the time when delivery was scheduled. It is not based on the time of actual delivery, even if the goods arrive later.

855. Article 576(1) of the Com. Code provides loss or damage to the goods and therefore does not cover delay, in which case, the Civ. Code applies (Article 416 of the Civ. Code).

856. In determining the amount of damages, freight charges and other costs that are not required to be paid by reason of loss or damage to the goods are deducted from the amount of damages (Article 576(2) of the Com. Code).

857. The purpose of Article 576 is to protect the carrier engaged in the mass and uniformed carriage of goods by limiting the amount of damages and to prevent disputes by standardizing the range of damages (Supreme Court Judgment of 20 April 1978, *Minshu*, Vol. 32, No. 3, 670.). Since the Article is intended to protect the carrier, Article 576(1) shall not apply if loss or damage to the goods has occurred with wrongful intent or gross negligence of the carrier (Article 576(3) of the Com. Code). Further, it is understood that Article 576(1) shall not also apply if the person assisting the carrier's performance has wrongful intent or gross negligence.

858. Article 576(1) stipulates a fixed amount of damages. This leads to the result that the statutory amount should be paid even if the actual damage is more than this amount, and the statutory amount should be paid even if the actual damage is less than this amount. The latter seems unjustified, but it is considered not unreasonable because the carrier is able to decide the freight based on the amount of damages fixed by the law. However, if there has been no damage at all, the obligation to compensate damages does not arise (Supreme Court Judgment of 20 April 1978, *Minshu*, Vol. 32, No. 3, 670).

859. For the carriage of goods by rail, the fixed amount of compensation for damages is strengthened. When the consignor consigns the goods for carriage, he may pay a certain indication fee and indicate the amount of the damages up to the price at the place of destination at the end of the period of delivery (Articles 11 of the ROA and 29 and 30 of the RRT). In the event of loss or damage, the railway is liable for all damages up to the amount of the compensation indicated, unless the loss or damage was caused by intentional action or gross negligence of the railway (Article 11-2 of the ROA). In the case of expensive goods (as specified in Article 28 of the RRT) or animals for which no compensation is indicated, the maximum amount of compensation is fixed, except for the damage caused by intentional action or gross negligence of the railway (Articles 11-2(2) of the ROA and 73 of the RRT).

860. The Com. Code does not set out a limitation of liability of the carrier. However, since the provisions of the Com. Code regarding the carrier's liability are discretionary provisions, it is assumed that the carrier makes a special agreement on the limitation of liability if necessary.

III. Special Provisions for Expensive Goods

861. A carrier is not liable to compensate for damages regarding a loss, damage or delay to cash, negotiable instruments of value, or other expensive goods unless the consignor notified the type and value thereof upon entrusting the carrier with the goods for transportation (Article 577(1) of Com. Code). This provision takes into account that expensive goods have a high risk of damage and that if the carrier needs to compensate for damage at the price of the goods, he will be obliged to pay an unexpected and large amount of compensation.

862. Expensive goods do not mean merely pricey goods but the goods which, in view of the foreseeability of the carrier, are significantly expensive from their volume and weight. This may include jewellery, furs, precious metals, and USB drives containing important information, but does not include the goods whose high value is apparent from their volume and weight. In a case where a polishing machine was damaged during land transport by truck, the Supreme Court held that the polishing machine in question is quite huge in terms of volume and weight, its high value is also apparent at first glance, and the polishing machine in question should not be regarded as an expensive goods stipulated by the said Article (Supreme Court Judgment of 21 April 1970, *Hanji*, Vol. 593, 87).

863. In rail transport, the RRT lists the types of expensive goods (Article 28(1) of the RRT). However, if the amount of compensation is indicated, the railway is liable for all damages up to the amount indicated and it does not matter whether it is an expensive goods or not (Article 11-2(1) of the ROA). If there is no indication of the amount of compensation, the limit of the amount of compensation for damage is directly stipulated (Article 11-2(2) of the ROA), except in case of wrongful intent or gross negligence of railway (Article 11-2(3) of the ROA). Therefore, in rail transport, special provisions for expensive goods of the Com. Code do not apply.

864. The notice must be given by the time the contract is concluded. This is because if the consignor notifies the carrier of the type and price of the goods by the conclusion of the contract, the carrier can take special measures or charge a higher freight rate. The aim of this provision is to give special consideration to the carrier according to the type and price of the goods, to inform the carrier of the maximum amount of damage, and therefore to protect its business (Tokyo D.C. Judgment of 25 November 1975, *Hanji*, Vol. 819, 87).

865. If the consignor does not notify the type and price of the expensive goods, it is considered that it is not possible to claim damages for such expensive goods as ordinary goods because determining the value of such expensive goods as ordinary goods is impossible.

866. However, special provisions for expensive goods shall not apply (i) if the carrier knows that the goods are expensive goods at the time of conclusion of the contract or (ii) if loss, damage or delay of the expensive goods has occurred by the wrongful intent or gross negligence of the carrier (Article 577(2) of the Com. Code). As to (i), if the carrier knows that the goods are expensive, even without any notice from the consignor, the carrier could have refused carriage or taken special measures. Therefore, it is not appropriate to deny the carrier's liability, and the carrier should be liable for damage as expensive goods. As to (ii), if the loss, damage, or delay of the expensive goods is caused by the carrier's wrongful intent or gross negligence, it would be unreasonable to release the carrier from liability. However, it is considered that the appropriate amount of compensation will be determined after taking a lack of notice into account.

867. The liability of the carrier when the actual price of the goods differs from the notified price is as follows: (i) if the notified price is lower than the actual price, the carrier shall be liable only for the notified price; and (ii) if the notified price is higher than the actual price, the carrier is liable for the actual price.

IV. Liability of the Carrier in Multimodal Transport

868. A multimodal contract of carriage is a contract in which two or more types of transport (land, marine, or air) are undertaken under a single contract. The liability of the carrier in multimodal transport shall be subject to the provisions of the laws and regulations of Japan or the Conventions concluded by Japan which shall apply to each carriage in the event of loss or other damage to the goods (Article 578(1) of the Com. Code). This provision applies *mutatis mutandis* to the case where land transport to which two or more different laws and regulations shall apply for each section is undertaken under a single contract (Article 578(2) of the Com. Code).

§4. The Legal Status of Consignor

I. Obligation to Issue an Invoice

869. A consignor must issue an invoice at the request of the carrier (Article 571(1) of the Com. Code). The invoice is a document describing the matter stipulated in the Com. Code and is not a requirement for the contract of carriage, but it should serve as evidence. The invoice is intended to inform the consignee of the contents of the shipment and to facilitate the identification of the shipment with its description. However, it is not understood that the invoice is the only evidence to prove the contract of carriage. Therefore, it is possible to argue the facts which are different from the description in the invoice.

870. In transport by rail, the consignor must issue an invoice when consigning the goods (Article 50(1) of the RRT). The railway may refuse to accept the carriage if the invoice is not issued (Article 6(1)(i) of the ROA).

871. The description of the invoice is stipulated in Article 571(1) item (i)–(v) as follows: (i) the type of the goods; (ii) the volume or weight or package of the goods, or the number of packages, and the marks of the goods; (iii) the type of packaging; (iv) the name or trade name of the consignor and consignee; (v) the places of departure and destination. No signature is required on the invoice.

872. In the case of transport by rail, further information is legally required (Article 50(2) of the RRT).

873. The invoice is a written document, but it is more convenient to send the matters by email or other electronic methods in many cases. Therefore, the consignor can provide the matters to be described in the invoice by electromagnetic method with obtaining the consent of the carrier (Article 571(2) of the Com. Code). In this case, the consignor shall be deemed to issue an invoice (Article 571(2) of the Com. Code).

874. It is not considered that the lack of any one of the descriptions listed in Article 571(1) denies the validity of the invoice as evidence. It is also possible to include information which is not required by Article 571(1), such as the freight rate or the place and date of preparation of the invoice.

875. If the consignor deliberately or negligently issues an incorrect or incomplete invoice and it results in loss or damage to the goods, the carrier may be exempted from liability for damages. Rather, if the carrier suffers damage as a result of such description, he may claim damages from the consignor.

876. In the carriage by rail, the consignor is liable to the railway for the description in the invoice, whether intentionally or negligently (Article 51 of the RRT).

II. Duty to Give Notice Regarding Dangerous Goods

877. If the carrier is unaware that the goods are dangerous goods, this could cause serious damage not only to the carrier but also to other parties involved. This could also have a significant impact on society. In addition, there are many types of dangerous goods, and the situations where dangerous goods must be handled have been increasing in recent years. Therefore, in order to ensure the safety of the carriage, the Com. Code imposes on the consignor a duty to give notice regarding dangerous goods.

878. If the goods are inflammable, explosive, or otherwise dangerous, the consignor shall, before delivery, notify the carrier of this fact and the name, nature, and other information necessary for the safe carriage of the goods (Article 572 of the Com. Code). Typical examples of dangerous goods are gunpowder and petrol. As there is no restriction on the method, oral notification is permitted.

879. Article 572 of the Com. Code imposes a duty to give notice to the consignor, but it is not a no-fault liability. When the consignor breached his duty to give notice, the Com. Code has no provision, and the Civ. Code applies. Therefore, if the carrier suffers damage due to the consignor's breach of the duty to give notice, the carrier shall be entitled to demand damages unless the consignor proves that there is no reason attributable to him (Article 415(1) of the Civ. Code).

880. The duty to give notice is not discharged even if the carrier knew or could have known that the goods were dangerous goods. However, if the carrier knew or could have known it, it may be a basis for offsets or denying causation.

881. Article 572 of the Com. Code is a discretionary provision. Therefore, the terms and conditions set out by the carrier have an important role in practice.

III. Right of Consignor

882. A consignor may request a carrier to stop transporting, change the consignee and otherwise handle the goods (Article 580 of the Com. Code). If, during the carriage of goods, the credit standing of the consignee, the buyer of the goods, or the economic situation changes significantly, the consignor may wish to change the consignee or stop the carriage. Therefore, in order to protect the consignor's interests, the consignor is entitled to dispose of the goods. The carrier is obliged to comply with this disposition. The right of disposal is intended to protect the consignor, but at the same time, it burdens the carrier. Therefore, it is considered that its content is restricted to some extent. The consignor cannot request any essential change in the original obligation assumed by the carrier, such as a return to the departure or an extension of the destination.

883. If the carrier accepts the consignor's request, the carriers, in return, may request payment of freight charges in proportion to transportation already completed, payment of accompanied cost, payment for monies it has paid on behalf of another person, and payment of costs arising from its other handling of the goods (Article 580, second sentence of the Com. Code).

§5. The Legal Status of the Consignee

884. The consignee is the person who is to take delivery of the goods from the carrier in his own name at the place of destination. However, the party to the contract of carriage is the consignor, and accordingly, it is the consignor who has rights and obligations under the contract of carriage. Thus, difficulties arise when the consignor and consignee are different. The Com. Code solves this issue by giving the consignee the same right of the consignor.

885. After the goods arrive at the destination or in the event of a total loss of goods, the consignee acquires the rights of a consignor arising pursuant to a transportation contract (Article 581(1) of the Com. Code). However, the consignor's rights and obligations shall not be extinguished. The rights of both parties co-exist, but in the relationship between the consignor and the consignee, the consignor's rights prevail. Therefore, if the consignor makes instruction regarding the carriage of goods (Article 580 of the Com. Code), the consignor will not be able to demand delivery of the goods. However, if the consignee requests delivery of goods or its compensation of damages, the consignor may not exercise such right (Article 581(2) of the Com. Code).

886. Once a consignee receives the goods, it bears the obligation to pay freight charges and other costs to the carrier (Article 581(3) of the Com. Code). On the other hand, the consignor is also obliged to pay the freight and other charges under the contract of carriage. Therefore, the consignor and consignee are jointly and severally obliged to pay them.

§6. Transport Document

887. The Com. Code prior to the amendments in 2018 provided for an inland B/L for land transport (Articles 571–575 and 584 of the Pre-Amendment Com. Code). These provisions were supposed to facilitate the disposal of goods during transportation, such as when the consignor obtains finance against the goods during transport. However, contrary to the time when the Com. Code was enacted in 1899, land transport takes very little time, and there is no need to facilitate the disposal of goods during transport. Even in practice, it is said that there were no examples issuing the inland B/L. Therefore, the amended Com. Code in 2018 abolished the inland B/L.

§7. Time Bar

I. General

888. With regard to the carrier's liability, the Com. Code provides for a special short-term statute of limitation. Since the carrier delivers large quantities of goods repeatedly and rapidly, it is not easy to secure evidence for each transportation. In addition, limiting the carrier's liability would lead to keeping freight rates low. Therefore, the Com. Code provides a special short-term limitation.

II. Extinguishment of Liability of Carrier by Lapse of Time

889. The liability of the carrier regarding loss, damage, or delay of the goods is extinguished if no judicial claim is made within one year since the day on which the consignee received the goods (in the case of a total loss of goods, the day to be delivered) (Article 585(1) of the Com. Code). This one-year period may be extended by mutual agreement of the parties only after the damage to the goods has occurred (Article 585(2) of the Com. Code).

890. In a case where the carrier has further consigned the transport of the goods to a third party, if the carrier indemnifies the damages or a judicial claim is made against him within the period specified in paragraph (1), the period for the liability of a third party to the carrier shall be deemed to have been extended until the expiration of three months from the date on which the carrier indemnifies or a judicial claim is made (Article 585(3) of the Com. Code). This provision aims to protect the carrier who has the right of recourse.

III. Extinguishment of Liability of Carrier by Receiving the Goods Without Reservation

891. The liability of a carrier is extinguished if the consignee receives the goods without reservation. However, this shall not apply if the goods contain a defect that cannot be immediately discovered or the goods are partially lost, and the consignee issues notice of this to the carrier within two weeks from the date of delivery (Article 584(1) of the Com. Code). This provision shall not apply if the carrier has knowledge of the defect or partial loss to the goods (Article 584(2) of the Com. Code).

892. In a case where the carrier has further consigned the transport of the goods to a third party, if the consignee issues a notice to the carrier within the period specified in paragraph (1), the period for the liability of a third party to the carrier shall be deemed to have been extended until the expiration of two weeks from the date on which the carrier receives the notice (Article 584(3) of the Com. Code). This is to protect the carrier who has the right of recourse.

893. Article 584(1) is for damages or partial loss to the goods and does not cover total loss and delay.

IV. Extinguishment of Carrier's Claim

894. A claim held by the carrier against a consignor or a consignee is extinguished by prescription if it is not exercised for a period of one year from the time when it may be exercised (Article 586 of the Com. Code).

§8. Successive Carriage

I. Definition

895. Successive carriage means successive land transport of the same goods by several carriers. It is not the case that the consignor contracts with each carrier individually, but several carriers undertake the carriage one after the other on a single invoice for the consignor.

II. Right and Obligation of Successive Carriers

896. If two or more carriers perform land transport in succession, the second or subsequent carrier bears the obligation to exercise the rights of the previous carrier in its stead (Article 579(1) of the Com. Code). This provision imposes an obligation on the latter carrier to exercise the right instead of the former carrier, because the carrier who has delivered the goods to the carrier of the next section is no longer able to exercise the right. In return, the second or subsequent carrier acquires the rights of the previous carrier once it performs its obligations to the previous carrier (Article 579(2) of the Com. Code).

III. Liability of Successive Carriers

897. In respect of a land transport undertaken by one carrier, if another carrier undertakes for a part of that land transport in succession for the consignor, they are jointly and severally liable to compensate for damage, loss, or delay of the goods (Article 579(3) of the Com. Code). By this provision, each carrier in the successive transport is jointly and severally liable for damages in case of loss, damage, or delay of the goods, even if the claimant does not prove in which sector the loss, damage, or delay occurred. However, this applies to the external relationship, such as the carriers against the consignee. Among carriers, each carrier is entitled to recourse against the carrier who carried the section in which the loss, damage, or delay of the goods occurred.

898. As this provision is discretionary, it can be excluded by a special agreement. Thus, it is important to pay attention to the terms and conditions of carriage.

§9. Cause of Action

899. Under the Com. Code, the carrier's liability is based on the default of the contract of carriage (contractual liability). On the other hand, if the carrier causes damage to the goods through his own or his employee's negligence, the requirements of tort would be satisfied because the ownership of the goods has been infringed (Article 709 of the Civ. Code). Thus, the question arises as to the relationship between the carrier's liability under the contract and in tort.

900. The Supreme Court held that the right to claim damages based on default of the contract of carriage and the right to claim damages based on tort co-exist (Supreme Court Judgment of 17 Oct. 1969, *Minshu*, No. 97, 35). Based on this Supreme Court's position, the provisions of Article 576 (Amount of compensation for damages), Article 577 (Special provisions for expensive goods), and Articles 584–585 (Extinguishment of liability of carrier) shall apply *mutatis mutandis* to tort liability regarding loss, damage or delay of the goods (Article 587 of the Com. Code). This is because if the above provisions were not applied to the carrier's liability in tort, the legislative purpose of these provisions in reducing the liability of the carrier would not be achieved. However, this shall not apply to the liability of the carrier against the consignee, where the carrier had accepted transport from the consignor notwithstanding that the consignee previously refused to accept the transport under the consignment of the said consignor (Article 587, second sentence of the Com. Code).

§10. Passenger Transportation

I. Definition

901. Article 589 defines the contract for carriage of passengers commonly applicable to land, marine, and air transport. It stipulates that a contract for carriage of passenger shall become effective when the carrier undertakes to carry a passenger, and the other party undertakes to pay the fare for its results (Article 589 of the Com. Code). The contract for carriage of passengers is a consensual and bilateral contract.

II. Liability of Carrier with Regard to Passengers

902. A carrier is liable for damage suffered by a passenger due to transportation unless the carrier proves that it is not neglected to exercise due care in transporting the passenger (Article 590 of the Com. Code). This provision applies to loss of life, bodily injury, and delay of a passenger.

903. A distinctive feature of the carrier's liability is the one-sided mandatory provision in respect of the life of the passenger. Any special provision exempting or reducing the carrier's liability for damages caused by loss of life or bodily injury to a passenger (except for damages mainly caused by delay) is void (Article 591(1) of the Com. Code). This provision makes contractual clauses such as limiting the amount of compensation for the carrier null and void.

904. However, the prohibition of such a special contract excludes damages mainly caused by delay (Article 591(1) brackets of the Com. Code). This is because, considering the impact on the mass transportation business, the validity of the exemption clause should be determined on a case-by-case basis in applying the Consumer Contract Act (Law No. 61 of 2000) or the Civ. Code rather than being uniformly invalid. It is also taken into account that it would be harsh for the carrier to deny any exemption in which the damage to the passenger is caused mainly by delay, which makes the carrier difficult to run a reasonable carriage business and might eventually lead to an increase of fares.

905. A special provision exempting or reducing the carrier's liability for damage to the passenger shall also be null and void in the following cases: (i) if a carrier performs transport in the event of a major fire, earthquake or other disaster, or threat of such a disaster; or (ii) if a carrier carries a person whose life or body is likely to be seriously endangered by the vibrations or other circumstances normally associated with the carriage (Article 591(2)(i)(ii) of the Com. Code). These include, for example, the transport of news reporters, evacuees from a disaster, or seriously ill people who have no choice but to use risky means of transport. In these cases, despite the social need for transportation, there is a concern that the carrier may be reluctant to undertake carriage because liability is not covered by insurance.

III. Liability of the Carrier with Regard to Checked Baggage

906. A carrier has the same liability as a freight carrier with regard to the baggage that passengers have delivered to it, even if the carrier does not claim any special freight charges for the baggage (Article 592(1) of the Com. Code). An employee of a carrier has the same liability as an employee of a freight carrier with regard to the baggage that passengers have delivered to it (Article 592(2) of the Com. Code). If a passenger does not request the delivery of his/her baggage within one week from the date of arrival at the destination, the carrier may deposit the object or put it up for auction after demanding that the passenger receive the baggage within a reasonable period of time. In such a case, once the carrier deposits the baggage or puts it up for auction, the carrier must issue notice of this to the passenger without delay (Article 592(3) of the Com. Code). If the price of the baggage is likely to decline for reasons such as damage, the carrier may put it up for auction without making the demand (Article 592(4) of the Com. Code). If a carrier puts the baggage of a sales transaction up for auction pursuant to the provisions of the preceding two paragraphs, the carrier must deposit the proceeds of the auction; provided, however, that this does not preclude the carrier from appropriating all or part of the proceeds to cover the freight charges (Article 592(5) of the Com. Code). If the passenger's domicile or residence is unknown, the carrier is not required to issue a demand or give notice to the passenger (Article 592(6) of the Com. Code).

907. In transport by rail, there are special restrictions on the baggage that may be checked by passengers (Article 37 of the RRT). Also, as in the case of the carriage of goods, the amount of compensation for damage is fixed except for the case of wrongful intent or gross negligence of the railway (Articles 11–13 of the ROA and Articles 29, 30, 73 and 74 of the RRT). If the passenger does not pick up the checked baggage within twenty-four hours from its arrival, the railway may charge a reasonable storage fee (Article 45 of the RRT). Checked baggage of which the owner is unknown shall be acquired by the railway if the owner cannot be identified within six months after public notice (Article 13-2 of the ROA). After that period, the railway may dispose of such checked baggage at its discretion.

IV. Liability of the Carrier with Regard to Unchecked Baggage

908. A carrier is not liable to compensate for loss or damage to baggage (including personal items) that a passenger has not delivered to it, unless there is negligence on the part of the carrier (Article 593(1) of the Com. Code). It would be disproportionate if the liability of unchecked baggage were heavier than that of checked baggage. Therefore, the provisions for exempting or reducing the carrier's liability apply to *mutatis mutandis* to the case that the carrier is liable to compensate damages for loss or damage to the unchecked baggage. In applying the provisions, the 'delivery of the goods' shall be changed to read as 'termination of carriage' (Article 593(2), last sentence of the Com. Code).

V. Right to Demand Fares

909. The contract for carriage of passengers is considered as a contract for work (Article 632 of the Civ. Code). Therefore, according to Article 633 of the Civ. Code, the remuneration for the carriage of passengers shall be paid after the work. However, in the carriage of goods, the goods may be retained, and a lien may be enforced on them. On the other hand, in the carriage of a passenger, there is nothing to retain. Therefore, when transporting an unspecified number of passengers, payment shall be made before the end of the transport, either before or after ride without delay according to the terms and conditions of a contract or commercial practice (Article 1(2) of the Com. Code). If a ticket is issued, payment shall be made in exchange for it.

910. With regard to rail transport, the passenger is not allowed to ride unless the fare is paid in advance and the passenger receives a ticket (Article 15 of the ROA). A passenger who rides without a valid ticket, or who refuses to have their ticket inspected, or who fails to hand over its ticket at the time of collection may be charged by the railway the equivalent fare for the ride as well as an additional amount not exceeding twice the equivalent fare for the ride (Article 18(1)(2) of the ROA and Article 19 of the RRT). If the entering station of passengers is not identified, the fare is calculated from the starting stop of the train (Article 18(3) of the ROA).

911. At least one child under the age of six accompanied by a passenger is carried free of charge per passenger (Article 10(1) of the RRT). A child under 12 years is carried at half of the adult fare, except for the child under 6 years without fare (Article 10(3)).

VI. Extinguishment of Liability of Carrier

912. With regard to the liability to passengers, the Com. Code does not provide any special extinguishment of liability for damages sustained by passengers stipulated in Article 590 of the Com. Code. Therefore, the Civ. Code applies, and, in principle, the claim is extinguished by prescription if it is not exercised for five years from the time when the claimant knows that it has become possible to exercise the right (Article 166(1)(i) of the Civ. Code).

913. With regard to checked baggage, a carrier has the same liability as a freight carrier with regard to the baggage that passengers have delivered to it, even if the carrier does not claim any special freight charges for the baggage (Article 592(1) of the Com. Code). Therefore, the liability of a carrier is extinguished if the passenger receives the baggage without reservation (Articles 592(1) and 584(1) of the Com. Code). Also, the liability of the carrier regarding loss, damage, or delay of the baggage is extinguished if no judicial claim is made within one year since the day on which the passenger received the baggage (in the case of a total loss, the day to be delivered) (Articles 592(1) and 585(1) of the Com. Code).

914. With regard to unchecked baggage, except for some provisions (Articles 576(2), 577, 584(2), 584(3), and 585(3)), the provisions of the contract of carriage of goods apply *mutatis mutandis* to the carrier's liability (Article 593(2) of the Com. Code). Therefore, the liability of a carrier is extinguished if the passenger does not complain by the end of the carriage (Articles 593(2) and 584(1) of the Com. Code). Also, the liability of the carrier regarding loss, damage, or delay of the baggage is extinguished if no judicial claim is made within one year since the termination of carriage (Articles 593(2) and 585(1) of the Com. Code).

VII. Extinguishment of Carrier's Claim

915. A claim held by the carrier against a passenger is extinguished by prescription if it is not exercised for a period of one year from the time when it may be exercised (Articles 594 and 586 of the Com Code). The claim in this context is considered to include not only a claim in respect of fares but also a wide range of claims arising in connection with the carriage.

Chapter 2. Air Transportation

§1. Introduction

916. International carriage by air is governed by the MC. In contrast, under the Com. Code prior to its amendment in 2018, domestic carriage by air was not governed by private law and was mainly dealt with the conditions of carriage of the carrier. The conditions of carriage shall be approved by the Minister of Land, Infrastructure, Transport and Tourism, as stipulated in Article 106(1) of the Civ. A.A. (Law No. 231 of 1952), which states that 'any domestic air carrier shall establish conditions of carriage and obtain approval from the Minister of Land, Infrastructure, Transport and Tourism'. The Minister of Land, Infrastructure, Transport and Tourism shall, when he/she intends to grant an approval, comply with the following standards: (i) the conditions of carriage have no possibility of adversely affecting the legitimate public interest and (ii) the conditions of carriage shall include the provisions at least defining the carrier's liability relating to fare and charge collection as well as transportation (Article 106(2) of the Civ. A.A.). Therefore, through the approval of the Minister, the conditions of carriage reflect the legitimate interests of the public.

917. However, in order to adapt to the changes in social and economic conditions since the enactment of the Com. Code in 1899, and in order to ensure legal stability, new regulations applicable to air transportation were introduced in 2018.

§2. Definition

918. The Com. Code defines air transport as the carriage of goods or passengers by aircraft under the provision of Article 2(1) of the Civ. A.A. (Article 569 of the Com. Code). Article 2(1) of the Civ. A.A. defines the aircraft as 'any aeroplane, rotorcraft, glider and airship which can be used for air navigation with a person on board and any other apparatus used for air navigation as may be specified by Cabinet Order'. Therefore, the term 'aircraft' under Com. Code means a manned aircraft and does not include unmanned aircraft (Article 2(22) of the Civ. A.A.) such as a drone. This is because the Civ. A.A. does not currently envisage the use of unmanned aerial vehicles for transportation business and the Com. Code follows this approach.

919. The Minister of Land, Infrastructure, Transport and Tourism shall register an aircraft in the Aircraft Register (Article 3 of Civ. A.A.). Any aircraft shall acquire Japanese nationality when registered (Article 3-2 of Civ. A.A.). No acquisition or loss or change of ownership of any registered aeroplane and rotorcraft may be duly asserted against a third party unless the aircraft has been registered (Article 3-3 of Civ. A.A. and Article 5 of Aircraft Mortgage Act (Law No. 66 of 1953)).

§3. SOURCE OF LAW

I. The Commercial Code

920. The provisions of Book II, Chapter VIII 'Transportation Business' of the Com. Code are applicable to all contracts of carriage, irrespective of the type of transport (land, marine, or air). Therefore, the provisions of Book II, Chapter VIII 'Transportation Business' of the Com. Code (Article 569–594) are applicable to transport by air.

II. The Montreal Convention

921. Japan has ratified the MC. 'The Convention applies to all international carriage of persons, baggage or cargo performed by aircraft for reward. It applies equally to gratuitous carriage by aircraft performed by an air transport undertaking' (Article 1(1) of the MC). 'The expression "international carriage" means any carriage in which, according to the agreement between the parties, the place of departure and the place of destination, whether or not there be a break in the carriage or a transhipment, are situated either within the territories of two States Parties, or within the territory of a single State Party if there is an agreed stopping place within the territory of another State, even if that State is not a State Party. Carriage between two points within the territory of a single State Party without an agreed stopping place within the territory of another State is not international carriage for the purposes of this Convention' (Article 1(2) of the MC). Accordingly, the MC shall apply the following cases: (i) according to the agreement between the parties, the place of departure and the place of destination are situated within the territories of States Parties of the MC; or (ii) the place of departure and the place of destination are situated within the territory of a single State Party and agreed stopping place is situated within the territory of another State whether it is a not a State Party or a State Party.

§4. DOMESTIC CARRIAGE OF GOODS BY AIR

I. Introduction

922. As stated above (§1), the 2018 amendment to the Com. Code has introduced regulations applicable to air transport (Articles 569–594). However, in domestic air transportation, the conditions of carriage is still important because the provisions of the Com. Code are very limited, and these provisions are, in principle, discretionary provisions, which can be excluded by the agreement.

II. Liability of the Carrier

923. The Com. Code stipulates that a carrier is liable to compensate for damage, loss, or delay of the goods unless it proves that it is not neglected to exercise due care in the receipt, delivery, storage, or transportation of the goods (Article 575). Thus, the carrier's negligence is presumed, and, in order to avoid liability, it must prove that it is not neglected to exercise due care.

924. All Nippon Airways Co., Ltd.'s (hereinafter 'ANA') Conditions of Carriage (effective March 1, 2021) stipulate that the Carrier is liable for damage caused by loss, damage or delay of the goods unless the Carrier proved that such damage has not been caused by the wilful misconduct or negligence of the Carrier (Article 42). Similar to the Com. Code, the carrier is presumed negligent.

925. Japan Airlines Co. Ltd.'s (hereinafter 'JAL') Conditions of Carriage (effective 28 March 2021) have the same provision as the ANA's (Article 39).

926. The conditions of carriage refer to the liability of delay. However, in the practice of air freight forwarding, it is well established that the carrier does not guarantee the date and time of commencement, completion and delivery of the cargo, unless there is a special agreement (*see* Article 27 of JAL's and ANA's Conditions of Carriage). Therefore, in air freight forwarding, delayed arrival is rarely a problem.

III. Amount of Compensation for Damages

927. The Com. Code stipulates as follows: The amount of damages in the event of the total loss or damage to the goods is determined based on the market price of the goods at the place and time at which the goods should have been delivered (or based on the commodity exchange price if such price is available); however, if such market price is not available, the amount of damages for the goods shall be determined by reference to the normal price of the goods of the same kind and quality at the place and time at which the goods should have been delivered (Article 576(1)).

928. ANA's Conditions of Carriage stipulate as follows: In the event that the carrier is liable to pay compensation for damage to the goods whose value is declared, the compensation shall be as follows: (i) in the case of a total loss, the declared value shall be the maximum; (ii) in the case of partial loss or damage, the declared value shall be multiplied by the proportion of price reduction calculated on the basis of the value at the place of arrival on the date of delivery (Article 43(1)). In the event that the carrier is liable to pay compensation for damage to the goods whose value is not declared, if the price at the place of arrival on the date of delivery or the date on which the goods should have been delivered is less than JPY 30,000 per item, the price at the place of arrival shall be deemed as the declared value, and if the price is JPY 30,000 or more, JPY 30,000 shall be deemed as the declared value, and each item of the preceding paragraph shall apply accordingly (Article 43(2)).

929. JAL's Conditions of Carriage have the same provisions as ANA's (Article 40).

930. Thus, both airlines' Conditions of Carriage stipulate different amounts of damages for the cargo whose value is declared or not. However, the value of the cargo is rarely declared in practice because, if the cargo is insured, the cargo is compensated by insurance proceeds even if the value is not declared.

IV. Exemption of Liability

931. The Com. Code has no provision for exemption of the liability of the carrier other than the expensive goods mentioned below.

932. ANA's Conditions of Carriage stipulate that the carrier shall not be liable for delay, loss, damage, or any other damage to cargo in the following cases: (i) the reasons stipulated in Article 26; (ii) alteration, wear and tear or defect of the cargo, or due to death or injury of the animal; (iii) inadequate packing, damage caused by packaging, insufficient packing tags, incomplete indications and descriptions of the waybill, or any other fault or negligence by the consignor; (iv) contact with other objects or other accidents likely occur in the aircraft; (v) rain, snow, strong winds or other bad weather, and the damage not caused by the carrier's negligence; (vi) false declaration of the waybill by the consignor (Article 44).

933. JAL's Conditions of Carriage stipulate the same (Article 41).

V. Provisions for Expensive Goods

934. The Com. Code stipulates as follows: A carrier is not liable to compensate for damage regarding a loss, damage or delay to cash, negotiable instruments of value, or other expensive goods unless the consignor notified the type and value thereof upon entrusting the carrier with the goods for transportation (Article 577(1)).

935. ANA's Conditions of Carriage stipulate as follows: No shipment having a declared value for carriage in excess of JPY 10,000,000 per single shipment will be accepted for carriage unless advance arrangement with the consignor therefor has been made (Article 20).

936. JAL's Conditions of Carriage have almost the same provisions as ANA's (Article 20).

937. In terms of these provisions in the Conditions of Carriage that the carrier will not accept the shipment in excess of JPY 10,000,000 without a special agreement, it is not appropriate for the carrier to seek exemption merely on the ground that the goods are expensive goods, as long as the carrier accepts the goods. Therefore, it is considered that it would be difficult to seek an exemption only for the reason of the expensive goods under the Com. Code.

VI. Extinguishment of Liability

938. The Com. Code stipulates as follows: The liability of a carrier is extinguished if the consignee receives the goods without reservation; however, this shall not apply if the goods contain a defect that cannot be immediately discovered or the goods are partially lost, and the consignee issues notice of this to the carrier within two weeks from the date of delivery (Article 584(1)). This provision shall not apply if the carrier has knowledge of the defect or partial loss to the goods (Article 584(2)).

939. ANA's Conditions of Carriage stipulate as follows: Claims for compensation of damages relating to cargo must be made in writing within the period referred to in the following paragraphs: (i) in case of partial loss or damage, within seven days from the date of receipt; (ii) in case of delay, within seven days from the date of arrival; (iii) in case of non-delivery, within fourteen days from the date on which the non-delivery could have been known (Article 45(1)). The carrier is not liable for damages unless a claim is made within the period referred to in the preceding paragraph (Article 45(2)).

940. JAL's Conditions of Carriage state the same (Article 42).

VII. Obligation to Issue an Invoice

941. The Com. Code stipulates that a consignor must issue an invoice at the request of the carrier (Article 571(1)). The description of the invoice is stipulated in Article 571(1) as follows: (i) the type of goods; (ii) the volume or weight or package of the goods, or the number of packages, and the marks of the goods; (iii) the type of packaging; (iv) the name or trade name of the consignor and consignee; (v) the places of departure and destination (Article 571(1)(i)–(v)). No signature is required on the invoice.

942. It is not considered that the lack of any one of the descriptions listed in Article 571(1) denies the validity of the invoice as evidence. It is also possible to include information which is not required by Article 571(1), such as the freight rate and the place and date of preparation of the invoice. Article 571(1) clarifies that the carrier is able to request the consignor to issue an invoice describing the matters required by law.

943. If the consignor deliberately or negligently issues an incorrect or incomplete invoice and it results in loss or damage to the goods, the carrier may be exempted from liability for damages. Rather, if the carrier suffers damage as a result of such description, he may claim damages from the consignor.

944. Contrary to the Com. Code, the conditions of carriage expressly provide that the carrier is not liable for damages caused by the incorrect or incomplete declaration of the consignor (Articles 8 and 9 of ANA's and JAL's Conditions of Carriage). In terms of ensuring the safety of aircraft operations, negligence of the consignor is not required.

VIII. Right of Consignor

945. The Com. Code stipulates that a consignor may request a carrier to stop transporting, change the consignee and otherwise handle the goods (Article 580).

946. ANA's Conditions of Carriage stipulate as follows: The consignor may, for his own convenience, give the following instructions upon presentation of the waybill: (1) cancellation of transport; (2) return to departure; (3) change of consignee; (4) change of destination (Article 30(1)). The instructions referred to in items (1), (3), and (4) of the preceding paragraph shall be valid only if they are given before the cargo is loaded on the aircraft, and the instructions referred to in item (2) shall be valid only if it is given before the cargo is delivered to the consignee named in the waybill (Article 30(2)).

947. JAL's Conditions of Carriage provide the same (Article 30(1) and (2)).

948. Therefore, according to the Conditions of Carriage, regarding the return of the cargo to departure, instruction should be given before the delivery of the cargo to the consignee. Regarding cancellation of transport, change of consignee and change of destination, the instruction should be given before the cargo is loaded on the aircraft.

§5. International Carriage of Goods by Air

I. Introduction

949. Japan has ratified the MC. The MC shall prevail over the rules of the Warsaw Convention (the Convention for the Unification of Certain Rules relating to International Carriage by Air signed at Warsaw on 12 October 1929) and other conventions and protocols (Article 55 of the MC). However, the MC does not oblige States Parties to denounce the Warsaw Convention and any other conventions and protocols. Therefore, with regard to carriage by air between a State Party and a non-State Party of the MC, the applicable Conventions and Protocols between the two States shall apply. Conventions and Protocols in force in Japan are the Warsaw Convention, the Hague Protocol, the Montreal Protocol No. 4, and the MC (as to the name of these conventions, *see* Article 55 of the MC).

II. Air Waybill

950. 'In respect of the carriage of cargo, an air waybill shall be delivered' (Article 4(1) of the MC). 'Any other means which preserves a record of the carriage to be performed may be substituted for the delivery of an air waybill. If such other means are used, the carrier shall, if so requested by the consignor, deliver to the consignor a cargo receipt permitting identification of the consignment and access to the information contained in the record preserved by such other means' (Article 4(2) of the MC). As per Article 4(2), electrical data instead of paper documents is permitted.

951. 'The air waybill shall be made out by the consignor in three original parts' (Article 7(1) of the MC). 'The first part shall be marked "for the carrier"; it shall be signed by the consignor. The second part shall be marked "for the consignee"; it shall be signed by the consignor and by the carrier. The third part shall be signed by the carrier who shall hand it to the consignor after the cargo has been accepted' (Article 7(2) of the MC). 'The signature of the carrier and that of the consignor may be printed or stamped' (Article 7(3)). 'If, at the request of the consignor, the carrier makes out the air waybill, the carrier shall be deemed, subject to proof to the contrary, to have done so on behalf of the consignor' (Article 7(4) of the MC).

952. 'The air waybill or the cargo receipt is prima facie evidence of the conclusion of the contract, of the acceptance of the cargo and of the conditions of carriage mentioned therein' (Article 11(1) of the MC). 'Any statements in the air waybill or the cargo receipt relating to the weight, dimensions and packing of the cargo, as well as those relating to the number of packages, are prima facie evidence of the facts stated; those relating to the quantity, volume and condition of the cargo do not constitute evidence against the carrier except so far as they both have been, and are stated in the air waybill or the cargo receipt to have been, checked by it in the presence of the consignor, or relate to the apparent condition of the cargo' (Article 11(2) of the MC). Contrary to a B/L, an air waybill is not negotiable. This is because, in air freight forwarding, the cargo arrives at the destination in a very short time, and there is no need to transfer the air waybill before the cargo arrives.

953. With regard to Article 11, there is a case (Tokyo C.A. Judgment of 19 January 2016, *Kouminshu*, Vol. 49, No. 4, 824). It was a case of air carriage of a car. The air waybill contained a statement that the consignor agreed that the goods described in the air waybill had been accepted in apparent good order and conditions for carriage. It also contained the name and the serial number of the car, as well as the words 'new car', and was signed by the consignor or his agent to the effect that he certified that the information contained in the waybill was correct. The Tokyo C.A. held, in summary, that (i) According to Article 11 of the MC, a statement on the waybill relating to the apparent condition of cargo is prima facie evidence, but its probative value is not absolute and can be overturned by counter-evidence. (ii) Based on the evidence, it is admitted that the air waybill contains a statement to the effect that transfer is prohibited ('Not Negotiable'), and a resolution of the International Air Transport Association prohibits the issuance of a negotiable air waybill. (iii) Considering the above, the air waybill is not a negotiable instrument of value but only an evidential document which has certain evidential value. (iv) Therefore, although the air waybill states that the car is in apparent good order and conditions for carriage, the description on the waybill does not have absolute probative value and is not the only definitive evidence. (v) In addition, it is impossible to immediately understand from the description 'the car in apparent good order and conditions for carriage' to mean that the car was in a completely undamaged condition, and the description does not prove that the car was completely undamaged before the transport. (vi) Therefore, the description that the car in apparent good order and conditions for carriage cannot be interpreted as meaning that the car was completely undamaged condition before the transport and cannot be found to be a false description as alleged by the appellant.

954. The Tokyo C.A. held that the legal nature of the description in an air waybill is different from that of a B/L, which is a negotiable instrument of value. Therefore, a fact which is different from the descriptions on the air waybill can be asserted.

III. Liability of the Carrier

955. 'The carrier is liable for damage sustained in the event of the destruction or loss of or damage to, cargo upon condition only that the event which caused the damage so sustained took place during the carriage by air' (Article 18(1) of the MC). 'The carriage by air within the meaning of paragraph 1 of this Article comprises the period during which the cargo is in the charge of the carrier' (Article 18(3) of the MC). 'The period of the carriage by air does not extend to any carriage by land, by sea or by inland waterway performed outside an airport. If, however, such carriage takes place in the performance of a contract for carriage by air, for the purpose of loading, delivery or transhipment, any damage is presumed, subject to proof to the contrary, to have been the result of an event which took place during the carriage by air. If a carrier, without the consent of the consignor, substitutes carriage by another mode of transport for the whole or part of a carriage intended by the agreement between the parties to be carriage by air, such carriage by another mode of transport is deemed to be within the period of carriage by air' (Article 18(4) of the MC). The carrier is liable for damage occasioned by delay in carriage by air of cargo (Article 19 of the MC).

956. 'However, the carrier is not liable if and to the extent it proves that the destruction, or loss of, or damage to, the cargo resulted from one or more of the following: (a) inherent defect, quality or vice of that cargo; (b) defective packing of that cargo performed by a person other than the carrier or its servants or agents; (c) an act of war or an armed conflict; (d) an act of public authority carried out in connection with the entry, exit or transit of the cargo' (Article 18(2) of the MC).

957. In addition, 'If the carrier proves that the damage was caused or contributed to by the negligence or other wrongful act or omission of the person claiming compensation, or the person from whom he or she derives his or her rights, the carrier shall be wholly or partly exonerated from its liability to the claimant to the extent that such negligence or wrongful act or omission caused or contributed to the damage' (Article 20 of the MC).

958. With regard to the amount of compensation, the contract of carriage by air does not adopt a fixed compensation. Instead, compensation for damages is made in the amount of the actual loss, within the limits of the declared value of the cargo or within the limits of the amount of liability set out in the MC. The MC states that 'In the carriage of cargo, the liability of the carrier in the case of destruction, loss, damage or delay is limited to a sum of 22 Special Drawing Rights per kilogram, unless the consignor has made, at the time when the package was handed over to the carrier, a special declaration of interest in delivery at destination and has paid a supplementary sum if the case so requires. In that case the carrier will be liable to pay a sum not exceeding the declared sum, unless it proves that the sum is greater than the consignor's actual interest in delivery at destination' (Article 22(3) of the MC).

959. It is said that in practice, the special declaration stipulated in Article 22(3) is rarely taken, and contrary to the Com. Code and the COGSA (*see* Article 577 of the Com. Code and Article 15 of the COGSA), the MC does not set out the exemption for expensive goods. Therefore, even if the consignor does not notify that the cargo is expensive goods, he may obtain compensation up to the declared value stated in the air waybill or up to the limit of liability set by the MC. This is because originally, in the carriage by air, expensive goods are often carried, and the carrier should be aware that the cargo is expensive. Also, requiring the declaration of value makes the carrier easier to reflect the risk of compensation in insurance premiums and freight rates.

960. 'If an action is brought against a servant or agent of the carrier arising out of damage to which the Convention relates, such servant or agent, if they prove that they acted within the scope of their employment, shall be entitled to avail themselves of the conditions and limits of liability which the carrier itself is entitled to invoke under this Convention' (Article 30(1) of the MC). This limit is an absolute limit of liability, which can be availed even if the damage was caused with intent to cause damage or recklessly and with the knowledge that damage would probably result (Articles 22(5) and 30(3) of the MC). The aim of this rule is to achieve prompt compensation for damages along with the carrier's strict liability (*see* Articles 18(1) and (2) of the MC).

961. Although it was a case of the Warsaw Convention, the Supreme Court decided on the relationship between the limitation of liability and the delayed interest (Supreme Court Judgment of 28 Jun. 1977, *Minshu*, Vol. 31, No. 4, 511). The Supreme Court held that delayed interest for damage to the cargo is outside the scope of the limitation of liability. The reason are, in summary, as follows: (i) Articles 22(2) and 24(1) of the Warsaw Convention limit the carrier's liability for damage caused by accident or delay during carriage by air in connection with the carriage of checked baggage and cargo under an international contract of carriage by air to a sum of 250 francs[5] per kilogramme. (ii) On the other hand, delay interest is a type of compensation for delay imposed on a debtor who is in default in the performance of a monetary obligation in addition to the original obligation on the basis of such default. (iii) Therefore, it is reasonable to interpret that the delayed interest imposed on a carrier who is liable for damages within the limitation of liability in the event of default is not limited by the aforementioned provision. (iv) Accordingly, the carrier shall be liable for damages to the extent of limited liability as provided for in Article 22(2) of the Warsaw Convention and shall also be liable to pay delayed interest until such liability has been completed. This judgment is considered applicable to the MC.

IV. Timely Notice of Complaints (Article 30 of the MC)

962. 'Receipt by the person entitled to delivery of cargo without complaint is prima facie evidence that the same has been delivered in good condition and in accordance with the document of carriage' (Article 31(1) of the MC). In the case of damage, the person entitled to delivery must complain to the carrier forthwith after the discovery of the damage, and, at the latest, within fourteen days from the date of receipt in the case of cargo. In the case of delay, the complaint must be made at the latest within twenty-one days from the date on which the cargo has been placed at his or her disposal (Article 31(2) of the MC). 'Every complaint must be made in writing and given or dispatched within the times aforesaid' (Article 31(3) of the MC). 'If no complaint is made within the times aforesaid, no action shall lie against the carrier, save in the case of fraud on its part' (Article 31(4) of the MC).

963. The aim of these provisions is to release the carrier from liability at an early stage because the carrier delivers large quantities of cargo in a short period and it is difficult to preserve the evidence.

V. Jurisdiction (Article 33 of the MC)

964. Article 33(1) of the MC, which follows Article 28 of the Warsaw Convention, establishes four jurisdictions: 'An action for damages must be brought, at the option of the plaintiff, in the territory of one of the States Parties, either before the court of the domicile of the carrier or of its principal place of business, or where it has a place of business through which the contract has been made or before the court at the place of destination' (Article 33(1) of the MC). Regarding Article 28(1) of the Warsaw Convention, the Tokyo D.C. ruled that the place of destination under the contract of carriage is Japan and that Japanese courts have jurisdiction (Tokyo D.C. Judgment of 15 July 1985, *Hanji*, Vol. 1211, 120).

5. Francs is a currency unit consisting of sixty-five and a half milligrams of gold of millesimal fineness nine hundred (*see* Article 22(5) of the Warsaw Convention as amended at The Hague 1955).

965. In addition, with regard to Article 28 of the Warsaw Convention, a court has ruled that it is possible to file an action separately in Japan and abroad for damage arising from a foreign airplane accident (Tokyo D.C. Interlocutory Judgment of 23 June 1987, *Hanji*, Vol. 1240, 27). The plaintiffs filed an action with the USA and Canadian courts and subsequently filed an action with the Tokyo D.C., in case the foreign actions were dismissed. The defendant argued that, according to Article 28(1) of the Warsaw Convention, an action for damages must be brought in the territory of one of the High Contracting Parties, either before the court having jurisdiction where the carrier is ordinarily resident, or has his principal place of business, or has an establishment by which the contract has been made or before the court having jurisdiction at the place of destination, and that the plaintiff should choose and bring their action before one of the four courts stipulated by the Convention. The court held that the purpose of Article 28(1) of the Warsaw Convention, which obliges an action to be brought against a Contracting State, is only to prevent the application of the Convention being avoided by bringing the action to a court in non-Contracting Party, and that, as the Convention lacks provisions for the recognition and enforcement of judgments between Contracting Parties, the provision cannot necessarily be interpreted as prohibiting international duplicate actions.

966. As such, the Tokyo D.C. admitted that actions could be brought separately in Japan and abroad.

VI. Limitation of Actions (Article 35 of the MC)

967. 'The right to damages shall be extinguished if an action is not brought within a period of two years, reckoned from the date of arrival at the destination, or from the date on which the aircraft ought to have arrived, or from the date on which the carriage stopped' (Article 35(1) of the MC). 'The method of calculating that period shall be determined by the law of the court seized of the case' (Article 35(2) of the MC).

968. As to the legal nature of this period, the Japanese court held that it is not a period of prescription but a period of limitation. The Tokyo D.C. held that the Convention does not set out any grounds for interruption or suspension of the time limit for filing an action, and it is difficult to interpret this time limit as a period of prescription (Tokyo D.C. Judgment of 2 December 2014, *Hanta*, Vol. 1414, 329). Under Japanese law, it is understood that a limitation period does not have the same interruption as in a prescription.

969. However, there is a case where the court did not apply Article 35(1) of the MC on the grounds that 'special circumstances' exist (Osaka D.C. Judgment of 12 December 2012, *Hanta*, Vol. 1398, 314). The Osaka D.C. held, in summary, that: (i) Article 35(1) of the MC cannot be interpreted as a provision that intends to apply the provisions for the interruption of prescription stipulated in the law of the place of jurisdiction. (ii) However, it is not considered that the two-year time limit must be formally applied in all cases. (iii) Considering the purpose of the Convention, it should be interpreted that this clause shall not apply when there are special circumstances which, if this clause applies, lead unreasonable conclusions and significant imbalances between the protection of consumers' interests in the international carriage and the development of international air transport services. (iv) The application of the clause exempting the carrier's liability due to the plaintiff's failure to bring an action within the two-year period, in this case, seriously disrupts the balance between the protection of consumers' interests in international air transport and the development of international air transport services and lead to an unreasonable conclusion. (v) Therefore, special circumstances exist.

970. Thus, the Osaka D.C. accepted an action brought after two years had passed from the date of arrival at the destination.

§6. Domestic Carriage of Passengers by Air

I. Introduction

971. Prior to the amendment in 2018, the Com. Code did not regulate the carriage of passengers by air. However, it was amended in 2018 and introduced general rules for the carriage of passengers commonly applicable to land, marine and air transport.

972. Article 589 of the Com. Code regulates the carriage of passengers commonly applicable to land, marine and air transport. It states that a contract for carriage of passenger shall become effective when the carrier undertakes to carry a passenger, and the other party undertakes to pay the fare for its result (Article 589 of the Com. Code). The contract of carriage for passengers is a bilateral and contractual contract and is regarded as a contract for work (Article 632 of the Civ. Code). The issuance of a ticket is not a requirement for the conclusion of a contract.

973. However, the Com. Code stipulates only a few matters and also most of them are discretionary provisions which can be excluded by the agreement. Therefore, the conditions of carriage prepared by the carrier play an important role in determining the contents of the contract.

974. Passenger transport is subject to stricter administrative regulations than freight transport in terms of entry, business planning, fares and conditions of carriage, in order to ensure the stability and safety of transport resources. The Civ. A.A. regulates operators who undertake the carriage of passengers in response to the demand of others and who use aircraft for such carriage. When the carrier provides transport services to a traveller by using transport services operated by another person, such carrier is regulated as a travel agency (Article 2(1)(v) of Travel Agency Act).

II. Liability of the Carrier with Regard to the Passengers

975. A carrier is liable for damage suffered by a passenger due to transportation unless the carrier proves that it is not neglected to exercise due care in transporting the passenger (Article 590 of the Com. Code). This provision presumes the negligence of the carrier and applies to loss of life, bodily injury and delay of a passenger.

976. A distinctive feature of the carrier's liability is a one-sided mandatory provision in respect of the life of the passenger. Any special provision exempting or reducing the carrier's liability for damages caused by loss of life or bodily injury to a passenger (except for damages mainly caused by delay) is void (Article 591(1) of the Com. Code). This provision makes contractual clauses such as limiting the amount of compensation for the carrier null and void.

977. However, the prohibition of such special contract excludes damages mainly caused by delay (Article 591(1) brackets of the Com. Code). This is because, considering the impact on the mass transportation business, the validity of the exemption clause should be determined on a case-by-case basis in applying the Consumer Contract Act or the Civ. Code rather than being uniformly invalid. It is also taken into account that it would be harsh for the carrier to deny any exemption in which the damage to the passenger is caused mainly by delay, which makes the carrier difficult to run a reasonable carriage business and might eventually lead to an increase of fares.

978. A special provision exempting or reducing the carrier's liability for damage to the passenger shall also be null and void in the following cases: (1) if a carrier performs transport in the event of a major fire, earthquake or other disaster, or threat of such a disaster; or (2) if a carrier carries a person whose life or body is likely to be seriously endangered by the vibrations or other circumstances normally associated with the carriage (Article 591(2)(i)(ii) of the Com. Code). These include, for example, the transport of news reporters, evacuees from a disaster, or seriously ill people who have no choice but to use risky means of transport. In these cases, despite the social need for transportation, there is a concern that the carrier may be reluctant to undertake carriage because its liability is not covered by insurance.

979. ANA's Conditions of Carriage (effective from 1 August 2021) states as follows: 'The Carrier shall be liable for any loss or damage arising in connection with the death or wounding of, or any other bodily injury suffered by, a passenger, if the incident or accident which causes such loss or damage takes place on board an aircraft or in the course of embarking or disembarking an aircraft' (Article 44(1)). 'The Carrier shall not be liable for such loss or damage as provided for in paragraphs 1 and 2 of this article, if it is proved that the Carrier and/or its Agent(s) have taken necessary measures to avoid such loss or damage or that the Carrier and/or its Agent(s) were prevented from taking such measures. The term "Agent(s)" as used in this chapter means any employee, representative, agent or contractor of the carrier who assists in the performance of the contract of carriage' (Article 44(3)). Similar to the Com. Code, the carrier is presumed negligent.

980. JAL's Conditions of Carriage (effective from 28 March 2021) have the same provisions as ANA's (Article 43(1) and (3)).

III. Amount of Damages with Regard to Passengers

981. Any special provision exempting or reducing the carrier's liability for damages caused by loss of life or bodily injury to a passenger (except for damages mainly caused by delay) is void (Article 591(1) of the Com. Code). Accordingly, as a principle, any clauses reducing or exempting the carrier's liability for damages are void. This is because the carriage of passengers carries passengers at high speed and it has a high risk for human life and body and also, until recently, some air carriers' conditions of carriage for passengers set out a limitation of the carrier's liability to JPY 23 million per passenger. Therefore, different from the carriage of goods (Article 576 of the Com. Code), the amount of compensation for damage to the passenger is not fixed and the carrier must compensate to the passenger for all the damages, including the lost profit.

982. As previously mentioned, however, the exemption clause ' for damages mainly caused by delay' is excluded (Article 591, brackets, of the Com. Code). Also, the following cases are excluded: (1) if a carrier performs transport in the event of a major fire, earthquake or other disaster, or threat of such a disaster; or (2) if a carrier carries a person whose life or body is likely to be seriously endangered by the vibrations or other circumstances normally associated with the carriage (Article 591(2)(i)(ii) of the Com. Code).

IV. Liability of the Carrier with Regard to Checked Baggage

983. The Com. Code stipulates as follows: A carrier has the same liability as a freight carrier with regard to the baggage that passengers have delivered to it, even if the carrier does not claim any special freight charges for the baggage (Article 592(1)). Therefore, the carrier is not exempted from liability for damages caused to the baggage unless he proves that he or his employee was not negligent (Articles 592(1) and 575, presumption of negligence), but at the same time, the amount of damages is fixed (Articles 592(1) and 576), and special provisions for expensive goods (Articles 592(1) and 597) are applicable.

984. An employee of a carrier has the same liability as an employee of a freight carrier with regard to the baggage that passengers have delivered to it (Article 592(2) of the Com. Code). Therefore Article 588 of the Com. Code applies and the same exemption from liability for the freight carrier is applicable (fixed amount of damages, limitation period, etc.).

985. ANA's Conditions of Carriage stipulate as follows: 'The Carrier shall be liable for any loss or damage arising in connection with the destruction or loss of, or damage to, any Checked Baggage or any other article of a passenger of which the Carrier takes custody, if an incident or accident which causes such loss or damage, takes place while such Baggage or article is in the custody of the Carrier' (Article 44(2)), 'The Carrier shall not be liable for such loss or damage as provided for in paragraphs 1 and 2 of this article, if it is proved that the Carrier and/or its Agent(s) have taken necessary measures to avoid such loss or damage or that the Carrier and/or its Agent(s) were prevented from taking such measures' (Article 44(3)). Similar to Article 592(1) and 575 of the Com. Code, this provision presumes the carrier's negligence.

986. Further, 'The Carrier shall not be liable for any loss or damage arising in connection with destruction or loss of, or damage to any Checked Baggage or any other article of a passenger that the Carrier takes custody of, if such damage is caused solely by any inherent defect, inadequate quality or flaw in the Baggage or the article' (Article 45). This is an exemption from liability for damage caused by inherent defects in baggage.

987. JAL's Conditions of Carriage for passengers are the same as those of ANA's (Article 43(2)(3)(4) and 44).

V. Liability of the Carrier with Regard to Unchecked Baggage

988. The Com. Code stipulates as follows: A carrier is not liable to compensate for loss or damage to baggage (including personal items) that a passenger has not delivered to it, unless there is negligence on the part of the carrier (Article 593(1)). Therefore, with regard to unchecked baggage, there is no presumption of negligence and the passenger claiming compensation bears the burden of proof. This is because unchecked baggage and personal items are not in charge of the carrier.

989. Also, it would be disproportionate if the liability of unchecked baggage were heavier than that of checked baggage. Therefore, the provisions for exempting or reducing the carrier's liability apply *mutatis mutandis* to the case that the carrier is liable to compensate damages for loss or damage to the unchecked baggage. In applying the provisions, the 'delivery of the goods' shall be changed to read as 'termination of carriage' (Article 593(2), last sentence).

990. ANA's Conditions of Carriage stipulate as follows: 'The Carrier shall be liable for loss or damage arising out of or in connection with the destruction or loss of, or damage to Unchecked Baggage or any other article carried or worn by a passenger only if it is proved that such destruction, loss or damage was caused by the negligence of the Carrier and/or its Agent(s)' (Article 44(4)). Similar to the Com. Code, the carrier's negligence is not presumed and that the passenger claiming compensation bears the burden of proof.

991. JAL's Conditions of Carriage provide the same (Article 43(4)).

VI. Amount of Compensation for Damages with Regard to Baggage

992. The Com. Code does not have any limitation of liability of the carrier in respect of checked and unchecked baggage.

993. ANA's Conditions of Carriage set out the limitation of liability. 'The Carrier's liability for the carriage of Baggage shall be limited to 150,000 yen per passenger, provided that if the passenger declares a value higher than the amount for the Baggage before the commencement of the carriage and an excess value charge is paid pursuant to the provisions of Article 42, the liability of the Carrier shall be limited to an amount equivalent to such declared value but shall not, under any circumstances, exceed the actual value of the Baggage' (Article 48(1)), 'The term "Baggage" as used in the preceding paragraph shall include Checked Baggage, any other article of a passenger that is placed in the Carrier's custody, Unchecked Baggage and any other article carried or worn by the passenger' (Article 48(2)). However, there is an exception for limitation of liability. 'The limitation of liability provided for in Article 48 of these Conditions of Carriage shall not be applicable if it is proved that the damage has been caused by the willful misconduct or gross negligence of the Carrier and/or its Agent(s), provided that if such damage is caused by willful misconduct or gross negligence of the Agent(s), it shall also be proved that the damage occurred while the Agent(s) was (were) performing his/her (their) duties' (Article 50).

994. JAL's Conditions of Carriage stipulate the same as those of ANA's (Articles 47 and 49).

VII. Deposit and Disposal of the Baggage

995. The Com. Code stipulates as follows: If a passenger does not request the delivery of his/her baggage within one week from the date of arrival at the destination, the carrier may deposit the object or put it up for auction after demanding that the passenger receive the baggage within a reasonable period of time. In such a case, once the carrier deposits the baggage or puts it up for auction, the carrier must issue notice of this to the passenger without delay (Article 592(3)).

996. ANA's Conditions of Carriage stipulate as follows: 'Checked Baggage that remains unclaimed for 7 days, calculated from the day following the date of its arrival at the destination, may be disposed of by the Carrier as appropriate. In this case, the passenger shall be liable for any damage or expenses incurred by the Carrier in connection with such disposal' (Article 34).

997. JAL's Conditions of Carriage have the same provision (Article 32).

§7. International Carriage of Passengers by Air

I. Liability of the Carrier with Regard to Passengers

998. 'The carrier is liable for damage sustained in case of death or bodily injury of a passenger upon condition only that the accident which caused the death or injury took place on board the aircraft or in the course of any of the operations of embarking or disembarking' (Article 17(1) of the MC). 'For damages arising under paragraph 1 of Article 17 not exceeding 128,821 Special Drawing Rights for each passenger, the carrier shall not be able to exclude or limit its liability' (Article 21(1) of the MC). 'The carrier shall not be liable for damages arising under paragraph 1 of Article 17 to the extent that they exceed for each passenger 128,821 Special Drawing Rights if the carrier proves that: (a) such damage was not due to the negligence or other wrongful act or omission of the carrier or its servants or agents; or (b) such damage was solely due to the negligence or other wrongful act or omission of a third party' (Article 21(2) of the MC).

999. As such, the MC has adopted a two-tier system of liability for the death or injury of passengers: (i) no-fault liability up to 128,821 SDR and (ii) presumed-fault liability in excess of that amount, which is discharged if the carrier proves that it is not negligent or other facts stipulated in Article 21(2). In addition, contrary to the Warsaw Convention, the MC does not have any provision for the limitation of liability of the carrier for death or injury to passengers.

1000. As to the meaning 'in the course of any of the operations of embarking' (Article 17(1) of the MC), there is a case on the Warsaw Convention (Tokyo C.A. Judgment of 24 March 1965, *Hanji*, Vol. 408, 11). The Tokyo C.A. held, in summary, as follows: As the contract of carriage, in this case, is an international contract of carriage governed by the Warsaw Convention, the carrier should, in accordance with the provisions of Article 17 of the Warsaw Convention, be liable for compensation if the accident which caused the damage so sustained took place onboard the aircraft or in the course of any of the operations of embarking. Although there are many different views as to the meaning of the term ' in the course of any of the operations of embarking', it is reasonable to interpret that the period of time during which a possibility of special danger to air carriage due to the various operations for getting passengers onboard the aircraft exists, in other words, from the time when the passenger enters the airfield after giving his or her ticket until the time when the passenger leaves the airfield after landing.

1001. It is understood that 'bodily injury' under Article 17(1) of the MC does not include pure mental injury and 'punitive, exemplary or any other non-compensatory damages shall not be recoverable' (Article 29 of the MC).

II. Liability of the Carrier with Regard to Baggage

1002. 'The carrier is liable for damage sustained in case of destruction or loss of, or of damage to, checked baggage upon condition only that the event which caused the destruction, loss or damage took place on board the aircraft or during any period within which the checked baggage was in the charge of the carrier. However, the carrier is not liable if and to the extent that the damage resulted from the inherent defect, quality or vice of the baggage. In the case of unchecked baggage, including personal items, the carrier is liable if the damage resulted from its fault or that of its servants or agents' (Article 17(2) of the MC). 'In the carriage of baggage, the liability of the carrier in the case of destruction, loss, damage or delay is limited to 1,288 Special Drawing Rights for each passenger unless the passenger has made, at the time when the checked baggage was handed over to the carrier, a special declaration of interest in delivery at destination and has paid a supplementary sum if the case so requires. In that case the carrier will be liable to pay a sum not exceeding the declared sum, unless it proves that the sum is greater than the passenger's actual interest in delivery at destination' (Article 22(2) of the MC). This provision 'shall not apply if it is proved that the damage resulted from an act or omission of the carrier, its servants or agents, done with intent to cause damage or recklessly and with knowledge that damage would probably result; provided that, in the case of such act or omission of a servant or agent, it is also proved that such servant or agent was acting within the scope of its employment' (Article 22(5) of the MC).

III. Liability of the Carrier with Regard to Delay

1003. 'The carrier is liable for damage occasioned by delay in the carriage by air of passengers, baggage or cargo. Nevertheless, the carrier shall not be liable for damage occasioned by delay if it proves that it and its servants and agents took all measures that could reasonably be required to avoid the damage or that it was impossible for it or them to take such measures' (Article 19 of the MC). 'In the case of damage caused by delay as specified in Article 19 in the carriage of persons, the liability of the carrier for each passenger is limited to 5,346 Special Drawing Rights' (Article 22(1) of the MC). This provision 'shall not apply if it is proved that the damage resulted from an act or omission of the carrier, its servants or agents, done with intent to cause damage or recklessly and with knowledge that damage would probably result; provided that, in the case of such act or omission of a servant or agent, it is also proved that such servant or agent was acting within the scope of its employment' (Article 22(5) of the MC).

1004. The MC does not define the term 'delay'. Therefore, the meaning of the delay and the scope of damages would be determined by the law of the jurisdiction.

1005. In relation to the Warsaw Convention, the Sendai D.C. held, in summary, as follows (Sendai D.C. Judgment of 25 February 2003, *Hanta*, Vol. 1157, 157): (i) The carrier shall be liable for default if the baggage is carried after an objectively reasonable period of time had passed from the time when the passenger was carried, in view of the whereabouts of the passenger and the baggage, the geographical relationship between them, the operation of aircraft in that area and other traffic conditions, the carrier's system for handling the baggage, and other factors. (ii) However, a passenger who has checked his or her baggage expects that the baggage will be carried at the same time with the passenger and normally plans his or her activities at the destination based on this expectation. (iii) Therefore, it is reasonable to conclude that, as a matter of good faith, if the carrier fails to carry the baggage simultaneously with the passenger due to its wilful misconduct or gross negligence, the carrier is liable for the damage caused by such failure, irrespective of whether or not an objectively reasonable period of time has passed.

IV. Jurisdiction

1006. An action can be brought in any of the four jurisdictions allowed for the carriage of goods. 'An action for damages must be brought, at the option of the plaintiff, in the territory of one of the States Parties, either before the court of the domicile of the carrier or of its principal place of business, or where it has a place of business through which the contract has been made or before the court at the place of destination' (Article 33(1) of the MC). In addition, 'In respect of damage resulting from the death or injury of a passenger, an action may be brought before one of the courts mentioned in paragraph 1 of this Article, or in the territory of a State Party in which at the time of the accident the passenger has his or her principal and permanent residence and to or from which the carrier operates services for the carriage of passengers by air, either on its own aircraft or on another carrier's aircraft pursuant to a commercial agreement and in which that carrier conducts its business of carriage of passengers by air from premises leased or owned by the carrier itself or by another carrier with which it has a commercial agreement' (Article 33(2) of the MC).

V. Limitation of Actions

1007. The time limits within which a passenger must bring an action for the carrier's liability are the same as in the case of carriage of cargo. 'The right to damages shall be extinguished if an action is not brought within a period of two years, reckoned from the date of arrival at the destination, or from the date on which the aircraft ought to have arrived, or from the date on which the carriage stopped' (Article 35(1) of the MC).

1008. In case of damage to checked baggage, the complaint must be made in writing to the carrier within seven days from the date of receipt and, in case of delay, within twenty-one days from the date on which the baggage has been placed at his or her disposal (Articles 31(2) (3) of the MC). 'If no complaint is made within the times aforesaid, no action shall lie against the carrier, save in the case of fraud on its part' (Article 31(4) of the MC).

Chapter 3. Multimodal Transportation

§1. General

I. Definition

1009. Prior to the amendment in 2018, the Com. Code had no provision regarding the liability of the carrier in a multimodal (combined) transport. Therefore, although the multimodal contract of carriage is widely used, it was not clear the liability of the carrier in multimodal transport and legal stability was lacking. Therefore, when the Com. Code amended in 2018, the new provisions for multimodal transport were introduced (Article 578). Under the Com. Code, a multimodal contract of carriage means a contract in which two or more types of land, marine, or air transport are undertaken under a single contract (Article 578(1)).

II. Types

1010. There are two main types of multimodal carriers: (1) one is the actual carrier (e.g., a shipping company) who undertakes the whole carriage and performs part of the carriage as an actual carrier and consigns the rest to another actual carrier; and (2) the other is a Freight Forwarder who does not have its own means of transport (non-vessel operating common carrier) and who undertakes the carriage and uses a subcontractor for the whole section of the carriage where two or more different modes of transport are carried out.

1011. Multimodal transport in Japan is mostly a combination of motor truck transport with rail, air, or marine transport. On the other hand, international multimodal transport is mostly a combination of marine transport with a motor track or rail transport (mainly for North America and Europe) or marine transport with air transport (mainly for Europe via North America or for Latin America).

§2. Source of Law

1012. The provisions of Part 2, Chapter VIII of the Com. Code are the general rule for the carriage of goods commonly applicable to land, marine, and air transport. Therefore, these general rules apply to the contract of multimodal carriage. In addition, Article 578 stipulates the liability of the multimodal carrier. These provisions also apply to international carriage as far as it is governed by Japanese law. However, these provisions are discretionary, and parties can exclude them by agreement.

1013. In addition, the amendments of Com. Code in 2018 introduced a new provision for multimodal transport B/L (Article 769(1) of the Com. Code).

§3. MULTIMODAL TRANSPORT B/L

1014. In practice, a multimodal (combined) B/L, a document representing the right to demand delivery of the goods, is issued for multimodal transport when the carrier undertakes land and sea transport in a single contract. However, prior to the 2018 amendments, the Com. Code did not contain any provisions governing the legal relationship with the multimodal B/L. Therefore, a new provision for multimodal transport B/L was introduced in 2018 (Article 769 of the Com. Code).

1015. When the carrier or Master has accepted the land and marine transport under a single contract, he shall, at the request of the consignor, without delay after the loading of the goods, issue one or more multimodal transport Bs/L describing that the loading was completed (Article 769(1)). In line with the practice, the Com. Code stipulates the description of the multimodal transport B/L as the description of the B/L as well as the place of departure and destination (Article 769(2)).

1016. Multimodal transport B/L referred to in Article 769 is issued when land and marine transport are undertaken under a single contract. Therefore, the Com. Code does not have a provision for a multimodal transport B/L involving air transport. This is because air carriage takes a short period, and there seem to be no cases of issuing the B/L.

§4. LIABILITY OF THE CARRIER

I. In Case the Section Is Identified

1017. When the section of the carriage where the damage of the goods occurred is identified, Article 578(1) is applicable. Therefore, the liability of the carrier in multimodal transport shall be subject to the provisions of the laws and regulations of Japan, or the Conventions concluded by Japan which shall apply to each carriage in the event of the loss or other damage of the goods (Article 578(1) of the Com. Code). This is because it is considered reasonable that the multimodal carrier should be liable in accordance with the contents of the laws and regulations or mandatory provisions stipulated by the convention generally applicable to each sector of carriage.

1018. Further, Article 578(1) shall apply *mutatis mutandis* to the case where land transport to which two or more different laws and regulations shall apply for each section is undertaken under a single contract (Article 578(2) of the Com. Code). This is because there are cases where different laws and regulations apply to different sections, even when the carrier undertakes only land transport. For example, when a carrier undertakes truck transport and rail transport, track transport is subject to the Com. Code and rail transport is subject to the ROA (Law No. 65 of 1900).

II. In Case the Section Is Not Identified

1019. Article 578 is applicable if it is proved that in which sector the cause of the damage of the goods occurred. There is no provision directly applicable to the case where it is not clear in which sector the cause of the damage of the goods occurred. In that case, the provisions of Part 2, Chapter VIII of the Com. Code (Article 570–588) are applicable, which are the general provisions for the carriage of goods.

1020. There were mainly two reasons why the 2018 amendments to the Com. Code did not directly stipulate the case. One is that assuming that the general provisions for the carriage of goods apply to multimodal transport, it was considered that it would be sufficient for the parties who wish to be treated differently to make a special agreement if necessary, and therefore there was little need for the law to provide any special rules. The other is that with regard to the determination of the carrier's liability, there are several foreign legislations such as (a) legislation that the regulation for the longest section of the transport applies, (b) legislation that the within the regulations which are applicable to the case, the regulation providing the highest amount of damages applies, and (c) legislation that as long as the marine transport sector is included, the regulation for marine transport applies. However, as to (a), the longest transport is mostly air transport but the damage to the goods rarely occurs during air transport and therefore its reasonableness is questionable. As to (b) and (c), it was considered difficult to find a reasonable reason why such regulation should be applied if there was no special agreement between the parties.

III. Terms and Conditions

1021. The provisions of the Com. Code are discretionary, and if there is a special agreement between the parties, the agreement prevails. In Japan, the Japan Shipping Exchange, Inc. and the Japan International Freight Forwarders Association Inc. issue standard terms and conditions for multimodal transport.

Selected Bibliography

§1. Books on Japanese Transport Law

The following are the leading books on Japanese Transport Law. They are written in Japanese.

Egashira, K. *Commercial Transaction Law.* 8th ed. Kobundo, 2018.
Fujita, K., S. Ochiai & T. Yamashita. *Commentary on the Convention for the Unification of Certain Rules for International Carriage by Air.* Yuhikaku, 2020.
Kobayashi, N. *New Commercial Maritime Law.* Shinzansha, 2021.
Ishii, T. *Commercial Maritime Law.* Yuhikaku, 1964.
Nakamura, M. & T. Hakoi. *Commercial Maritime Law.* Revised ed. Seibundo, 2013.
Shigeta, T., et al. *Commercial Maritime Law.* Seirin Shoin, 1994.
Sakamoto, T. & S. Miyoshi. *New International Air Law.* Yushindokobunsha, 1999.

§2. Books on Japanese Laws

The following are the books on Japanese laws written in English. One can also search English version of Japanese transport law in the internet site of MLIT (Ministry of Land, Infrastructure, Transport and Tourism). https://www.mlit.go.jp.

Sato, K. (ed.). *The Commercial Code & The Corporation Law of Japan.* EHS Law Bulletin Series, 2020. Tokyo: Eibun-Horei-Sha, Inc.
Sato, K. (ed.). *The Civil Code of Japan.* EHS Law Bulletin Series, 2020. Tokyo: Eibun-Horei-Sha, Inc.
Sato, K. (ed.). *The Law Concerning International Carriage of Goods by Sea of Japan.* EHS Law Bulletin Series, 2018. Tokyo: Eibun-Horei-Sha, Inc.
Sato, K. (ed.). *Marine Transportation Law.* EHS Law Bulletin Series, 2021. Tokyo: Eibun-Horei-Sha, Inc.
Sato, K. (ed.). *The Code of Civil Procedure of Japan.* EHS Law Bulletin Series, 2021. Tokyo: Eibun-Horei-Sha, Inc.
Sato, K. (ed.). *The Arbitration Law of Japan.* EHS Law Bulletin Series, 2019. Tokyo: Eibun-Horei-Sha, Inc.
Sato, K. (ed.). *Road Traffic Law of Japan.* EHS Law Bulletin Series, 2020. Tokyo: Eibun-Horei-Sha, Inc.

Index

The numbers here refer to paragraph numbers.

1910 Collision Convention, 512

Air transport, 23, 916–1008, 918
  domestic carriage of goods by air, 922–948
  domestic carriage of passengers by air, 971–997
  international carriage of goods by air, 949–970
  international carriage of passengers by air, 998–1008
Act on General Rules for Application of Laws (Law No. 78, 2006), 38
Act on Port Regulations (APR), 558
Act on Prevention of Marine Pollution and Maritime Disaster (APMPMD, Act No. 136 of 1970), 599
Air waybill, 950–954
Arbitration, 44
Assistance, 394
Athens Convention Relating to the Carriage of Passengers and their Luggage by Sea, 1974, 808

Baggage, 815
Bareboat charters, 279–284
  effect against third parties, 281
  liability to third parties, 283–284
  responsibility for repairs, 282
Bill of lading, 302–313
  arbitration agreements, 344
  definition, 302
  characteristics, 307–313
  charter parties and, 327–329
  choice of governing law, 338
  statutory contents, 327–329
  electronic, 326
  functions, 303–306
  Hague Rules, 158
  Hague Visby Rules, 158
  jurisdiction agreements, 340–343
  types, 314–329
  clean and foul bills, 320
  master and house bills, 321
  multimodal transport, 1014–1016
  received and shipped bills, 319
  surrendered bills of lading, 322
  to-order, straight and bearer bills, 315–318
Bunker Oil Convention, 597

Captain, 126–141
  authority of, 128–131
  appointment, 133
  definition and qualifications, 126
  dismissal and termination, 141
  duties, 132
  liability for acts of seamen, 140
  representation of the shipowner, 135–137
  right to dispose of and use carried goods, 138–139
  substitute and acting, 134
Carrier, 162, 845
  definition, 845
  liabilities, 172–173, 345–352, 897–900
  claim valuation, 178–180, 353
  high value goods, 181, 357, 861–867, 934–937
  exclusions for international carriage, 177
  error in navigation or management, 347
  excepted causes, 349–350
  fire, 347

due care, 172–173, 346, 348
limitation of liability in international carriage, 182, 354
loss, damage or delay, 175
partial loss
notice for international carriage, 184, 359
objection for domestic carriage, 183
special agreements, 187–188
unseaworthiness, 174, 345
time bar for cargo claims against the carrier, 185–186, 360, 888–894
title to sue, 176, 358
tort, 189
obligations, 162–171
discharging and delivering the goods, 171
keeping custody of the goods with due care, 169
loading of goods, 167
obligation to comply with shipper or charterer's instructions, 170
performing the voyage, 168
warranty of seaworthiness, 163–166
rights, 191–194
dangerous and illegal goods, 191, 362
retention against the goods, 125, 192
time bar of claims by the carrier, 193
Case law, 36
Charter parties, 264–265
bareboat charters, 279–284
time charters, 285–301
voyage charters, 157, 161, 266–278
Charterer, 160
Civil Aeronautics Act (Law No. 231, 1952), 32
Civil Code of Japan 1896, 25
Class I Specified Vessels, 705
Class II Specified Vessels, 706
Code of Civil Procedure 1996 (Law No. 109, 1996), 40
Collision, 91, 217, 230, 240, 283, 289–292, 379, 390, 391, 511
Commercial Code of Japan 1899, 25
Common Risk Avoidance Disposition, 473
Consignee, 160, 205–212
identification of, 205–206
obligations, 207–208
payment of freight and other costs, 207
taking receipt of the goods, 209
rights, 212
Consignor, 160
Consigned Freight Forwarding Business Act (Law No. 82, 1989), 34
Constitution of Japan, 2
Consumer protection, 39
Convention Concerning International Carriage by Rail of 9 May 1980, 848
Convention for the Unification of Certain Rules of Law respecting Assistance and Salvage at Sea, 1910 (1910 Salvage Convention), 394
Convention Internationale pour l'unification de certainesreglesconcernant les Immunites des naviresd'Etad, 525
Convention on the Contract for the International Carriage of Goods by Road done at Geneva on 19 May 1956, 848
Contracts for the carriage of goods by sea, 156, 212
definition, 159
parties, 160
semi-mandatory provisions in international carriage, 365–370
types
for the carriage of individual goods, 157
voyage charters, 157, 161, 266–278
Court execution officer, 728

Dangerous goods, 191, 198–200, 298, 362–364, 877–881

Exclusive economic zone, 602

Fire, 177, 182, 189, 347, 634
Flag of conveniences, 16
Freight forwarder, 845

General average, 466
General average adjuster, 504
General average statement, 504
General passenger liner service operator, 810
Grounding, 478

Harmful water ballast, 606
Hazardous liquid substances, 603

Illegal goods, 191, 364
Immediate appeal, 731
International Carriage of Goods by Sea Act (Law. No, 172, 1957), 29, 156

International Convention for the Unification of Certain Rules Relating to Civil Jurisdiction in Matters of Collision, 525
International Convention for the Unification of Certain Rules Relating to the Arrest of Sea-going Ships, Brussels, 1952, 716
International Convention on Arrests of Ships, 1999, 716
International Convention on Salvage, 1989, 394
international fund, 676
International Regulations for Preventing Collisions at Sea, 1972, 557

Japan Coast Guard, 602
Japanese Ships, 58–60
privileges, 59
requirements, 60
Jurisdiction, 40
Jurisdiction clause, 42

Limitation of shipowners' liability, 213–263
1957 International Convention relating to the Limitation of the Liability of Owners of Sea-Going Ships, 213
breaking limitation, 246
claims ineligible for limitation, 240–244
claims subject to limitation, 229–239, 451
Convention on Limitation of Liability for Maritime Claims, 1976, 213
counterclaims, 245
limits of liability, 248–263
parties entitled to limitation, 219–223
shipowner etc., 220–221
salvor, 222
servants etc., 223
proceedings, 253–263
claims against the limitation fund, 261–262
commencement, 259–260
deposit, 257–258
distribution of fund and closing of proceedings, 263
jurisdiction, 254–256
ships eligible for limitation, 227–228
Limitation of Shipowners Liability Act (Law No. 94, 1975), 29
Loss of earnings, 561
Loss of profits, 538

Maritime transport, 12
Maritime liens, 82–108
claims giving rise to, 90–95
enforcement of, 122–124
extinguishment, 105–108
governing law, 85–89
International Convention for the Unification of Certain Rules of Law Relating to Maritime Liens and Mortgages, 1926, 83
International Convention on Maritime Liens and Mortgages, 1993, 83
object of, 104
order of priority among other security interests, 98–103
Maritime Traffic Safety Act, 558
Minister of the Environment, 604
Minister of Land, Infrastructure, Transport and Tourism, 608
Ministry of Land, Infrastructure, Transport and Tourism (MLIT), 9
Civil Aviation Bureau, 15
Maritime Bureau, 12
Road Transport Bureau, 14
Montreal Convention (Convention for the Unification of Certain Rules for International Carriage by Air), 916, 921
Motor Truck Transportation Act (Law No. 83, 1989), 31
Multimodal transport, 868, 1009–1021

No cure no pay, 412

Objection to execution, 731
Offshore facilities, 627
Oil Pollution Damage Act (law No. 95, 1975), 29
Oil pollution damage of general vessels etc., 684
Oil record book, 602

Passenger transportation, 901–915
Personal injury, 580–585
Pilotage, 374–378
fees, 377
licences, 375
obligations of the captain and pilot, 378
relationship between the pilot and captain, 379–380
relationship between the pilot and shipowner, 381
zones, 376
Port of registry, 61–62

Index

Prevention of Collisions at Sea Act, 557
Private international law, 38
Protocol of 2002 to the Athens Convention Relating to the Carriage of Passengers and Their Luggage by Sea, 1974, 808
Provisional seizure, 715

Railway Business Act (Law No. 92, 1986), 30
Railway Operation Act (law No. 65, 1900), 30, 846
Railway transport, 19
Regulations on Railway Transport (Order of Ministry of Railways No. 3 of 1942), 846
Road transport, 21

Salvage, 395
Salvage contract, 432
Salvage remuneration, 447
Salvor, 398
Seamen, 142–155
  hiring contract, 145–150
  rights and duties, 154–155
Sea waybills, 324
Ship
  acquisition or loss of, 67–69
  commercial home port, 62
  Japanese nationality, 58–60
  legal definition/general meaning, 46–57
  legal nature, 56–57
  register of small-sized vessels, 66
  sale of, 70–74
  shipbuilding contracts, 75
  ship's ledger, 65
  ship registry, 64
Ship leases, *see* bareboat charter
Shipbuilding contracts, 75
Shipper, 160, 194–204
  obligations, 195–200
  dangerous goods, 198, 362
  delivery of documents, 196
  delivery of shipping label, 197
  payment of freight, 195
  rights, 201–204
  cancellation of carriage, 202–204
  disposal of the goods, 201
Ship mortgage, 109–121
  effect against third parties, 113
  enforcement of, 122–124
  object of, 110–112
  order of priority among other security interests and bareboat charters, 114–117
  special types of, 118–121
Ship sale, 70–74
Ship's husband, 81
Ship's ledger, 65
Shipowner
  co-ownership, 78–81
  external relations, 80
  internal relations, 79
  ship's husband, 81
  definition, 76
  liabilities, 77
Ship registry, 64
Special compensation, 441
Specified underground seepage water, 619
Successive carriage, 895–898
Supplementary fund, 680
Supreme Court, 6

Tanker oil pollution damage, 655
Territorial waters, 602
Time charter, 285–301
  charterer's right to give instructions, 288–295
  charterer's liability for collision, 289–292
  responsibility for costs, 296
Time charterer, 535
Total volume control standards, 617
Tow, 382
Towage contract, 382
  external relations, 391–393
  internal relations, 386–390
  types, 382–384
  contracts for towage work, 382
  employment-type tow contracts, 382–384
  carriage-type tow contracts, 383
  towage contracts in the narrow sense, 383
Transport laws in Japan, 25
Transport by road and rail, 843–915
Type I Specified Vessel, 692
Type II Specified Vessel, 693
Tug, 382

Vessel Act, 53, 58–60, 410
Voyage charter, 157, 161, 266–278
  cancellation, 276–278
  departure and voyage, 272–273
  discharge, 275

disposal of the goods, 274
loading and laytime, 270–271
parties, 268
warranty of seaworthiness, 269

Water Pollution Prevention Act (WPA, Act No. 138 of 1970), 600
Wreck Removal Damage, 700

York Antwerp Rules, 471

Index

www.ingramcontent.com/pod-product-compliance
Ingram Content Group UK Ltd.
Pitfield, Milton Keynes, MK11 3LW, UK
UKHW020138290926
15471UKWH00003B/556

9 789403 517162